For the Library

THE FORTUNES

OF EPIC POETRY

THE FORTUNES

OF EPIC POETRY

A Study in English and American Criticism

1750—1950

Donald M. Foerster

The Catholic University of America Press

1962

59073

Donald M. Foerster died on March 2, 1961, at age forty-seven. A minimum final revision of the manuscript was made by his father,

N.F.

Preface

In ancient Greece, as everyone knows, Homer was the "Bible" of the people. In ancient Rome, it is said, Virgil was the favorite of emperor and clown. In Elizabethan England, the Graeco-Roman epic was considered indispensable for the training of princes and gentlemen. In the England of Cromwell and Charles II, the epic seemed to Milton, as poet, the best means of explaining how evil came into the world. In the England of Anne and the Georges, as in the America of Thomas Jefferson, no man could pretend to be educated unless he knew large portions of Homer and Virgil by heart, and no poet, it almost seemed, could hope for laurels unless he had published an *Epigoniad* or a *Columbiad*.

But in our world, the epic has fallen upon evil days. What remains of its high prestige? Critics affirm that heroic poetry is an anomaly in our unheroic age, that science has destroyed man's love for the mythical and supernatural, that global warfare and modern political beliefs have made us indifferent to the aristocratic Greek chieftain and his small-scale battles beneath the walls of Troy. Other critics observe that the tempo of twentieth-century life precludes reading of long narratives in uniform verse, or that new concepts of the nature of poetry have led readers to prefer the modern lyric, intellectualized and tightly complex, to rambling epics of adventures on land and sea, of struggles between an autocratic Hebrew God and an altogether too human Satan, of trials of the soul in its ascent into the Christian empyrean. Still others imply that the day of poetry—all poetry—has apparently come to an end, that the mushrooming of natural, psychological, and social sciences has established the realistic novel as the appropriate literary form for the contemporary mind.

Has a revolution in taste actually occurred? If so, why and when did it begin? What have been the stages in its development? Which critics have depreciated the epic and what arguments have they used? On the other hand, was the change perhaps illusory, at least far from complete? May it be that critics have continued to find pertinent the views of poetry held by Aristotle, Horace, Sidney, Pope, Johnson? Is it not possible that the far-reaching efforts of scholarship and criticism during the past half century have added to our understanding and appreciation of the major epics? Why have the *Divine Comedy* and *Paradise Lost* survived as acknowledged world masterpieces, and why are translations of Homer's poems outselling many "best-sellers" of our day? In a word, is it conceivable that even in our age of prose and science the prestige of epic poetry is fully as high as ever?

These are not trifling questions. They raise significant issues with which scholarship will be concerned in the future, issues pertaining not only to the history of epic criticism but also to the complex history of literary aesthetics as a whole. I cannot pretend to have discussed them with finality in this book.

Up to the present, studies of epic criticism have not gone beyond the year 1800: Romantic opinion finds no place in books such as Georg Finsler's *Homer in der Neuzeit*, H. T. Swedenberg's *Theory of the Epic in England, 1660-1800,* and my own *Homer in English Criticism.* To be sure Paget Toynbee reprinted a vast assortment of Romantic comments on Dante, and Logan Pearsall Smith and latterly Robert Martin Adams are among those who have summarized some of the salient features of the twentieth-century controversy over Milton. But there has been no attempt to come to grips with the shifting concepts of the epic as a genre following the disintegration of neo-classicism, to study the rivalry of the epic and the other genres, and to show how fundamental changes of taste since Wordsworth's time have favored first this heroic poet and then that one. The present volume makes such an attempt.

Because of the scope of the subject, it has not been my intention to provide more than a survey. In the opening chapter on the period from Dryden to Johnson, I have borne in mind that the neo-classical view is already sufficiently clear to most scholars, and that the implications of the historical approach around 1750 have been adequately examined in books like René Wellek's *The Rise of English Literary History*. And I have concluded with an "Epilogue," in which it seemed to me premature to do more than touch lightly upon the diversity of twentieth-century opinion, not yet arrived at completion. Throughout the book, it has been necessary to use only the most pertinent materials, sometimes to ignore important critics because their statements bearing on the epic were unimportant, and conversely, to pay heed to many minor critics, because they happened to say something illuminating. It will be observed that I have focused attention upon critical estimates of the four greatest epic poets, Homer, Virgil, Dante, and Milton. To consider the superabundance of comments on scores of other poets—Indian, Norse, Portuguese, Slavic, South American—and multitudes of poets who wrote hybrid epics of all sorts would lead, it appeared to me, to a cluttering of evidence that might well obscure more than it would reveal. A fairly close analysis of critical opinion on the four poets just mentioned promises to be the most effective way to elucidate the several shifts in literary taste over the past two centuries.

This book is neither a history of epic poetry nor a critique of the epic as a literary genre, but simply a study of changing attitudes toward heroic poetry.

In three chapters of the book I have condensed or expanded material which first appeared in *PMLA, Studies in Philology,* and the *Philological Quarterly*. Thanks are due the publishers of these journals for permission to reprint.

I wish to acknowledge the courtesies of the library staffs of the College of William and Mary and of Yale University. And I take this opportunity to express my gratitude to friends who kindly read part of the manuscript, especially Seymour M. Pitcher and René Wellek.

DONALD M. FOERSTER

CONTENTS

1 Homage and Doubt in the Neo-classical Period

A HEROIC POEM, truly such, is undoubtedly the greatest work which the soul of man is capable to perform."[1] To Dryden it perhaps seemed as if he were expressing an axiom of the ages, a truth too self-evident ever to be questioned. Little did he suspect that the time would arrive when critics would honor the lyric at the expense of the epic or prose fiction at the expense of both the lyric and the epic. Little did he imagine that literary theorists could ever argue, as some few of them do today, that there is no such thing as "greatness" in art.

What led Dryden to pay such homage to the epic? To answer the question, we must remember his basic conception of literature. For him as for all neo-classicists, the central intention of a true literary work was not the dispassionate recording of the particulars of daily living or the baring of the author's soul: these are intentions that were to be recognized by later generations of critics. Dryden believed that all serious literature must be directed at man's whole being, intellective as well as emotional. Its chief function, he held, is to instruct through the medium of pleasing fiction, and conversely, to please by satisfying one's innate desire to acquire knowledge. It attains these dual aims instantaneously, and it does so in two ways. On the one hand, the true literary work minimizes transient appearances, the ever-changing, kaleidoscopic aspects of human experience, emphasizing instead the real that underlies ordinary phenomena, the real in the sense of the central and the ideal, of the objective towards which life collectively is ever striving; in the words of Dryden

1

himself, a great poem presents "images more perfect than the life in any individual."[2] On the other hand, the work of art seeks to be an ideality within itself, to be an objectification of the same rational pattern that is presumably implicit in the operations of nature—in short, to be organically perfect. It must have an absolute unity of all parts, an inner consistency and harmony, for without these it will be no work of art, of Nature in its ideal sense, but merely an accidental phenomenon reflecting the failures and shortcomings of all individual phenomena.

In theorizing about the epic, Dryden of course joined company with most neo-classicists in modifying this Aristotelian point of view. The purpose of the heroic poem, he intimated, is perhaps not so much to mirror human nature in its totality as to exhibit through concrete illustrations the ideal of ethical conduct. An epic is written in order "to form the mind to heroic virtue by example".[3] the epic poet desires to teach, to enlighten the soul so that it will automatically choose the good. Reading between the lines, one gathers that Dryden had no such high opinion of the lyric, that he probably questioned, above all else, its usefulness as a vehicle for ethical instruction. But there can be no question as to how he ranked tragedy and epic. In "A Discourse concerning the Original and Progress of Satire," he observes that the epic requires greater genius and more learning ("universal learning"), and that it has a greater action, more dignity, and more variety.[4] In the "Dedication of the Aeneis" he says that "tragedy is the miniature of human life; an epic poem is the draught at length." The former is directed at the passions rather than at man's rational nature; its effects are "too violent to be lasting."[5] Granted that tragedy "puts off a fit, like the quinquina," and relieves one for a time, an epic poem is superior because it effectively "roots out the distemper, and gives a healthful habit."[6] Hence in Dryden's opinion Homer and Virgil have surpassed all writers of tragedy; they have excelled particularly in displaying through narrated action the great potentialities of man as an ethical being, in instilling a love of virtue and a hatred of vice. Often as he may mention the cohesion and the formal perfection of their art, Dryden stresses most of all their didactic value.

"Homer's moral was to urge the necessity of union," to set forth "the ruinous effects of discord";[7] it is a moral of the utmost importance. Aeneas is described as the "thoroughly virtuous" hero, as a leader who exhibits for our edification "piety to the gods and a dutiful affection to his father, love to his relations, care of his people, courage and conduct in the wars, gratitude to those who had obliged him, and justice in general to mankind."[8]

In several of his essays Dryden suggests how he believes the more important heroic poets should be ranked. Homer and Virgil are of course peerless, but though Dryden hesitates to choose between them, it is fairly apparent that he prefers Virgil. In the "Dedication of Examen Poeticum," for example, he grants that Homer is perhaps more to be "admired," but he finds him rather too talkative and digressive, and rather too barbarous in his outlook on life. Homer, Dryden observes, "can move rage better than he can pity"; "he forms and equips those ungodly man-killers, whom we poets, when we flatter them, call heroes."[9] As for the other principal heroic poets, each seemed to Dryden to have his own limitations. For example, he observes that Spenser "aims at the accomplishment of no one action," that Tasso "confesses himself to have been too lyrical," and that Lucan "is wanting both in design and subject."[10] *Paradise Lost* is a noble and sublime epic, says Dryden; but in "A Discourse concerning the Original and Progress of Satire" he objects, among other things, to the subject of the poem, to an action which is not "prosperous" (Adam and Eve are punished), to Milton's making Satan his hero, and to the introduction of only two human actors among a host of supernatural beings.[11]

What generalizations can be made regarding Dryden's attitude towards the epic? In the first place, it seems certain that his praise of that type of poem was sincere, that he was not merely saying what his readers expected him to say. In writing "Annus Mirabilis" he admitted that he had derived much from Virgil; later of course he made a translation of the *Aeneid,* which, for all its faults, exhibits more careful workmanship and more capable scholarship than has sometimes been allowed; he acknowledged that his *State of Innocence and Fall of Man* was heavily indebted to *Paradise Lost*. Moreover, at one time he contemplated writing an epic of his own, and his heroic plays, as he himself observed, were in a sense epics written in a dramatic framework: "an heroic play ought to be an imitation, in little, of an heroic poem."[12] In the second place, something can certainly be said for his estimates of epic poetry. True, he is often unoriginal: many things that he said had been said before by Aristotle, Horace, Sidney, Boileau, Bossu, Segrais, and other critics ancient and modern. But Dryden deserves credit for wide and careful reading, for weighing the opinions of other critics, and for adopting only those opinions in which he could truly believe. Today we may have little respect for some of his pronouncements—as, for example, the one derived from Bossu, that the epic poet first selects his moral, then his fable, then his characters, and so on—but we should at least admit that he had a wider perspective than many of the neo-classicists. He did not often attempt to dictate, he had little patience for Italian and French critics who thought only in terms of the "rules," and he made a vigorous plea for the freedom of the imagination when he attacked those who objected to hippocentaurs and chimeras in poetry, also when he defended the appearance of the ghost of Polydorus in Virgil, the enchanted wood in Tasso, and the Bower of Bliss in Spenser.

Critics in the time of Queen Anne were not generally inclined to quarrel with Dryden's opinions. When Pope proclaimed that "Unerring Nature, still divinely bright" is "At once the source, the end, and test of Art," he was of course merely reaffirming the neo-classical view that good art, like the Cartesian universe, is rational and orderly, that it is subject to certain fixed laws. In the *Essay on Criticism* at least, he tended to minimize the importance of sensation, self-expression, individuality, and various other qualities which Romantics in Wordsworth's day were especially to prize; in fact, it might not be going too far to say that he regarded such qualities as belonging to inferior art. Pope put heavy stress instead upon judgment, common sense, restraint, imitation, universality, and the rules. He evidently believed in a system of fixed genres, a system so firmly established from the beginning of time, so defensible on rational grounds, that he saw no hope of success for the modern poet who dared to modify existent literary forms, who thought for a moment about the possibility of creating new ones. Though some of his contemporaries argued for the supremacy of the tragic drama, Pope, like Dryden, awarded the epic the highest rank. "Be Homer's works your study and delight." Throughout the *Essay* the implication is that Homer, along with Virgil, is the ideal teacher of immutable truth, the immortal genius who exposes through art the central features of human nature, the impeccable model for every aspiring poet. This is also the implication, we might add, of some portions of the preface which Pope wrote for his translation of the *Iliad*. Discussing the characters who appear in the poem, he declares that "nothing can be more exact than the Distinctions he has observ'd in the different degrees of Virtues and Vices."[13] Pope seems to feel that Homer deliberately set out to epitomize for all ages not only the nature of courage but also the many sub-species of courage: "that of *Achilles* is furious and intractable; that of *Diomede* forward, yet listening to Advice and subject to Command: We see in *Ajax* an heavy and self-considering Valour, in *Hector* an active and vigilant one: The Courage of *Agamemnon* is inspirited by Love and Ambition, that of *Menelaus* mix'd with Softness and Tenderness for his People."[14] Turning to the technique of the *Iliad*, Pope adopts the usual neo-classical procedure of segmenting the whole into what were supposedly its principal constituents. He bestows unrestrained praise upon the three modes of Homer's fable—the "probable" (which recites "Actions as tho' they did not happen, yet might, in the common course of Nature"), the "allegorical" (which adumbrates "Secrets of Nature and Physical Philosophy"), and the "marvellous" (which "includes whatever is supernatural, and especially the Machines of the Gods"). Pope also discusses at some length the appropriateness of the speeches, then the "sentiments," then the descriptive passages, images, and similes, then the "expression," and finally the versification.

A second important Augustan to honor the epic was Joseph Addison. Granted that his enthusiasm for Milton indicates a departure from extreme neo-classicism and perhaps an instinctive attempt to widen the bounds of epic, one can scarcely contend that Addison's criteria of great literature were radically different from Dryden's and Pope's. If he does not say categorically that *Paradise Lost* is an epic poem, it is, one assumes, because there is genuine doubt in his mind that any heroic poet is entitled to modify the tradition of Homer and Virgil, to ignore one or more of the "requirements" of Aristotle. As in Pope's preface, so in Addison's initial essays on *Paradise Lost,* there is the assumption that the epic is the supreme kind, that it is an imitation of men in action, and that it is a significant imitation only if it conveys immutable truths and ideals of conduct to the mind of the reader. Examining Milton's fable first of all, he praises its oneness, its completeness, its "greatness," concluding with strictly neo-classical remarks on the length of time covered by the action. Then he turns to the characters. Unlike Dryden, Addison holds that Adam and Eve are the true protagonists (elsewhere he suggests the Messiah), but it would appear that his espousal of the rules makes it difficult for him to justify the prominence which Milton gives to some of the supernatural personages in the poem; in fact, Sin and Death are "of such a chymerical Existence" that they do not seem "proper Actors in an Epic Poem."[15] Other neo-classical proclivities, other indications that Addison adjudged the epic supreme, are manifest in subsequent essays in which he speaks of the appropriateness of the sentiments and of the language employed in *Paradise Lost.* "It is requisite," he observes, "that the Language of an heroick Poem should be both perspicuous and sublime." Milton is praised for "shunning the common Roads of Expression" through his careful selection of metaphors, Latinisms, Graecisms, inversions, redundancies,[16] through all the devices that were to seem to later critics so deplorably artificial. If Addison did not place *Paradise Lost* on quite the same high level with the *Iliad* and the *Aeneid,* the reason was of course that the poem sometimes violated the neo-classical canons.

Since the time of Wordsworth the early eighteenth century approach to the epic has often been described as rigid, narrow, and arbitrary. One must realize, however, that if the English Augustans tended to stress the rules, conscious artistry, universality, structural arrangement and ethical import, they were also inclined to make abundant allowance for the poetic qualities which were to be so highly esteemed by later schools of critical thought. It might be said, in fact, that neo-classical theory contained the seeds of its own destruction, that it pointed the way for the eventual repudiation of its own basic tenets. To illustrate how this was true let us turn again to Pope. In the *Essay on Criticism,* as it has been suggested above, Pope emphasized skill and judgment, reason and common sense, imitation and the following of Nature. But he was not one to "write dull receipts how poems may be made," to fail to see that art is many-sided. Throughout the *Essay* he recognizes the need for "wit" (a term often implying imagination or creativeness), and in Part I he suggests that "Some beauties yet no Precepts can declare," that in poetry, as in music, there "Are nameless graces which no methods teach," that Pegasus may occasionally deviate from the common track and "snatch a grace beyond the reach of art." If the *Essay* may seem to dwell upon the need for restraint and calm judgment, one must remember, of course, that Pope was primarily addressing critics rather than poets, also that he was, rightly enough, emphasizing the point that art can all too easily become undisciplined and chaotic when free rein is given to the imagination and emotions.

In his Preface to the *Iliad* Pope's estimate of poetry and specifically of the epic would seem to be somewhat different. It is an estimate that is certainly neither narrow nor arbitrary, that gives ample recognition to originality, the emotions, and the imagination. At the outset he proclaims that "It is the Invention that in different degrees distinguishes all great Genius's: The utmost Stretch of human Study, Learning, and Industry, which masters everything besides, can never attain to this."[17] Referring to Homer, he says that invention is "the great and peculiar Characteristick which distinguishes him from all other Authors." Pope dwells upon the originality of the Greek poet with respect to his fable, characters, images, battles, speeches, and so on. He also speaks in some detail about Homer's sublimity, his animation and rapture and fire. For example, in comparing Homer with Virgil, he observes that *"Homer* hurries and transports us with a commanding Impetuosity, *Virgil* leads us with an attractive Majesty: *Homer* scatters with a generous Profusion, *Virgil* bestows with a careful Magnificence: *Homer,* like the *Nile,* pours out his Riches with a sudden Overflow, *Virgil* like a River in its Banks, with a gentle and constant Stream." On the whole, one feels that Pope has modified his point of view; he pays far more attention to "wit" and invention than to judgment and restraint. This is to be expected, of course, since he is now writing about a great poetic genius, not advising critics and aspiring young poets. In any event, the Preface clearly shows that a neo-classicist like Pope could recognize and give approval to some of the chief qualities that were to be ascribed to the Greek epic in the time of Wordsworth and beyond, that his theory of literature was comprehensive enough for him to see that slavish adherence to the "rules" will not assure one of writing a great epic, that in poetry at its best there is some element of the irrational and the inexplicable.

In yet another way did poetic theory, hence epic theory, avoid becoming rigid, static, and mechanical. Concomitant with the growth of Baconian and Cartesian science was the attainment, on the part of critics, of a degree of historical perspective, of an awareness of the manifold particularities present in literary works, of an apparent consecutiveness and pattern in the development of literature. It is beside our purpose to discuss here the inception of the Battle of the Ancients and Moderns in France, the quarrels between Perrault and Fontenelle, later between La Motte and Madame Dacier, or the echoes of these quarrels in English critical writings around 1700. Suffice it to say that on both sides of the Channel the intellectual milieu was such that no theorist was tempted to treat lightly the conditions under which a literary masterpiece had come into being, the state of morality or of religion or of society as a whole at the time of its composition, and even the character and experience of its author. In England this historical-biographical approach had little immediate impact upon epic theory; it seems to have been utilized at first largely for the purpose of explication rather than criticism. If Dennis suggested that the Christian concept of God might inspire the creation of

modern epics greater than Homer's, the majority of critics saw
in this new approach merely the possibility of overriding the
whims and prejudices of contemporary readers. Thus for page
after page Dryden sought only to explain how circumstances in
ancient Rome had helped to shape the *Aeneid*.[18] Thus too when
Pope recommended that a critic

> *Know well each ancient's proper character;*
> *His fable, subject, scope in every page;*
> *Religion, country, genius of his age*

he was certainly not implying that particularities should be al-
lowed to serve as a criterion of aesthetic worth; he was only sug-
gesting that a thorough understanding of backgrounds is pre-
requisite to competent judgment. Nor in practice did Pope fail
to follow the advice which he had given. Discussing the era of
Homer in his preface to the *Iliad*, he intimates that his basic
intention is to explain away for his readers the "seeming Defects"
of the poem. These defects—for example, the extreme brutality
of Homer's warriors—"will be found upon Examination to pro-
ceed wholly from the Nature of the Times" in which the Greek
poet lived, of a period when "a Spirit of Revenge and Cruelty
reign'd thro' the World, when no Mercy was shown but for the
sake of Lucre, when the greatest Princes were put to the Sword,
and their Wives and Daughters made Slaves and Concubines."
Pope protests against Madame Dacier's "strange Partiality" for
Homeric manners, her blind admiration for every aspect of
classical antiquity, but he does concede that "there is a Pleasure
in taking a view of that Simplicity in Opposition to the Luxury
of succeeding Ages," in reading, for example, about princes
tending sheep and princesses fetching water. But if Pope and
other English neo-classicists put the heaviest stress upon the
timelessness of the classical epic, it is not hard to see how mere
elucidation might tend to slip over and become actual judg-
ment of a literary work (as in the case of Madame Dacier), how
doctrines of social progress might increasingly insinuate them-
selves and give rise to doctrines of literary progress, how Homeric

morality might begin to seem too primitive to some critics, how the classical epic might come to be characterized as an early and essentially outmoded type of poetry. The prestige of the epic was secure for the time being. It was to remain secure only as long as adherence to a single, supposedly immutable standard precluded or discouraged relativism and progressivism, as long, too, as literary creation was regarded mainly as a rational process, the ultimate purpose of which was to communicate the unchanging ethical ideal.

In his *Elements of Criticism* (1762), Lord Kames declared that epics, like dramas, are intended either "to move the passions and exhibit pictures of virtue and vice" or "to illustrate some moral truth, by showing that disorderly passions naturally lead to external misfortunes." In any event, action is definitely the fundamental part of them all. In making such statements, Kames may have seemed to some of his contemporaries rather too dogmatic and traditional, rather too emphatic about moralism in poetry, about the preceptive and ethical character of the epic and the drama. But it is doubtful that most critics found his pronouncement antiquated and unpalatable, for down to the end of the eighteenth century the neo-classic approach of Dryden, Addison, and Pope continued to prevail. It was used by Sir William Jones, who, in spite of his approval of the lyric and the irregular heroic poetry of India, affirmed that it is to the great credit of European epics that "examples of heroes and kings were introduced, to illustrate some moral truth, by showing the loveliness and advantages of virtue, or the many misfortunes that flow from vice."[19] It was also used by Hugh Blair in many sections of his highly popular *Lectures on Rhetoric and Belles Lettres* (1783), and by William Melmoth when he stated that "the principles of criticism are as certain and indisputable even as those of the mathematics."[20] As for Dr. Johnson, a far more important critic of course than any of the above, the traditional neo-classical point of view manifests itself when he has Imlac say in *Rasselas* that it is the poet's business "to examine, not the individual, but the species" (a statement also made by Fielding in *Joseph Andrews*); "to remark general properties and large appearances" rather than to "number the streaks of the tulip."[21] Moreover, in his life of Milton, Johnson examines in the customary fashion the various components of *Paradise Lost*—the subject, the characters, the machinery, the episodes, the sentiments, and so forth. And certainly neither Dryden nor Pope (nor, for that matter, Sidney and other Renaissance critics) would have objected to Johnson's observation that "Poetry is the art of uniting pleasure with truth, by calling imagination to the help of reason. Epic poetry undertakes to teach the most important truths by the most pleasing precepts, and therefore relates some great event in the most affecting manner."[22] We must remember, however, that Johnson was a liberal and broadminded neo-classicist, that he believed Bossu wrong in saying that all epic poets choose a "moral" before considering their fable and characters, that he criticized Dryden for holding that Adam was not an epic hero "because he was overcome," that he again opposed Dryden when he defended the less sublime parts of *Paradise Lost,* and that he did not censure Milton for finding "reality . . . a scene too narrow for his mind."[23] If Johnson found serious defects in the poem, if there have been protests against his statement that "We read Milton for instruction, retire harassed and overburdened," it must surely be granted that his attitude toward epic poetry is more justifiable than that of numerous French and English critics at the beginning of the eighteenth century. At least he did not dwell upon the "rules" or assume that the slightest departure from the practice of Homer and Virgil was highly undesirable.

Though the neo-classical approach was the dominant one, there can be no blinking the fact that the period after 1750 was in a very real sense a period of transition, one in which it became less and less customary to think of the genres as having been fixed since time immemorial, of great poetry as an imitation of action and best exemplified by the classical epic and possibly the classical drama. Criticism was in the process of removing literature from the vacuum in which it had been placed: instead of fixity and rules, theorists were accentuating more and more the time and place in which a thing is written, the infinite diversities and uniquenesses of works of art, the principle of growth and change, and perhaps most significant of all, the emotional rather than the intellectual aspects of literature—the poet's emotions as the cause and the reader's emotions as the target of the poem. Since these emphases were now far stronger than in the Age of Pope, they naturally began to effect a partial reassessment of the epic—only partial, of course, because neo-classic theory was still ascendant.

First of all, there was intensified interest in poems other than epics. As the British empire expanded into Pacific and Asiatic waters, as scholarship developed and political and "conjectural" history took on new meaning, attention was increasingly paid to the literature of distant, often primitive lands, to that of Peru, of Lapland, of India, of Otaheite, and even of the wildernesses of America. Moreover, with the rise of nationalism came the "discovery" of Britain's literary past and a greater zest for Chaucer and Spenser, Elizabethan lyrics and folk-songs, the romances of the Anglo-Norman courts and the sonnets of Wyatt and Surrey: the writings of Gray, Walpole, Chatterton, and Thomas Warton bear ample evidence of an antiquarianism that did not focus upon the ancient epics of Greece and Rome. Still more important was the upsurge of enthusiasm for Shakespeare. For the most part, earlier neo-classicists had found it embarrassingly difficult to justify their instinctive admiration for the Elizabethan dramatist: the only logical argument seemed to be that he had not heard about the rules of Aristotle, that his eccentricities were to be forgiven because they were attributable to the crudity of the age in which he had lived. However, now that the rules were themselves suspect, now that one was more free to pass over or even relish the illogicalities of art, Shakespeare became a figure with whom the epic masters of old were obliged to share a fair portion of their prestige. If asked to make a definite choice between Homer and Shakespeare, Dr. Johnson might well have sat silently deliberating for some time before beginning with his customary appellative, "Sir, . . ."

Another factor that militated against the automatic equating of great poetry with the epic poetry of the ancients was the liberalization and extension of the whole concept of "epic." In part this was due to skepticism that the genres were really fixed after all, to a growing consciousness of the gradual evolution of poetic types; in part it was due to a general acknowledgment of the diversity that obtains within any one type. One might even go so far as to say that it was prompted by all the changes that were occurring in the critical outlook as a whole. To be sure, Dr. Johnson and other critics analyzed *Paradise Lost* in a manner not dissimilar to Addison's, but in general there was rather less tendency to praise the poem insofar as it complied strictly with basic neo-Aristotelian principles, or, in other words, with what seemed to be the poetic practice of Homer and Virgil. Thus William Warburton made a special appeal for Milton when he proposed a tripartite division of the epic as a genre: Homer, he declared, had taken possession of "the province of Morality, Virgil of Politics, Milton of Religion. . . . These are the *three species* of the Epic poem; for its largest sphere is HUMAN ACTION; which can be only considered in a *moral,* a *political,* or *religious* view."[24] And William Duff, for all his traditionalism, was hardly measuring Milton by Homer when he lauded him as one of the greatest original geniuses in all literature; he believed Milton great largely because *Paradise Lost* was not in any real sense an imitation of the *Iliad,* because in its essentials it manifested no slavish adherence to the precepts of Aristotle. The trouble with following the rules, Duff remarked, is that it "ties the mind down to the observance of them, perhaps at the very time that the imagination is upon the stretch, and grasping at some idea astonishingly great."[25] Elsewhere Duff agreed with Addison that the allegorical figures of Sin and Death appeared to be out of place in an epic, but, he added, "it is the privilege of a great Genius to break through certain rules which will be binding for ever on persons of lesser abilities, not only with impunity, but sometimes with applause."[26] On the whole, what many of the critics admired most in Milton was the boldness and sublimity of his language, the novelty and picturesqueness of his images and descriptive touches, the grandeur of some of his conceptions—

in short, the separate "beauties" rather than the form, the theme, or even the outlook on life implicit throughout the poem.

There were yet more significant efforts to widen the bounds of epic and in the process of so doing to stress poetic qualities which earlier critics had been prone to underrate. Richard Hurd, for instance, attempted to justify the label of "epic" for the *Faerie Queene* by subdividing the genre into the equivalent of the somewhat later Schlegelian "classical" and "romantic." His argument was that "when an architect examines a Gothic structure by Grecian rules, he finds nothing but deformity. But the Gothic architecture has it's own rules, by which when it comes to be examined, it is seen to have it's merits, as well as the Grecian."[27] More specifically, "judge of the *Faery Queen* by the classic models, and you are shocked with it's disorder: consider it with an eye to it's Gothic original, and you find it regular."[28] Neither Hurd nor any of his contemporaries was bold enough to call Dante's *Divine Comedy* an epic—people usually agreed with Voltaire that the poem was too irregular and barbarous—but Hugh Blair did not hesitate to assign the denomination of "epic" to such little-known and rule-breaking poets as Lucan and Camoëns. Though the *Pharsalia* seemed no "perfectly regular Epic Poem, yet it were the mere squeamishness of Criticism, to exclude it from the Epic Class. The boundaries, as I formerly remarked, are far from being ascertained by any such precise limit, that we must refuse the Epic name to a Poem, which treats of great and heroic adventures, because it is not exactly conformable to the plans of Homer and Virgil."[29] And Blair and many others were fully convinced not only that Ariosto and Tasso should be recognized as bona fide epic poets but also that they were great ones in their respective ways. Speaking of them both, Elizabeth Montagu asserted in the manner typical of the transition period that "however these poets, by the severe and frigid critics may have been condemned for giving ornaments not purely classical, to their works; I believe every reader of taste admires, not only the fertility of their imagination, but the judgment with which they availed themselves of the superstition of the times, and of the customs and modes of the country, in which they laid their scenes of action."[30] Finally, there was that noble savage, Ossian, a great favorite in Scotland during the sixties and seventies, a poet to be admired, so it was said, because his epics were so thoroughly spontaneous and "natural," because he had never heard of Homer and Aristotle. Of Ossian we shall have more to say in just a moment.

On the surface these mid-century tendencies in criticism would appear to have lent new prestige to heroic poetry. At least one was in a somewhat better position than earlier critics to justify his enjoyment of a fairly wide range of epic verse; at least one did not feel compelled to deprecate the individuality and the extravagant fictions of a poet such as Ariosto. It is obvious, on the other hand, that transition theory was inadvertently generating within itself some serious threats to the reputation of the epic as a kind: that as the limits of the epic were enlarged it was becoming harder to attribute an identity of aim and method to all members of the species; that originality and emotionalism would seem to be just as discoverable, perhaps even more so, in both lyrical and dramatic poetry; that a critical relativism might easily emerge as a result of the stress upon diversity; and that Shakespeare, Chaucer, Spenser, and other native poets were clearly beginning to distract attention from the heroic poets of antiquity. In fact, what had appeared to be the basic excellences of the Graeco-Roman epic, its perfection of form and its universal ethical import, were tending to become obscured to a certain degree.

A challenging question suggests itself at this point: granted that the neo-classic approach continued to prevail, were there any specific and unmistakable indications of a new attitude toward Homer and Virgil, towards the two poets long believed to have virtually pre-empted the whole realm of literature for themselves? Frequently it was asseverated without any qualification whatsoever that Virgil was entitled to a place among the three or four best poets of all time. As late as 1785 a writer in the *Critical Review* confidently described the *Aeneid* as "the most judicious and respectable form of the epos."[31] Though rather less enthusiastic, Blair refused to commit himself to the common opinion that Virgil is inferior to Homer; merely suggesting that each is different from the other, he credited the Roman not only with a delectable "sweetness and beauty" in his numbers but also with an "exquisite sensibility," a "pathetic spirit" that is most fully realized in the "family-pieces" of Aeneas, Anchises, and Creusa, and in the account of the love-affair between Aeneas and Dido.[32] However, it is clear that a widespread revolt against Virgil was in the making. Unlike Pope, who had praised "young Maro" for discovering that Nature and Homer are the same, many transition critics belabored the Roman poet for his reluctance or his inability to "invent" anything of his own. They felt that the *Aeneid* is but a faulty, slavish, and inanimate reproduction of the *Iliad*. Thus, a reviewer observed that "Virgil servilely followed Homer in his plan, in his characters, and in his adventures"—in almost every way possible;[33] and Blair could not refrain from admitting that "in many places" Virgil "has not so much imitated, as he has literally translated" the *Iliad*.[34] None of the many admirers of original genius believed that the *Aeneid* is a truly great poem: it was not to be mentioned in the same breath with the plays of Shakespeare or *Paradise Lost* or even the *Orlando Furioso*. Virgil, said John Brown, had "all the *secondary Qualities* of an *Epic Poet*" but he "wanted that all-comprehensive Genius which alone can conceive and strike out a great original Epic Plan, no less than that independent Greatness of Soul which was quenched by the *ruinous Policy* of the Times, and which alone can animate true Genius to a full Exertion of its Powers in the Cause of *public Virtue* and *Mankind*."[35] Though far more outspoken and hostile than most critics, John Pinkerton raised a question that must have been in many people's minds: "Why should I be condemned to follow Virgil thro all his feeble imitations of Homer, in the plan and conduct of the Eneid?" And he proceeded to animadvert in the following manner: "Virgil's storm is Homer's, tho Homer would not have begun with it. The conversations of the gods are all Homer's, . . . Homer hath games: Virgil hath games; his very ships, which he introduces as a novelty, prove him incapable of originality, for their accidents are from Homer's races. Homer's ships are on fire, Virgil's are on fire. If Ulysses goes to hell, Eneas goes to hell. . . . Wonderful poet! Judicious imitator!" Only the style of the Roman, "the pickle that has preserved his mummy from corruption," seemed to Pinkerton at all noteworthy.[36]

Thus there were essentially two ways of regarding the *Aeneid*: either as a highly successful imitation of the *Iliad* and therefore of Nature, or as a painstaking and worthless reproduction of an inimitable original. Opinion of Homer, on the other hand, was vastly more complex. The prevailing view, to repeat once again, was that the Greek epics are irreproachable with respect both to form and to the "lessons" they impart, that in a very real sense they are contemporaneous in all ages and societies. On the whole, however, Homeric criticism after 1750 was rapidly becoming less authoritarian and less homogeneous. As the newer historical approach gained ground, as the local and particular assumed greater importance in critical theory, it began to appear that the epics of Homer did not actually belong to some sphere outside of and above time and place but rather that they were, to an eminent degree, documentations of a primitive way of life, an epitome of the cultural ideals of an early people. For some critics, Homer himself was not to be measured by poetic principles extracted from Aristotle but by the traits of his heroes and the kinds of deeds they performed. And the traits and deeds selected as evidence were invariably the more brutal ones. John Jortin, for instance, spoke of Achilles as "a boisterous, rapacious, mercenary, cruel, and unrelenting brute,"[37] apparently forgetting how resolutely this Greek warrior faced certain death, how loyal he was to Patroclus, how compassionate towards the bereaved Priam. Commenting on the fierce battles in the *Iliad,* another critic, a physician, remarked that "a slaughterhouse or a surgery would not seem proper studies for a poet." Homer and his successors, he added, "dwelt with a savage pleasure upon every idea of pain and horror that studied butchery could excite." Often the Homeric heroes were compared to the primitive peoples described by Kames and Ferguson in their conjectural histories of man, to the American Indians, the Peruvians, and African tribesmen. A writer in

the *Monthly Review,* after emphasizing the "ignorance and bar-
barity" of the Homeric era, reached the conclusion that the
Greeks at Troy did not differ greatly from the redskins in the
New World: both made it a practice to "insult their vanquished
enemies" and to "sing and dance round them, and mortify them
with every kind of brutal raillery."[38] Others objected to the pirati-
cal habits of the Greeks, to the "indelicacy" involved in Paris's
theft of Helen, to the unromantic relationship of the sexes, to the
way in which the heroes gorged on beef, even to the unpleasant
episode in which the infant Achilles is said to have vomited wine
upon the clothes of Phoenix. Interestingly enough, the primi-
tivist John Brown assailed one of the basic tenets of neo-clas-
sicism when he questioned Homer's capacity as a teacher of
moral truth: "Where is *Virtue* praised? Is it in the Conduct of the
natural *Greek,* who looked upon *no means* as *base* to escape
Danger? . . . Is it in the Conduct of AGAMEMNON, who de-
clared his *Passion* for a *Capitive,* and his *Neglect* of his *Queen,* in
the *Face* of the *whole Army?*"[39]

To the twentieth century way of thinking, there is little to be
said for such analyses of Homer. They appear to reflect shallow-
mindedness and mere prejudice, a tendency to confuse the
essence of poetry with its externalities and accoutrements, to
treat a poetical work as if it were simply an historical text that
might just as well have been written in prose. Moreover, even if
one were willing to allow that Homer might be judged by his
characters, it was decidedly unfair to neglect the fact that one
of Homer's poems, the *Odyssey,* does not honor brutality at all,
that the protagonist of this poem is a civilized being, the very
soul of courage, self-reliance, endurance, and loyalty. But if we
look at the matter closely, we can perhaps account for this aber-
rant tendency in Homeric criticism. On the one hand, it would
seem that a sense of past and present naturally invites a judgment
of past and present, a comparison of what was with what is.
And if this sense is sufficiently strong, there will always be un-
discriminating people who are ready to construe all change as
progress. Fully recognizing the remoteness of the age of Homer
and the differences between the manners of ancient Greeks and

modern Englishmen, some critics after 1750 jumped to the un-
warranted conclusion that remoteness necessarily implies bar-
barism, a way of life far inferior to their own. They condemned
early Greek civilization; hence they depreciated, if they did not
quite condemn, the poetry that "expressed" it. On the other hand,
it would appear that at least some of the disapprobation of Homer
was prompted by the revolt against authoritarianism and its pre-
dilection for the classical epic. One of the most promising lines
of attack against the Aristotelian code was to call into question
the universality of Homer by showing that the purely local and
particular was conspicuous throughout his poetry. However this
may be, we should not forget that the progressivist approach was
only in the process of forming. It was not to become firmly en-
trenched until the time of Wordsworth, until vast social and
cultural changes had ushered in essentially new ways of regard-
ing literature, until a conjunction of Romantic theories had com-
pletely displaced traditional neo-classical theory.

Even in the mid-eighteenth century, however, historical inter-
pretation of Homer did not always tend to undermine his pres-
tige. The rise of literary scholarship, a growing dissatisfaction
with the sophistication and artificiality not only of contemporary
art but also of contemporary life as a whole, the new stress upon
individuality, self-expression, and emotionalism as requisites in
poetry—these were obviously instrumental in developing a critical
theory capable of withstanding the incursions of progressivism.
A highly polished state of society, it was suggested, discourages
and may even preclude the creation of great art: inspiration is
thwarted by professional criticism, and proper poetic subjects
are inaccessible because life is too thoroughly regulated and
monotonous and degenerate, because most human behavior com-
plies with an arbitrary social code. Actually there was scant
agreement as to when the greatest poetry had been written: if
clearly not in the eighteenth century, then possibly in the Age of
Elizabeth, or, as earlier Ancients had said, in the Age of Pericles,
or in several periods of history, or in the span of time between
Homer and Virgil. But one of the commonest points of view—
one that would be shared by few persons today—was that poetry

had attained perfection, from the sheer force of circumstances, in times when men were barely beginning to relinquish their barbaric mode of life. One of the first and most influential critics to espouse this theory was a Scot, Thomas Blackwell. In his *Enquiry into the Life and Writings of Homer* (1735), Blackwell maintains that the Greek poet was fortunate enough to live in an age when he could compose the most immortal of all verse simply by representing "things both in his own and other Countries, *almost as he heard them talked of.*"[40] Had he come into the world sooner, "he could have seen nothing but Nakedness and Barbarity"; had he come later, he would have found the states of Greece lazily enjoying the fruits of peace or carrying on well-disciplined struggles against one another. In the one case his poetry would have been altogether crude; in the other it would have been too artificial. As it was, Homer was able to portray men who had discovered some of the arts of civil life yet spoke and acted naturally, "without other Restraint than their own native Apprehensions of *Good* and *Evil, Just* and *Unjust,* each as he was prompted from within."[41] Also, Homer had at his disposal an ideal language for poetry, one which still retained "a sufficient Quantity of its *Original, amazing, metaphoric* Tincture" but had not acquired the enervating refinement that obliges poets to express themselves in a *"Set* of courtly Phrases."[42] Blackwell then points out how other things militated in favor of Homer: the religion of the early Greeks, their taste for the marvelous, and their erroneous conception of geography. As for the identity of Homer himself, Blackwell sometimes speaks of him as a kind of court poet who "resorted to the great Feasts and high Solemnities all over *Greece,* to assist at the Sacrifices, and entertain the People";[43] at other times as a man of learning, a teacher and philosopher; but generally as a "wandering indigent Bard." In the role of a rhapsodist, Homer would sing extemporaneously before large audiences: while he was "personating a *Hero;* while his Fancy was warming, and his Words flowing; ... like a Torrent, he wou'd fill up the Hollows of the Work; the boldest Metaphors and glowing Figures wou'd come rushing upon him."[44] Summing up the argument of his book, Blackwell says that Homer became the greatest poet in the world by "the *united* Influence of the happiest CLIMATE, the most natural MANNERS, the boldest LANGUAGE, and most expressive RELIGION: When *these* were applied to so rich a Subject as the War between Greece and Troy, they produced the ILIAD and ODYSSEY."[45]

The mid-century brought a deluge of studies more or less resembling Blackwell's. Most of them sought to establish the importance of environment as an efficient cause of individuality in literature, to explain the slow evolution from primitive song in praise of deity to more elaborate religious-heroic poetry, and eventually to dramatic representation. Most of them argued for an efflorescence and perfection of poetry in rude periods when intense emotionalism prevails and a subsequent decline when society becomes fully organized, when philosophy and reason take precedence over the imagination and the feelings, when spontaneous poetic creation gives way to a cautious following of rules and conventions. Most of them tended to minimize, sometimes to ignore, the element of deliberate art in Homer and to discover in his epics a high degree of exuberance, a most commendable naturalness and simplicity, a delightful waywardness of fancy, a true spirit of romance. In these studies, Homer is not only an ideal noble savage but also the ideal poet of all time. Nevertheless, primitivistic criticism was not completely homogeneous: emphases differed from book to book and so too did the conception of Homer. Whereas Blackwell had characterized the Greek poet as semi-civilized and learned, Robert Wood placed him a stage further back in point of time by depriving him of any ethical purpose, of any knowledge of the sciences, of Egyptian religion, and most significant of all, of the art of writing. Critics had previously averred that Homer was an unlettered bard—actually the view is traceable to classical antiquity—but Wood was the first of the moderns to examine the evidence with any real thoroughness. He declared that Homer had lived at a time when poetry was still "entirely addressed to the ear,"[46] that he was a mendicant singer, almost a mere balladist, that he composed his verse in detached pieces, and that these pieces remained unassembled until the age of Pisistratus. As we have shown elsewhere,[47] Wood's exposition of the matter attracted the attention of Herder, Heyne, Goethe, and Wolf, and was thus indirectly responsible for the long controversy over Homeric origins.

Most of the Scottish critics were rather less interested than Wood in Homer's method of composition; they chose to emphasize instead the sheer emotionalism of the poet and his poetry. Thus, John Pinkerton could find nothing censurable in the fact that Homer was little more than a barbarian. The "youth of society," he said, is "lost in tempestuous passions, which call forth extraordinary exertions of mind. Such exertions form the very life and soul of poetry. . . . Violent actions, and sudden calamities of all kinds, are the certain concomitants of uncivilized life: to these we owe a poetry warm, rapid, and impetuous, that, like a large river swelling from a bleak mountain, carries the reader along in the barge of fancy, now by vales, fragrant with wild flowers, now thro woods resounding with untaught melody."[48] Similarly, Adam Ferguson felt that the very earliest poets, of whom Homer was one, had merits that far outweighed their lack of craftsmanship. Because the primitive bard is "simple and vehement in his conceptions and feelings, he knows no diversity of thought, or of style, to mislead or to exercise his judgment. He delivers the emotions of the heart, in words suggested by the heart: for he knows no other. And hence it is, that while we admire the judgment and invention of Virgil, and of other later poets, these terms appear misapplied to Homer."[49] Though not so thoroughgoing a primitivist as Ferguson, William Duff visualized the Homeric age as "uncultivated," as a period when "the manners, sentiments, and passions are (if we may use the expression) perfectly ORIGINAL. They are the dictates of nature, unmixed and undisguised. . . . The Poet in describing his own feelings, describes also the feelings of others."[50]

How are we to account for this new conception of Homer? Certainly one factor was the reaction to Aristotelianism, the ever more pressing demand for cognizance of the emotional element in great poetry. Another factor was undoubtedly the rise of the historical approach, an approach that made much of the sequential nature of literature in general, of the chronological place of

each work of art. There is, on the other hand, a special signifi-
cance in the fact that critical primitivism made almost no head-
way at all within the borders of England itself. Edward Young
may have pleaded for originality of poetic composition, Clara
Reeve may have praised what she regarded as the wild and
romantic fictions of Homer, and Joseph Warton may have
sentimentally admired the *Odyssey,* in the fashion of Rousseau,
for its depiction of a wholesome, idyllic way of life contrasting
sharply with that of modern times. But one can find no evidence
whatsoever that any Englishman other than Wood conceived of
Homer primarily as an unlettered singer who poured forth his
woodnotes without any attempt at restraint; and even Wood
himself, as a matter of fact, seems to have been more impressed
by Homer's talent for photographic reproduction of concrete
detail than by his spontaneous expression of intense feeling. Prim-
itivistic theory was therefore almost wholly Scottish in origin.
It was stated first in Blackwell's *Enquiry;* it appeared again in
the writings of some of the men whom Blackwell instructed at
Aberdeen. Influential as this professor of Greek may have been,
the main cause of its propagation was, however, the startling
"discovery" around 1760 that Scotland had a great primitive
poet of her own, a bard whose glories every patriotic Highlander
was eager to publish to the world. That bard was of course
Ossian—singer, warrior, chieftain, all in one.

There is no occasion to discuss here the intricacies and con-
volutions of the heated controversy that began almost as soon
as *Fingal* appeared, the grounds for argumentation between
Englishman and Scot, and the many repercussions that were even-
tually felt from one end of Europe to the other; our concern is,
rather, the way in which the "discovery" helped to shape epic
criticism in general and Homeric criticism in particular. Scot-
tish chauvinists realized well enough that little was to be gained
merely by rhapsodizing about the wonders of Ossianic poetry
per se, that current opinion was already predisposed towards the
more decorous verse of the Greeks and Romans. Under the leader-
ship of Hugh Blair, such critics as James Macpherson, Lord
Kames, and Ewen Cameron—indeed almost every Scottish critic

except David Hume—were therefore resolved to win prestige for Ossian by appropriating some of the views expressed by Blackwell in his *Enquiry*. If Ossian was an early bard, was not Homer also one? Would it not redound to the credit of Scotland if her "new" poet were compared to Homer himself? Hence essay after esssay was written in order to point out the many parallels between the two. Both had lived in primitive societies, it was said; both had sung extemporaneously, had described natural, unsophisticated heroes, had used figurative language because abstract terms were as yet non-existent, and had enhanced their narratives by utilizing systems of supernatural machinery. But such boldness on the part of the critics quickly led to still greater boldness. Did it not seem that Ossian had actually surpassed Homer in certain respects? Hugh Blair was positive that he had. Turning to the poets' use of machinery, Blair declared that "Ossian's mythology is, to speak so, the mythology of human nature; for it is founded on what has been the popular belief, in all ages and countries. . . . Homer's machinery is always lively and amusing; but far from being always supported with proper dignity. The indecent squabbles among his gods, surely do no honour to epic poetry."[51] Ossian's heroes were often considered superior: Fingal, Duff observed, is braver and more amiable than any of Homer's warriors; he "has all the qualities that can ennoble human nature; that can either make us admire the hero, or love the man."[52] Ossian appeared to be eminently more "refined" than Homer. According to Cameron, he did not describe brutal scenes "below the Dignity of an Epic Poem" but "the Bravery and Generosity of Heroes; the Tenderness of Lovers; the Attachments of Friends, Parents, and Children."[53] "This is indeed a surprizing Circumstance, that in Point of Humanity, Magnanimity, and virtuous Feelings of every Kind, our rude *Celtic* Bard should be distinguished to such a Degree, as not only the Heroes of *Homer,* but even those of the polite and refined *Virgil,* are left far behind by those of *Ossian.*"[54] Small wonder that Walpole, Hume, Johnson, and many others were skeptical about the authenticity of the Highland poems!

Scottish critics around 1750 were thus utilizing an approach that threatened to revolutionize epic theory completely. In maintaining that the greatest poetry is primitive, spontaneous, original, and natural, they were obviously questioning the worth of Virgil's *Aeneid*. In discovering crudities in the *Iliad* that were absent in *Fingal* and *Temora,* they were also casting some doubt upon the supremacy of Homer. Even the prestige of Milton was none too secure, for, as Duff pointed out, *Paradise Lost* was at best a notable exception to the rule, the only modern poem that evinced true originality and lofty imagination. As we shall see, primitivism was eventually to infiltrate Romantic criticism both in England and on the Continent, to help to establish the distinction between "natural" poetry and "artificial" poetry, to provide a new basis for estimating the place of the epic in the wide realm of literature. But one important thing remains to be said about Scottish theory in the mid-eighteenth century, namely, that it was on what appears to us as the horns of an embarrassing dilemma. In a sense it was at war with itself. No matter how enthusiastically each critic pursued the primitivistic approach to Homer and Ossian, he could not bring himself to the point of thoroughly repudiating neo-classical judgments and standards. Whether from fear of being derided or from plain conviction, he would have it that the early heroic poets were not only children of nature but also true artists, not only ebullient singers but poets whose works exemplified the soundest aesthetic principles. And in attempting to explain this dualism, his arguments were, to say the least, of an ingenious sort. Thus James Macpherson, having asserted that Ossian was an unlettered bard, proceeded to declare that *Temora* "resembles Homer" in adhering closely to the unities of time, place, and action, in skillfully describing events that had transpired prior to the main events of the poem, in opening *in medias res,* and in following the law of probability.[55] Since Ossian had no way of knowing the Greek rules of composition, the similarity between him and Homer "must proceed from nature."[56] Each poet had lived in a primitive era, each poet had copied directly from the life round about him, and each poet had thus achieved a high degree of artistry without really being aware of the fact. Likewise, Hugh Blair examined *Fingal* with care and announced

that this rhapsodic poem rarely departed from the principles of
Aristotle: "it will be found to have all the essential requisites of
a true and regular epic."[57] "All the incidents recorded bear a con-
stant reference to one end; no double plot is carried on; but the
parts unite into a regular whole: And as the action is one and
great, so it is an entire or compleat action." Blair insisted, in fact,
that "unity is indeed observed with greater exactness in Fingal,
than in almost any other Epic composition. For not only is
unity of subject maintained, but that of time and place also."[58]
Though unwilling to go along with Bossu, Blair explained that
a "general moral" could be extracted from the poem, specifically
that "Wisdom and Bravery always triumph over brutal force."[59]
The reason for this artistry, the reason too for an equivalent
degree of artistry in the primitive epics of Greece, was that
"Aristotle studied nature in Homer. Homer and Ossian both
wrote from nature. No wonder that among all the three, there
should be such agreement and conformity."[60]

Conceivably we may appear to have concentrated too long
on the various estimates of Homer, of Homer in comparison to
Ossian, and not long enough on the estimates of the other heroic
poets. There is justification, however, for this obvious lack of
proportion. Though Milton exercised a tremendous amount of
influence upon the English poets of the mid-eighteenth century,
one could scarcely claim that he evoked any highly significant
or original epic criticism during the many decades between Addi-
son's papers on *Paradise Lost* and Johnson's *Lives of the Poets*.
Such judgments as were passed did not differ substantially
from Addison's: they pertained to the effects of Milton's learning
upon his poetry, to his grandeur in general, to the boldness and
vividness of his conceptions, of specific lines and images, and to
the sublimity of the character of Satan. If *Paradise Lost* was
really beginning to come into its own, if the wider recognition it
received was tending to modify and liberalize the traditional con-
cept of "epic," one must grant nevertheless that neither Milton
nor Virgil nor Tasso nor Ariosto was so central a figure as Homer
in the literary criticism of the period, so prominent in the strug-
gle between old and new ideas, between neo-classical theories on

the one hand and primitivist, progressivist, and emotionalist theories on the other. Homer has always been the poet to come to mind the moment that discussion begins to focus upon the epic. It was certainly true in the span of time between the Renaissance and the end of the Age of Pope, for the chief criteria of literature as a whole were of course derived from Homer by way of Aristotle and Horace and Boileau. And it was still largely true in the era just prior to the appearance of the *Lyrical Ballads*. The reputation of the *Iliad* and *Odyssey* was a fairly accurate measure of the reputation of the epic as a kind; moreover, the way one estimated these poems indicated clearly the nature of one's basic critical proclivities. Openly to attack the Homeric epic or to quibble about its more barbarous manners was in essence to display a lack of faith in some of the fundamental assumptions of neo-classicism, to magnify the importance of the local and particular and to make it an artistic criterion. To admire Homer, and Ossian with him, as an ideal primitive bard singing from the depths of his heart was perhaps not to question Homer's prestige, but it was certainly to cast some doubt upon the validity of the neo-classical approach, to imply that the traditional concept of the epic, indeed the traditional concept of poetry in general, should be subjected to a complete reappraisal. During the mid-eighteenth century, in short, Homeric criticism indicates no sudden or radical departure from long-established values, but it evidences more clearly than the criticism of any one of the other heroic poets the direction which aesthetic theory, including epic theory, was destined to take with the arrival of the Age of Wordsworth.

Throughout the nineteenth century it was of course customary to vilify the Augustan critics, to belittle their insistence upon adhering to the rules, their idolatry of Homer and Aristotle, their way of dissecting poems into infinitesimal fragments, their emphasis upon the intellective aspects of art, and their distrust of emotionalism. Today, though much of this hostility appears to have evaporated, we are hardly more sympathetic than the Romantics with the bulk of the theories once advocated by the neo-classicists—with the view that all true epics conform rather

stringently to the pattern of the Homeric epic, that the time of
the action in a narrative poem should not extend much more than
a year, that the first book of an epic should begin quietly and
should contain few if any long similes, that a heroic poet should
carefully select a moral lesson and then an appropriate fable
to illustrate that lesson. Yet we can too easily forget that the
excesses and defects of the neo-classical approach were reasonably
well balanced by its virtues. At least there was a centrality in
Augustan criticism, a ground for agreeing about the chief aims
of an epic, a recognition of the poet's obligations to the society
in which he lived, of the factors that contribute to make a poem
ephemeral or immortal. At least the neo-classicist felt that he
knew what an epic is and how it differs in scope, purpose, and
value, from other kinds of verse. At least he understood the im-
portance of content (no great poem was simply an expression of
self) and of form (no great poem was merely "thrown together"
without any thought about its structure). Was it, after all, so
tyrannical and arbitrary to regard the *Iliad* as a work of art
superior to a two-line epigram or a fourteen-line sonnet that re-
flected at best some small item or facet of human experience?
Was it so wrong to insist upon precise standards of criticism, to
attempt to look beyond the purely local, the often meaningless
flux and change that is bound to manifest itself in art as in all
things that are organic? Certainly if we examine the critical devel-
opments around 1750, we can hardly say with any real confidence
that the new approaches marked a substantial advance over the
old neo-classical one. Perhaps we can approve of the extension of
the limits of epic, of the greater heed paid to backgrounds, to the
continuity which undoubtedly exists in literary history, to the
imagination and the emotions as efficient causes of poetry, to the
considerable merits of works of a non-heroic and non-dramatic
kind. At the same time, if we direct our attention to some of the
chief pronouncements that were made about the epic *per se*, we
cannot escape the general conclusion that the use of new criteria
failed to put an end to dogmatism and arbitrariness. It was illog-
ical and obviously narrow-minded to denounce Virgil simply
because he had followed Homer in planning the *Aeneid,* to over-

look completely the specific intention of the Roman epic and
what we would now call its unique vision of life. Also, as we
suggested earlier, the condemnations of Homer as a barbarian
were entirely unwarranted. They were the result of a deplorable
tendency that is still with us today: the tendency to assume that
the degree of social progress reflected in a literary work is a more
or less valid measure of its aesthetic worth. (Perhaps, too, Homeric
warfare seemed rather alien to the spirit of the eighteenth cen-
tury salon.) But little more can be said for the attitude of the
primitivist. In Blackwell we find a determinism almost as rigorous
as that of Taine a century later: it is hard to believe that Greek
climate, religion, manners, and the like, were more responsible
than Homer for the creation of the *Iliad* and *Odyssey*. It is
equally hard to believe that Ferguson and many others were not
being arbitrary when they asserted that primitive poetry is by
all odds the best poetry, that technical skill is unimportant,
that sheer exuberance is the only mark of vitality in art, that long
poems such as Homer's sprang into being almost on the spur of
the moment. And there can be no discountenancing the fact that
prejudice born of patriotism, an intentional blinding of oneself
to the truth, was responsible for the militant Scottish campaign
for Ossian, for the comparisons of Homer and Ossian which seem
so utterly ridiculous today. In fine, although the neo-classical
dispensation had shortcomings that needed attention, it was
evidently being undermined around 1750 by a variety of new
systems with new shortcomings of their own.

2 English Romantic Concepts of the Epic and Criticism of Dante and Milton

In the early nineteenth century, criticism in England lacked a real center, a principal focus. It was comprised of many foci, many strands of dissimilar opinion. Fundamental ideas were often in palpable conflict, or they impinged upon or merged with other ideas. Because of this complexity, antagonism, and fusion, scholars have found it impossible to give a succinct yet comprehensive description of "romanticism," and it is equally impossible, in the present study, to epitomize what critics in Wordsworth's day thought of epic poetry. It will be necessary, in fact, to approach our subject from a multiplicity of angles, to follow the rather artificial procedure of singling out key ideas, issues, and developments, and of treating each one separately even though it may be closely linked with others.

Just what is an epic? Earlier theorists had assumed that they knew, but theorists after 1800 often implied that they were by no means certain. Generally speaking, they were unsure because the traditional concept of a hierarchy of genres, after some modification during the preceding century, was now in a state of almost complete collapse. The historical approach, with its stress upon development and uniqueness, had demonstrated once and for all that many basic rather than merely the superficial characteristics of a literary work are determined by time and place, that two works are alike only insofar as the circumstances under which they are written are alike. The related biographical approach had

30

proved that creative literature grows out of and is therefore appreciably shaped by specific events that have occurred in authors' lives. And the psychological approach, if indeed it can be distinguished from the biographical, had shown that one's mental traits, one's inborn way of feeling and thinking about life, also condition what he writes. More and more it appeared that the emotions themselves, or at least the emotions as springing from or giving rise to thought, are the prime mover to literary composition. In a world that now seemed typified by change, by difference, by growth and decay, it was inconceivable that literature could be set apart from other products of the human spirit and treated as though it alone were subject to immutable principles. Neo-Aristotelian laws and formulae—emphasizing architectural construction from without in place of evolution from within, objective presentation of external action in place of psychological reaction or emotion and thought as they blend and interanimate one another, sharp, logical distinction in place of biological nuance—were now regarded not as being founded on the nature of things but as being really contrary to it.

This should not, of course, be taken to imply that "epic" ceased to have any denotation or use whatsoever. To treat every literary work exclusively as a unique entity unfolding according to its own inherent laws is tantamount to adopting the relativist view that critical judgment should yield to mere appreciation, and the Romantics, obviously enough, did not wish to go as far as that. They found good use for the term "epic"; they compared and evaluated heroic poems of various sorts. But there were attempts on all sides to re-define and to find new bases for classifying and estimating. In Germany, Friedrich Schlegel applied the term broadly to objective poetry as a whole, and his brother, though he sometimes came perilously close to the relativistic point of view, spoke of the epic as *the* classical genre, as "the calm, quiet representation of an action in progress."[1] In England a minor critic, Mrs. Barbauld, divided poetry into two kinds, placing the lyric in one category by itself and the epic, drama, and descriptive verse in a second category. Wordsworth referred to Narrative as a general class separable into six sub-classes: Epopoeia, His-

toric Poem, Tale, Romance, Mock-Heroic, and "if the spirit of
Homer will tolerate such neighbourhood, that dear production of
our days, the metrical Novel";[2] whereas Shelley employed "epic"
to denote any poem (specifically those of Dante and Homer)
which bears "a defined and intelligible relation to the knowledge
and sentiment and religion" of the particular era in which it is
written.[3] At the same time, critics usually held that poetic
types cannot be completely isolated, that the genres tend to shade
into one another. Hence there were discussions of heroic ballads,
epical dramas *(Samson Agonistes),* pastoral epics, and of course
romantic epics. A writer in the *Retrospective Review* of 1823
echoes Richard Hurd when he observes "how absurdly have the
critics undertaken to fix the number of species or classes";[4] they
have done injustice to Ariosto because, "having admitted no
species of epic but the heroic, they had no choice but that of
condemning the *Orlando.*" The pressing question for the age, he
adds, in agreement with many Renaissance theorists, is whether
"the poet, who has the genius to do so," can or cannot "trace out
a new line for himself, and invent a species of poetry unknown
to his predecessors."[5] Often critics' definitions were inclined to be
somewhat vague. Henry Hallam attributes the ridiculous practice
of comparing Homer and Milton to "a lax application of the word
epic" to their poems; he does not think the two have much in
common but he carefully avoids saying to what genre *Paradise
Lost* would seem to belong.[6] Likewise, Coleridge shows some
uncertainty when he speaks of several "epic poems of great merit"
written in Charlemagne's time, then decides to call them "heroic
tales" extracted from a cycle of "minstrelsies."[7] Percival Stockdale
at least assumes that an epic is a poem with some sort of fable,
a hero, and a supernatural agency, but he also believes that a
poet should have a right to vary these "agreeably to the infinite
diversity of the powers and operations of the human mind."[8] For
John Foster, on the other hand, "epic" is "a denomination about
which there has been, among critics, a vast deal of superstition—
a denomination as fairly applicable . . . to any narration of the
great military transactions that have decided the destiny of a
state, as to the *Iliad.*"[9] And there were one or two critics who

apparently despaired of arriving at any suitable definition. Though
it is not quite clear what he means, George Dyer says that tragedy,
satire, and epic "are all foreign terms";[10] while Bryan Procter
made a highly interesting comment of a similar sort in one of
his essays on English literature. After denouncing all the "rules"
of the Augustans, he declares that there is no point whatsoever
in trying to separate poetry into genres, that it matters little
whether a poem "be called an epic or a romance, an epistle or
a dirge, an epitaph, an ode, an elegy, a sonnet, or otherwise."
All he insists upon—here he reveals the frequent Romantic
subordination of form—is that the poem "be full of the material
of poetry."[11]

If such general pronouncements would have distressed theorists
in Pope's day, so too would many of the early nineteenth century
remarks about particular poems. Thus a writer in the *Reflector*
elevates Firdusi almost to Homer's level despite the fact that
the Persian poet had disregarded those "minuter excellences" of
the epic, the fable and the unities;[12] and Hallam, in the same
breath that he says *Paradise Regained* is really "a drama of primal
simplicity" and the *Odyssey* is not "a legitimate epic," calls it
pure pedantry to refer to the *Orlando Furioso* as a romance
rather than an epic simply because it lacks a protagonist and a
continuity of action.[13] Form seemed to matter so little that the
Iliad was freely compared (Addison having prepared the way)
to early English ballads, to parts of Chaucer, to primitive war
songs, and even to prose romances. And there is the curious par-
allel between Wordsworth and Milton which was drawn by
Henry Crabb Robinson. Wordsworth, he allows, cannot right-
fully be called an epic poet, but "it is also true that what lives in
the hearts of readers from the works of Milton is not the epic
poem. Milton's story has merit unquestionably; but it is rather a
lyric than an epic narrative."[14] Once again we see how radically
emphasis was being transferred from action and plot to emotion-
alism.

Most critics were as unwilling as Robinson to speak of the
Excursion as "heroic," but they were ready enough to award this
adjective to other contemporary verse. Anna Seward, for in-

stance, finds the *Lay of the Last Minstrel* a truly original epic poem, "one of the most exquisite effusions of poetic fancy" in the English language, and she thinks that *Madoc* surpasses Southey's other "noble epic," the *Joan of Arc*.[15] Prejudiced as usual against Homer and Virgil, Coleridge wrote highly enthusiastic letters about *Madoc,* assuring its author that it had none of the glaring faults of the *Aeneid*. Similarly, William Erskine calls *The Vision of Don Roderick* an epic poem; "it is enough for us, and it would, we believe, have been enough for Aristotle," he says with a liberality typical of the time, "that a narrative should have plot, and interest, and action and pathos."[16] Nor did Sir Egerton Brydges see any reason to remonstrate about a view which he avers was then current, namely, that "Lord Byron is almost always *epic;* for he is almost always narrative";[17] and, like Southey, Byron himself spoke of *Joan of Arc* and the *Curse of Kehama* as genuine epic poems. For that matter, he explained rather facetiously, "if you must have an epic, there's *Don Juan* for you. I call that an epic; it is an epic as much in the spirit of our day as the *Iliad* was in Homer's. . . . I shall make my hero a perfect Achilles for fighting,—a man who can snuff a candle three successive times with a pistol-ball: and depend upon it, my moral will be a good one; not even Dr. Johnson should be able to find a flaw in it!"[18] Finally, there is Joseph Cottle, who introduced his *Alfred: an Epic Poem* to the world with the explanatory statement that episodes of high drama had been substituted for the usual horrifying accounts of battles and treacherous deeds.[19]

Comments like these were by no means exceptional; they occur abundantly in English critical writings after 1800. Some were casually made in order to supply a poem with a certain aura of grandeur that presumably emanates from the very word "epic," but all of them point to one significant fact: that in rejecting the old concept of the genres, in refusing to separate form from content and to treat it as a main basis for classification, critics were becoming quite uncertain as to the implications of "epic." They were bold enough in using the term; they thought it should mean something. However, they did not demand that a so-called epic poem should have formal unity or a certain length, a great or an important action, a mighty or even a principal hero, a race of gods or any other invisible agency. Often all that was expected was a slender thread of narrative detectable here and there in a moderately long poem, and sometimes merely an elevation of style, lofty imagination, or a nobility of spirit. True, more traditional definitions were not lacking in the Romantic period, but the frequent indecision of which we have spoken, the vagueness and broadness of conception, were rendering the term less meaningful. And this tendency, together with the tendency to prostitute "epic" by conferring it upon many poems that were far from grand or serious or in any sense permanently valuable, was clearly encouraging disrespect for the genre as a whole.

Rejection of neo-classical assumptions and dicta had another and possibly an even more important effect upon epic criticism. The way was now open for new systems of classification, systems which helped to lower rather than raise the prestige of heroic poetry. To be sure, separation of poetry into merely three basic kinds (epic, drama, and lyric) did not always militate against the epic, especially in Germany. But the Schlegelian division of Romantic (subjective) and Classical (objective), which we shall discuss in detail later, caused a pronounced reaction in some quarters against the Greek and Roman epic, and an indirect one against the heroic tradition as a whole. Moreover, the new methods of classifying entailed new critical emphases which were very largely inimical to the epic in general. For various reasons it was widely believed that the drama is superior to the epic. Thus in the writings of A. W. Schlegel, tragedy emerges as the most picturesque, and to the modern world, the most pertinent of the kinds. In England, Hazlitt waxed absurdly poetic about all sorts of verse, but his view of poetry as primarily the expression and communication of strong emotion, and his reference to the drama as filling one with "terror and pity" and the epic as creating "admiration and delight" would seem to suggest that he preferred a good tragedy even to a sublime and emotive epic like Milton's. In fact, the drama's immediacy of appeal, its "vehemence" as A. W. Schlegel called it, was widely cited as a chief reason for its superiority. Thomas Campbell, much as he enjoyed Homer, admitted that the typical epic only "calls us to be hearers of an amusing narrative";[20] while a writer in the *Edinburgh Review,* obviously influenced by German criticism, takes a rather different view of the matter. "A narrative poem," he says, "is perhaps more tempting in its shape than a play, and may fix the attention more deeply in the closet; but it is addressed to a more limited class, and necessarily affects our sympathies less forcibly; for a Drama is an embodying of the present, while an Epic is only a shadow of the past."[21] Coleridge's approach was both historical and philosophical. After describing the evolution of the drama from the epic, he joins Goethe and Schiller in preferring the drama because it represents fate as conflicting with and finally conquering the human will but not, as in the case of the epic, dominating it from beginning to end.[22] Nor was Coleridge the only one to eulogize Shakespeare at the expense of Homer and Virgil. Apparently accepting the dichotomy of Classical and Romantic, many writers lauded the intricate analysis of human nature typical of the Elizabethan drama and deplored the objective and superficial way in which character was depicted in the ancient epic. According to Anna Seward, for example, no sensible person could possibly prefer Homer's "score of heroes, who, Hector, Priam, and Telemachus excepted, are not much else besides heroes, to Shakespeare's masterly display of every character, every situation, and every scene in many-coloured life."[23] We are a very long way indeed from Sidney's and Pope's reverence for Achilles and Ulysses!

A more fundamental reason for Romantic depreciation of heroic poetry was of course the mounting interest in the lyric. Patently enough, it was now believed almost universally that plot is not a requisite in great poetry, that, as Hazlitt said, the real mission of the poet is the forceful communication of emotion, or, as Wordsworth put it, the communication of emotion recollected in tranquillity. The lyric seemed ideal as a vehicle, unsurpassable for the embodiment of one's feelings about the world of nature or of man; its sheer brevity, Mill suggested, gave it a special intensity. In comparison, the epic appeared too coldly statuesque and grand, too much the product of the conscious mind or of emotions that had lost most of their strength. Even the drama, because of its elaborateness and because of the interposition of the characters, did not permit any very intimate communication between the poet and his audience.

In England, at least, most of the Romantic comparisons between epic and lyric were implied rather than stated. They can best be detected in recurring complaints about the long-windedness of regular heroic poems and the patience that was required to read them from beginning to end. For example, Reginald Heber declares that an age "which has rioted so much in the richness of original productions" looks with "something more than weariness on the long and regular narratives" from which readers in the previous century had "derived years of calm and deep enjoyment."[24] In one of his prefaces, Thomas Musgrave says that the plan of the *Lusiad* should cause no distress for the simple reason that, while the modern reader may possibly return to the "beautiful or interesting passages" of an epic poem, he is rarely tempted to re-peruse the poem as a whole.[25] Even with England's own Milton people were obviously finding some fault, for Byron speaks of those "great epics that nobody reads,"[26] and Wordsworth complains "how few, how very few" read *Paradise Lost* except as a "religious book."[27] But there is one statement in the *Edinburgh Review* of October, 1809, which perhaps sums up best the current distaste for long and ponderous epics; it occurs in a review sometimes attributed to Francis Jeffrey. Having launched an attack on Barlow's *Columbiad,* the writer asserts that it is highly doubtful "whether *any* long poem of the Epic character will ever again be popular in Europe." There is "so much of imitation about them"—they seem so artificial—that the average reader cannot resist the impulse to turn elsewhere for entertainment. Homer, Virgil, and Milton perhaps stirred the interest of previous generations, the reviewer concludes, but "in the present state of society, we require, in poetry, something more natural or more impassioned, and, at all events, something less protracted and monotonous than the sober pomp and deliberate stateliness of the Epic."[28]

The lyric was of course a relatively new rival of the epic while the drama was not. But it was not always purely a matter of competition between the two or three basic kinds of poetry, for an especially potent and an essentially new challenger was the novel. In the mid-eighteenth century, we will recall, Fielding's *Tom Jones* had not only belittled many of the devices of the epic but had also proclaimed itself an epic of the modern sort. Much later Friedrich Schlegel actually placed some modes of the novel ahead of both the drama and the epic. And in England at about the same time, the efflorescence of prose fiction and the tremendous popularity of Scott in particular did much to lower esteem for long and formal narratives in verse, to make regular epics seem largely outmoded. In exalting Scott, one reviewer says that the novel of the present time can rightly be regarded as "an accommodation of the ancient epic to the average capacity of the numberless readers of modern times."[29] Epics are for the learned few; novels are for everybody. In a somewhat different vein, a commentator on Godwin's *Mandeville* writes that the epic had represented its hero as contending with "the worst attacks of external enmity, treacheries, and wrath," while the hero of modern prose fiction has to combat, usually without success, his own "wishes, prejudices, principles, and passions." "The march of human thought has been slow," he continues, "but its effects are sufficiently perceptible, and the most trivial of novelists does not weave his flimsy web of fiction without bearing testimony to the progress we have made. What was darkly hinted by the profound philosophers of old, is now familiarly illustrated by the popular creations of female fancy."[30] Knowledge had supposedly advanced so much that even romantic authoresses could now hope to compete with Homer.

This tendency to think of the modern novel as a substitute for the traditional epic was complemented by another important tendency. Great poets, truly great poets, will probably have a following in any era, but it is doubtful that a genre *as a genre* will continue to be so highly esteemed once successful works are no longer being added to it; it will become to some extent a mere historical curiosity. To be sure, authors still composed epic poems in the early nineteenth century (Southey immediately comes to mind), and there was optimistic talk about still greater epics in the future (Schelling), about the legends of India and Scandinavia, about the heroes of Britain, about Columbus, Cortez, and William Penn as possible subjects for aspiring heroic poets in coming generations. But there were also many comments which suggested that the day for writing worthwhile epics now lay in the rather remote past. Though Southey's republican and moralistic "heroic poems" enjoyed a momentary vogue, most literary magazines deplored such "epics" as Barlow's *Columbiad,* Cottle's *Alfred,* Cumberland's *Calvary,* and Hole's *Arthur;* and Englishmen called Klopstock, author of the *Messiah,* "the Birmingham Milton." Typical is a review of F. A. Parseval's *Philippe-Auguste: Poëme Héroïque, en Douze Chants* (1826): "M. Parseval has put mankind in possession of one more unquestioned epic, . . . crammed full of similes, visions, and prophecies; heroes of the most spotless magnanimity, and cowardly giants ten feet high; . . . charms, invocations, sorcerers, demons, enchanted bowers . . . and great battles of 200,000 on a side, in which the fate of the day is uniformly decided by some phenomenon from the clouds, . . . in a word, all the old 'materias vatum.' "[31] Mickle, a translator of Ariosto, observed that subjects for epics "are perhaps exhausted";[32] and Thomas Campbell complained that "the world is too old to afford us any thing original; nothing is left but to display our skill in and taste in cooking up a Refacimento."[33] Others suggested that materialism and science threatened the extinction of the poetic spirit in general, or had exploded the lingering belief in the marvelous and rendered both pagan and Christian myth unsuitable for modern poems. A rather different reason for skepticism about the future of heroic poetry was given by John Foster in one of his magazine articles. "Our times are unfavorable, to the last degree, to the writers of that kind of poetry commonly called epic." The great turmoil of the modern world, with its revolutions and military conquests, had made epic tales of war seem quite insipid. "We read or talk, over our wine or coffee, of some great battle that has recently decided the fate of a kingdom with an emotion nearly as transient as of an old bridge carried away in our neighbourhood by a flood."[34] Epics were for times when people needed to be stimulated by fictitious stories.

In discussing Romantic concepts of the epic and of its place among literary types, we have of course selected some of the newer and more radical points of view. In doing so we may have seemed to intimate that the prestige of heroic poetry was suddenly and completely destroyed as soon as, or soon after, Wordsworth, Scott, and the German critics became well-known in England. But this was clearly not the case. For one thing, more conservative and traditional opinions survived throughout the Romantic period, and today some are still being sanctioned in certain quarters. Neither Wordsworth nor Coleridge entirely repudiated neo-classical tenets; Leigh Hunt, differing with the common German and English view, said that the epic is the highest poetic type, "for it includes the drama, with narration besides";[35] Henry N. Coleridge referred to the epic as speaking "in the all-pervading language of essential human nature";[36] and Jeffrey, though his opinions were not steady or precise, could advocate common sense, morality, and propriety as basic standards for literature. Sounding very much like a comment from a critical essay of the early 1700's is one that appeared in the *Athenaeum* in 1807: "the small number of performances admitted into the rank of perfect epic poems, tends to inspire us with a high idea of the difficulty of this species of writing."[37] For a goodly number of critics, a heroic poem was still properly an invaluable imitation of men in action, a unified narrative revealing fundamental human traits; it was still largely a product of judgment and inventiveness, of uncanny craft, of wide knowledge. Moreover, one should not forget that the lyric was frequently denounced as having become sentimental and excessively introspective; it seemed too much concerned with moods and personal eccentricities. And the novel, however popular it might be, was often accused of corrupting morals, of being wasteful of a man's time. But none of this offsets the fact that the whole climate of opinion—the rejection of older definitions and estimates, the new esteem for other literary types, the increasing stress upon emotionality and subjectivism—was doing a great deal to make the epic seem rather out-of-date, to make it seem rather elementary and even primitive.

In Pope's day references to the epic as a definite species had been extremely frequent for the simple reason that only one kind of epic, the Homeric or classical, was generally recognized. The *Gierusalemme Liberata* had been approved only insofar as it seemed to conform to the Homeric pattern, and the *Orlando Furioso* had been thought at best a rather undesirable aberration from that pattern. In the Age of Wordsworth, on the contrary, sweeping statements and allusions regarding the species were comparatively rare; indeed, considering the fact that the genres no longer seemed at all fixed, that there was so much emphasis upon individuality, organicism, historical locus, and the like, one is rather surprised to discover that epics were discussed collectively as often as they were. However that may be, it was a much more usual procedure after 1800 to ignore entirely the matter of classification, to consider the *Iliad* or *Paradise Lost* as a poem in isolation and to judge it by itself on the basis of emotionality or some other favored criterion; or, with the same or a similar criterion in mind, to compare it broadly to another epic, to a play, a romance, or a ballad. In such cases criticism of course amounted to little more than criticism of particular poems as poems. Also quite customary was a practice traceable ultimately to the Battle of Ancients and Moderns and derived more recently from German as well as English theory, that of dichotomizing into traditions or broad types—into pagan and Christian, Classical and Romantic, ancient and modern, or simply original and derivative, primitive and civilized. Sometimes the division was made rather unconsciously and subtly; it was insinuated by the way in which critics spoke of specific literary works. Sometimes, too, it led to nothing more than generous recognition of the respective values of the two traditions or types, and thus of the epics and other poems belonging to each. But in making a dichotomy, of whatever sort and whether implicitly or explicitly, writers were very often inclined to take sides, to find, for instance, the Homeric epic better than the Miltonic or the Miltonic better than the Homeric. Since these procedures were the prevailing ones, we must now turn from the broad pronouncements on the epic as a species to Romantic discussions of its sub-species and of particular epic poems and epic poets. These discussions, based as they were on a variety of critical assumptions, and conflicting with one another as they so often do, are not only valuable to a study of epic criticism but are at the same time indicative of the almost unbelievable heterogeneity of Romantic criticism in general.

Following the lead of critics after 1800, we too will make a dichotomy, treating first what was said about modern epics, and then about primitive and classical epics. Obviously, since the number of heroic poems written in the Christian era is so vast, it would be almost impossible to examine Romantic appraisals of each and every one, and in any event an attempt to do so would result in a complete loss of focus. Hence, the judgments passed on contemporary verse narratives will be largely neglected; it is doubtful, anyway, whether we today think of them as bona fide epics. Nor would there seem to be a cogent reason to pay much heed to criticisms of Tasso and Ariosto, for they were not especially numerous and the majority were rather disposed to echo estimates made by critics in the latter half of the eighteenth century. Dante and Milton were the central figures. Long deprecated in England because of the "irregularities" of the *Divine Comedy,* Dante emerged around 1800 as one of the principal heroic poets. Now that "the old imperial code of criticism" had been fully discredited, Boyd said that Dante's poem could be rightly called a genuine epic; and Hunt, Shelley, D'Israeli, Robert Morehead, and others proceeded to speak of it as one or at least to compare it freely with the *Iliad* and *Paradise Lost.* Milton had of course been "discovered" long ago, but during the Romantic period he was imitated right and left, and his prestige rose to greater heights than ever. Of all the world's important poets, only Shakespeare was generally conceded to be more important than he.

Much as Romantic critics were interested in the evolution of literature, in the effects of time and place, it is unthinkable that they would overlook or reject universality as a chief quality of literary masterpieces. There was, however, some disagreement about the way or ways in which the heroic poetry of Dante and Milton was presumed to have transcended the local and particular. Well aware that neither poet had tried to depict human nature by means of outward action, that the neo-Aristotelian concepts of universality did not seem to apply, some persons took the view which Boyd expressed in the preface to his translation of the *Inferno*. Boyd said that while the *Iliad* could be of real value only to a Greek—an opinion that would have appeared heretical to any neo-classicist—Dante's poem is an epic that will appeal "wherever the natural love of virtue and justice, and the notion of a moral Governor of the Universe prevails; wherever the notion of Providence is found; . . . wherever the power of conscience, and the idea of right and wrong, and of future rewards and punishments governs the human breast."[38] In short, Homer interests not all men, but the patriotic citizens of one nation; Dante interests not one nation, but all men who are Christians. Shelley, on the other hand, does away with any such sharp distinctions. Though he assumes that literature is perpetually changing in its outward forms and may also reflect the individuality of an author, his neo-Platonic idea that every great poet "participates in the eternal, the infinite, the one," and that a poem, instead of being merely a copy of a copy, is "the creation of actions according to the unchangeable forms of human nature, as existing in the mind of the creator," suggests that the timelessness of Dante is for him essentially identical with that of Homer. These two poets are universal in the same way and perhaps to the same extent. But quite unlike the neo-classicist, who held that the value of great poetry is always more or less the same for all educated persons, Shelley also thinks that different ages will continue to discover new and different facets in a poet like Dante. "His very words are instinct with spirit; each is a spark . . .; and many lie covered in the ashes of their birth, and pregnant with a lightning which has yet found no conductor."[39]

Naturally, Shelley speaks in a similar way of Milton. But most critics defined the universality of *Paradise Lost* in a somewhat different fashion. Going beyond the position of Boyd yet not so far as Shelley, Coleridge suggests on one occasion that the "interest" in Milton's epic "transcends the limits of a nation; . . . [it] is wider than Christianity; . . . nay, still further, . . . it contains matter of deep interest to all mankind, as forming the basis of all religion, and the true occasion of all philosophy whatsoever."[40] Elsewhere Coleridge speaks of the poem as a "translation of reality into the ideal," and again, following Schelling, he refers to it as striving for the infinite.[41] Similarly, Hazlitt observes that Milton interests to a considerable extent because he calmly "abstracts" circumstances "from the world of reality to that of contemplation," thus giving them a "permanence and universality."[42] Hartley Coleridge agrees with his father; Milton's ideals, he says, "seem more substantial, more real, than any actual reality."[43] And a reviewer, in commenting about Milton, declares that "nothing was ever so *unearthly* as his poetry." Echoing Samuel Johnson's words but intending praise rather than blame, he adds that "nothing like any part of it had ever been matter of human experience."[44]

Clearly, all of these comments point to a concept, or more correctly, concepts, of universality uncommon in the preceding century. The modern epic, it was now implied, does not achieve immortality through the deliberate operation of the poet's imagination in recalling and combining, or through purposeful illustration of ethical truths that are valid according to human reason and human reason alone, or through the portrayal, by means of a sequence of outward actions, of the central motives and passions of all men—of wrath as personified in Achilles, for example. Permanence of interest lies, variously, in a seeking for the infinite; in vivid representation of the Christian ideal, or of the ideal of religion as a whole, or of the ideal of truth or beauty either as present in the mind of the poet, or as reflected in the actual and grasped intuitively by the imagination of the poet. Critics were not in agreement as to how the poet seized upon any of these ideals, but they did concur in the opinion that great art must transfigure and bring into harmony the ordinary objects of the everyday world and the ordinary experiences of life. And here it might be well to reiterate a point which can easily be obscured, namely, that however strongly intuition, originality, and sheer emotionalism may have been stressed around 1800, theorists did not always imply that untutored genius could produce the greater works of art. Sometimes it was said that emotion had to be filtered through the mind and transformed into what we today would call emotionalized thought. At other times it was argued that to write a truly fine poem one needed first to gain an understanding of the past, of its literature and philosophy. Dante was thus often thought of as bridging the ancient and modern worlds and Milton was applauded as a poet who had synthesized in his epic poetry the valuable heritage of classical antiquity and of the Renaissance. Nor did all this emphasis upon idealism and intellectuality merely mean higher prestige for the modern epic. It gave greater credence to the notion, going back to the seventeenth century, that art tends to be progressive. Whatever funds of knowledge Homer may have had, his funds were bound to seem scanty compared to those of Dante and Milton, his pagan ideals could not be said to rival those of the Christian era, nor was he able, as Stockdale put it, to benefit from "the gradual, general, and collateral improvements of the human mind" itself.[45] He appeared to be much too mundane and unphilosophic, much too concerned with the outward aspects of nature and of man. Here, then, was an indication that praise of modern epics could easily imply dispraise of classical and primitive ones.

Though estimates emphasized the matter of timelessness, a second main point urged in favor of the Italian and English epic was its extreme subjectivity. As we have intimated again and again, critics in the Romantic period openly dissented from the Augustan opinion that human reason plays a principal role in poetic creation. Believing instead that the basic factor is emotion, they became more deeply interested than earlier theorists in the psychological make-up of an author, his states of mind, the more impressive events in his life, and, in fact, the whole social milieu into which he had been born. Explanations of how a literary work came into being were easily transmuted into actual judgments of that work, and one's personal estimate of Dante and Milton, of Ariosto and Tasso, as reached through study of their poetry often became an estimate of the poetry itself. Thus one critic praises Ariosto's "fine animal spirits," his "heroic sensibility mixed with vivacity," and his "eye for nature."[46] In a sense the poem and the poet become one; they seem almost indistinguishable. Hazlitt admired the *Divine Comedy* in part because of "the continued earnestness of the author's mind," and he visualizes Dante as "power, passion, self-will personified," standing on the brink of the modern world, "bewildered" and "lost in wonder." "He interests," Hazlitt adds, "by exciting our sympathy with the emotion by which he is himself possessed."[47] Boyd, totally unresponsive to the objectivity of Homer, observes that Dante presents the reader "with a nearer and inward view of the man";[48] while Hunt emphasizes the "constant detail of thought and feeling" exhibited in the *Divine Comedy,* and the "passion" of the poet as he tells his story.[49] Arthur Hallam thinks of Dante as pouring forth his emotions, and speaks with high approval of the poet's "deep-drawn aspirations," his "fervent thoughts," and the "reverential feeling which seemed to possess the poet's imagination."[50] Rather more interesting, however, are some of Coleridge's remarks about *Paradise Lost.* Strongly influenced by German conceptions of "romantic" literature as subjective (personal, intense) and of "classical" literature as objective (impersonal, calm), Coleridge bluntly condemns Homer because he did not express his own feelings about the fall of Troy and then eulogizes Milton because he allowed *Paradise Lost* to mirror his personality, convictions, and emotions. In the English epic, he observes, "it is Milton himself whom you see; his Satan, his Adam, his Raphael, almost his Eve—are all John Milton; and it is a sense of this intense egotism that gives me the greatest pleasure in reading Milton's works. The egotism of such a man is a revelation of spirit."[51] On another occasion Coleridge notes that in Christian poetry in general "the reflective character" is predominant. Despite the stress he sometimes placed upon impersonality, good sense and judgment, he could add that "in the *Paradise Lost* the sub-limest parts are the revelations of Milton's own mind, producing itself and evolving its own greatness; and this is so truly so, that when that which is merely entertaining for its objective beauty is introduced, it at first seems a discord."[52]

But proponents of the modern epic often went further, per-mitting biographical data drawn from external sources—from tradition, records, and earlier lives—to color their judgments of *Paradise Lost* and the *Divine Comedy*. Just as Byron's poetry was often sanctioned or execrated, depending upon what one thought of the man, so expressions of admiration for Dante and Milton enhanced the good opinion of their epics. Hallam, for instance, speaks sympathetically of Dante as "the embittered exile, the man worn out by the world's severest realities, who knew how sharp it was to mount another's stairs, and eat another's bread, in his old age."[53] And William Godwin declares that the Italian poet is "one of those geniuses who in the whole series of human existence most baffle all calculation, and excite unbounded astonishment." Living in a dark age of danger and strife, "he trampled upon those disadvantages, and presents us with sallies of imagination and energies of composition, which no past age of literature has excelled, and no future can ever hope to excel."[54] There seemed to the admirers of Milton something particularly inexplicable, some-thing paradoxical and challenging about the English poet. A writer in the *Edinburgh Review* declares that "everything about Milton is wonderful; but nothing is so wonderful as that, in an age so unfavourable to poetry, he should have produced the greatest of modern epic poems."[55] Milton was like Socrates, Cole-ridge intimates; both had flourished "whilst pestilence, with a thousand furies running to and fro, . . . was shooting her darts of fire and venom all around";[56] and Stockdale, characterizing him as a "comet of rare appearance," finds it clear proof of Milton's exceptional genius that he rose above "the coarseness and vulgar-ity" of the age.[57] Again and again critics spoke of his isolation with the deepest respect; for them he became one of the "mis-understood" poets, an object of sympathy, an example of true poetic genius which, it was often believed in the Romantic period, ever finds itself at odds with its environment. Shelley declares that "Milton stood alone, illuminating an age unworthy of him,"[58] John Wilson, that he was obliged to draw "his poetry from the depths of his own spirit brooding over nature and human life,"[59] Hazlitt, that he "lived apart, in the solitude of his own thoughts,"[60] Campbell, that he was "alone and aloof above his times, the bard of immortal subjects."[61]

If Milton's isolation qualified him for the role of "ideal poet" as many critics conceived of that role, his blindness evoked the most highly sympathetic and even sentimental comments. Nathan Drake says that for "the divine and hallowed Milton, . . . blind, and aged, and forsaken, . . . an added tear must fall";[62] and Brydges, in a similar vein, that "blind, poor, exposed to insult and threatened with frightful dangers . . .; he threw off the incumbent weight like a giant, and behold the *Paradise Lost* broke out in all its splendour."[63] Especially one should not forget Wordsworth's great sonnet to Milton in 1802, or his famous reference in the *Prelude:*

> *Yea, our blind poet, who, in his later day,*
> *Stood almost single, uttering odious truth,*
> *Darkness before, and danger's voice behind;*
> *Soul awful! if the earth has ever lodg'd*
> *An awful Soul.*[64]

Sympathy for a sublime, self-reliant, and unfortunate soul could hardly help meaning admiration for the verse in which that soul expressed its most intimate feelings and beliefs. Far from being merely a "maker" or contriver, the poet is now in the poem. As suggested before, he *is* the poem, and the two cannot be considered separately.

Another reason people liked these modern epics concerned the kinds of characters they portrayed. For the neo-classicist, human beings like Achilles or Ulysses had always seemed more deserving of attention than Circe or Calypso or Polyphemus, but for many writers around 1800 Ariosto was a great poet because not a few of the actors in his epic (as also in Spenser's *Fairie*

Queene) were supernatural rather than human—weird monsters, dragons, goblins, fictions of the creative imagination rather than realities of nature. Leigh Hunt was not alone in praising the way Ariosto had handled his "wild story of a cannibal necromancer, who laughs at being cut to pieces, coming together again like quicksilver, and picking up his head when it is cut off, sometimes by the hair, sometimes by the nose!"[65] Such "romantic" tales were not merely for children; adults found them surprising, awe-inspiring, a means of escape from their dull everyday world. In the *Divine Comedy,* on the other hand, it was of course the protagonist of the poem, Dante himself, who seemed most interesting, and to a lesser degree Paolo, Francesca, and Ugolino, and other characters whose fate shocked or saddened one. But the characters of *Paradise Lost* were no less popular. Exhibiting the common Romantic tendency to judge on the basis of sheer "imagination" and the emotional sublime, critics frequently spoke of Satan as the most wonderful character not only in all epic poetry but in all literature. Thus Hazlitt refers to the rebel angel, in virtually the same words that he had referred to Dante himself, as "the abstract love of power, of pride, of self-will personified"; Satan is "the most heroic subject" ever chosen by a poet.[66] In Landor's *Imaginary Conversations,* Southey praises him because he is so "energetic;"[67] while Coleridge says that Satan represents the "alcohol of egotism," that around him Milton "has thrown a singularity of daring, a grandeur of sufferance, and ruined splendour, which constitute the very height of poetic sublimity."[68] According to Shelley, Satan "as a moral being" is superior to the God of *Paradise Lost;* he perseveres in spite of adversity, while God "in the cold security of undoubted triumph inflicts the most horrible revenge upon his enemy."[69] Surely this remark must have shocked many of those people who read *Paradise Lost,* so Wordsworth said, purely as a "religious book." But Procter paints an even more glowing picture of Milton's Devil. The rebel chief, he thinks, "is the most magnificent creation in poetry.... He is not like Macbeth or Lear, real in himself, literally true, and only lifted into poetry by circumstance: but he is altogether moulded in a dream of the imagination.

Heaven and earth and hell are explored for gifts to make him eminent and peerless. He is compounded of all; and at last stands up before us, with the starry grandeur of darkness upon his forehead, but having the passions of clay within his heart."[70] That Satan was Milton himself was an idea occasionally suggested in the Romantic period. Blake declared that the two were almost identical, while Chateaubriand, Shelley, Keats, and Coleridge ascribed to Milton the traits of several of the characters in *Paradise Lost.*

Adam and Eve were no rivals for Satan. They did not really seem like human beings; they reminded one of the rather insipid folk of the mythical Golden Age, or perhaps of the too-innocent Phaeacians of the *Odyssey.* But a few critics in Wordsworth's time did speak out in defense of Adam and his spouse. In direct answer to the charge that *Paradise Lost* lacks human interest, Hayley points to "the delicious tranquillity of innocence, the tormenting turbulence of guilt, and the consolatory satisfaction of repentance."[71] Stockdale, thinking of the pair in the Garden, asserts that Milton was "as much a master of the tender, and beautiful, as he was, of the striking and sublime."[72] Similarly, Procter declares that "nothing can be more beautiful than his pictures of our 'first parents' breathing the fragrant airs of Eden, communing with superior natures, dreaming in the golden sun, feeding upon nectareous fruits, and lying 'imparadised' in one another's arms, on pillows of violet and asphodel."[73] Nor is Hazlitt less adulatory. Replying to the objection that there is insufficient action in the later books of Milton's epic, he exclaims, "What need was there of action, where the heart was full of bliss and innocence without it!" Adam and Eve "were as yet alone in the world, in the eye of nature, wondering at their new being, . . . with the voice of their Maker walking in the garden, and . . . winged messengers from heaven like rosy clouds descending in their sight."[74] It seems apparent, however, that Romantic critics were more deeply impressed by the sublime and rebellious than by the idyllically happy characters of the epic.

Another main basis for approval of the modern epic grew out of its emphasis not on "defects" in the eighteenth century manner but on vaguely admired isolated "beauties." While emotionalism appeared to critics after 1800 a prime ingredient of poetry, there was difference of opinion as to the extent to which and the manner in which it should manifest itself in a poem. An extreme view was that emotionalism should reign throughout: Henry Crabb Robinson and John Stuart Mill both held that a literary work like *Paradise Lost* is effective only insofar as it is lyrical rather than epic by nature, and Poe in America of course branded Milton's poem a host of detachable lyrics with "unpoetical" matter thrust in between. The usual opinion, however, was rather less extreme. Many critics acknowledged the merits of narrative as narrative at the same time that they relished the "happiness" of a part, an image, a simile, the brief bursts of sincere passion in the segments of a poem, or the vividness of a phrase, a line, or a series of lines—parts which mysteriously yet unmistakably evoked feelings of pleasure or ecstasy in the sensitive reader. If such feelings appeared to be frequent enough and, above all, intense and "elevating" enough, the critic believed it his privilege or duty to call attention to their source and to base his evaluation of a poem to some extent upon them, or as was often the case with Lamb, Hunt, and De Quincey, almost entirely upon them. Ariosto's "wild fancies" were commonly pointed out, and Romantic estimates repeatedly concern the sublime images and highly "imaginative touches" rather than the structure of the *Divine Comedy,* the many evidences of Dante's "bold" language and his vivid or awesome expressions rather than the indications of his skill as a contriver. William Godwin speaks of Dante's ability in certain passages to make "a man's flesh creep upon his bones,"[75] and T. J. Mathias asks, "from what other Poet, ancient or modern, could I draw forth such expressions?"[76] Likewise, appraisals of Milton, especially Hazlitt's, were full of phrases of a highly enthusiastic sort—phrases like "unmeasurable domains of fancy," "captivating forms and majestic motion," "one continued tension of imaginative strength," "creative opulence," "copiousness," and "the thunder and lightning of poetry." Obviously, such phrases are generalizations about recurring experiences of pleasure, experiences one might have in reading not only modern epics but other kinds of poetry as well. In fact, a Beethoven symphony could produce a similar effect.

Viewed as a whole, these appraisals clearly point to the enormous popularity of modern epics. But no era, surely, gives anything like unanimous approval to any poet, and the Romantic period, with its great diversity of critical approaches and attitudes, did not quite make idols of Dante and Milton, Ariosto and Tasso. The latter two were often censured for their manifold irregularities, their glittering images, and their artificialities; the former two, for supposed defects of various kinds. There were objections to Dante's style, his allusions to long-forgotten persons and events, the obscurity of his allegory (especially in "Purgatorio" and "Paradiso"), and his infusion of burlesque. Robinson said that only about one-seventieth of Dante is "good,"[77] a remark which shows how much attention was being paid to parts rather than the whole. Preferring Milton, Landor observes that Dante's characters "are without any bond of union, any field of action, any definite aim. There is no central light above the Bolge; and we are chilled in Paradise even at the side of Beatrice."[78] But the letters of Anna Seward perhaps sum up best the complaints usually made about the Italian poet, complaints one would expect to come from addicts of the novel. Thinking only of the *Inferno,* the part of Dante's epic most commonly read in that day, Miss Seward declares that "there is little for the heart, or even for the curiosity as to story"; there is "terror, terror, nothing but terror." She calls Dante "this fire and smoke" poet, a monotonous egotist; and avers that the "terrible graces" of the *Inferno* "lose all their dignity in butcherly, gridiron, and intestinal exhibitions."[79] It is obvious enough why Henry Cary, the translator of Dante, wrote to her in reply, "abuse him, if you dare."[80]

Milton was not usually treated so roughly, but the objections made were rather similar. "Out of the admirers of the Paradise Lost," H. N. Coleridge asked, "what is the proportion of those who receive *pleasure* from it, or have even read that divine poem *through?*"[81] Some persons thought Milton's epic too "elevated": "How few can thoroughly relish the great productions of Milton —while the poetry of Bloomfield generally pleases!"[82] Others found Milton himself too austere, too idealistic; they insisted, as one critic put it, "upon his grieving like a man of this world, though he lived in a world of his own."[83] According to Robinson, the Irish orator, Curran, called *Paradise Lost* the "worst poem in the language. Milton was incapable of a delicate or tender sentiment towards woman";[84] and Charles J. Fox, in a similar vein, said the poem has "too much of the grand and terrific, and gigantic, without a mixture of any thing, either tender or pleasant, or elegant" except in the scenes in Paradise.[85] With still others it was Milton's religious views. While Byron remarked that he would be "very curious to know what his real belief was,"[86] Henry Hallam noted that the poet's Arianism had decreased his popularity "in this rigid generation";[87] and Hartley Coleridge believed that "many pious persons are wounded by the intermixture of human inventions with the words of revelation."[88] But to show how very differently Romantic critics could regard the same poem, we might take the comments of Arthur Hallam on the one hand and Leigh Hunt on the other. Hallam spoke exuberantly of *Paradise Lost* as "one continued tension of imaginative strength, never relaxed for a moment, active on all sides"; Milton's epic might be compared "to the glorious streams of music that gushed from the soul of Haydn or Mozart, vital throughout as with the ubiquitous expansion of one plastic mood."[89] So far could "appreciative" criticism go. Hunt, on the contrary, said that he preferred Milton's minor poems to his epic because they are joyous and healthy; he explained that the "wit" of *Paradise Lost* is "dreary," the erudition and grandeur "oppress" one, and "a gloomy religious creed" removes Milton "still farther from the universal gratitude and delight of mankind." The poem "does not work out the very piety it proposes."[90] Opinions like Hunt's may partially explain why the novel and the Elizabethan drama were often thought to be superior to heroic poems: one felt more willing to accept their subtle, sympathetic treatment of ordinary human passions and motives, their lifelike portrayal of the infinite complexity of the mind of ordinary mankind.

Surveying broadly all that has been discussed, we are immediately impressed by what looks like a paradox in Romantic thinking. There certainly appeared to be such a thing as the epic, for even if not quite sure what it was, many critics were free enough in their disapprobation of the genre, in suggesting that it had become outmoded. Almost without exception, any generalizations made about heroic poetry as a whole were of an adverse sort. Yet when it came to criticizing modern epics like those of Dante and Milton, comments were, again almost without exception, of a highly favorable kind. People could usually express nothing but praise for the idealism, the subjectivity, and the "beauties" which they found in these poets. Was there a real or merely a seeming paradox?

Any basic inconsistency appears rather unlikely. For one thing, newer concepts had not completely obliterated from critics' minds the older concept of the heroic poem as a narrative concerned with men in action. The word "epic" could hardly fail to make one think immediately of Homer, of Aristotle, of the traditional rules which were supposedly calculated to stifle creativeness, of neo-classical servility to the ancients, of Blackmore and Glover and Wilkie, whose poems seemed but feeble shadows of the *Iliad*. In short, it is probable that sweeping condemnations of the genre as a whole were largely owing to a reaction, conscious or unconscious, against the dogmatic criticism and the prejudices of the eighteenth century, and against poetry characterized by external action, savage warfare, and ridiculous gods who fought among themselves and slew or protected mortals. Moreover, this antagonism towards the epic—specifically the classical epic—was nearly always coupled with praise of other literary forms. Compared to the lyric with its intensity, the novel with its direct analysis of human behavior, and the drama with its seeming actuality, the *Iliad,* the *Aeneid,* and all epics in the Greco-Roman tradition appeared to a modern rather less interesting, pertinent, and valuable.

For their part, Dante and Milton were sometimes disparaged as too austere, too grand, and too long-winded; they were, as they have always been, above the intellectual grasp of the generality of readers. But it is doubtful that the categorical denunciations of the epic were in any way aimed at them. Coleridge, for instance, could speak depreciatingly of the heroic tradition but he was always enthusiastic about Dante and Milton. Apparently, critics were becoming less and less aware of the fact that the modern epics were actually epics. They were treating them simply as poems, as important works belonging to the Romantic tradition rather than specifically to an heroic tradition. Dante and Milton were to be compared not to Homer or Virgil but to Shakespeare. For the time being this, of course, meant that their prestige was secure, and it was to remain secure as long as sublimity, subjectivity, and idealism (Christian or neo-Platonic) were to seem the principal characteristics of great poetry. But as it will presently appear, the partial rejection of classical standards and emphases, the minimization of the importance of form, and the tendency to eulogize poetry which transcended ordinary human life were to lead to a significant reaction against Romantic points of view. This reaction, when it did occur, was to restore some of the balance between the ancient epic and the modern or Romantic epic.

3 The Early Epic in the Age of Wordsworth: Homer, Ossian, and Virgil

The TERM "ART-EPIC" did not become common currency in England until well along into the nineteenth century, until the theories of the Grimm brothers began to infiltrate literary criticism. Nevertheless, Romantic theorists were of course well aware that the modern epic, far from being the product of pure spontaneity, involved imaginative meditation and conscious craftsmanship. If they tried to show why a poem like *Paradise Lost* deserved its fame, they did not fail to mention that Milton had been an omnivorous reader, that he had pondered long the riddle of the cosmos, and that he had chosen and fashioned with extreme care the fable that appeared best suited to his over-all purpose. Furthermore, in the selection of imagery, language, and rhythm, he was believed to have proceeded with great circumspection and deliberation. "Milton," observed Wordsworth, "talks of 'pouring easy his unpremeditated verse.' It would be harsh, untrue, and odious, to say there is anything like cant in this, but it is not true to the letter, and tends to mislead. I could point out to you five hundred passages in Milton upon which labour has been bestowed."[1] To about the same degree, *Paradise Lost* and the *Divine Comedy* as well appeared to be both spontaneous and "conscious."

No such generalization could be made at that time about pagan epics. These poems belonged to various times, various nations, and various stages in social and literary development. Also there was a wide range of opinion as to their respective values. Virgil, having written in a highly refined era, was boldly attacked for the very reason that Pope and the English Augustans had praised him—because he had regarded Homer and nature as the same and had therefore followed Homer. To the Romantics this meant out-and-out plagiarism and manufacture; everything in Virgil seemed derivative and synthetic. With regard to Ossian, the skeptics charged Macpherson with bombast and bathos, while those persuaded, at least briefly, of the authenticity of the poems discovered the true sublime instead of bombast and tremendous pathos instead of bathos. And Homer, depending on one's critical pre-conceptions, was either made a legislator of the world or condemned summarily as a barbarian. In brief, attitudes towards pagan epics mirror even more clearly than those towards modern epics the composite and miscellaneous character of Romantic criticism as a whole. Since we are thus faced once again with complexities and contradictions, at least as many as in the previous chapter, we shall begin by considering first the grounds on which pagan epics were approved.

"Poetry is more the language of nature than is sometimes believed."[2] This declaration, made by George Dyer, a third- or fourth-rate poet of the period, can scarcely strike one as profound or original. The point of view had of course been an integral one in the Aristotelian-primitivistic theory of earlier Scottish critics. It had been largely dissevered from neo-classicism by somewhat later students and critics of ancient ballads and bardic songs, by the conjectural historians, by many who persisted in pleading the cause of Ossian; and it had then been completely dissevered in the primitivistic writings of Herder. Early in the nineteenth century, this concept of the emotional genesis of poetry seemed not only fully authorized by history— primitive verse the world over appeared to be highly spontaneous —but also well-suited as an instrument for eradicating the architectonic approach to literature developed by the previous century. If emotion had spurred the earliest bards to sing extemporaneously, was it not logical to think that even in civilized ages poetry ought primarily to be a vehicle for communicating emotion and hence should be judged on its power to do so?

Primitivism, the belief that the earlier the verse the more exuberant and better it is likely to be, is present here and there in critical writings after 1800. It appears sometimes in Hazlitt, Hunt, and Campbell. It is evident in Wordsworth when, on several occasions, he uses it to buoy his contention that the modern poet ought to dispense with stereotyped phraseology and adhere to the language of ordinary speech. But it plays an especially significant role in Romantic criticism of the pagan epic. If ill-calculated to win friends for the sophisticated Virgil, it did help greatly to justify admiration for Ossian, and it was responsible for the popularization of the concept of Homer formed by the Aberdeen critics around 1750. Rejecting the neo-classical view of Homer as an artist in whom good sense and judgment were happily balanced by phenomenal powers of invention, many Romantic critics came to regard him as the ideal example of the unlettered and wholly spontaneous bard. One should realize, however, that there is some danger in using the term "primitivism," some danger of creating misapprehension. To think as Herder usually seems to have done that the acme of poetry was reached in the supposedly uninhibited effusions of a Homer is one thing. Merely to assume that early poetry tends to be highly emotional and that all poetry should strive to do the same is quite another; it is not, strictly speaking, to be a true primitivist. Unquestionably, Wordsworth's point of view is the latter, and it is the point of view of many whom, for the lack of a better term, we today loosely call "primitivists." If we bear this distinction in mind, perhaps the matter of nomenclature is not particularly vital.

Though the flurry of excitement over Ossian lay well in the past, intensive investigations of Scottish antiquities, together with the testimonies published by Henry Mackenzie in 1805, had convinced many persons that a great bard had lived and fought and composed patriotic verse at least vaguely resembling that "translated" by Macpherson. As glimpsed through *Fingal* and

Temora, he became a symbol not so much of courage and valor, the chief Homeric virtues, as of misfortune and suffering; like Dante and Milton, he was an example of genius misunderstood and mistreated, of unhappy genius with whom an era of sensibility was only too eager to sympathize. Thus Wordsworth, though he was inclined to sneer at the Scottish epics, conceded that one's interest in Ossian is "connected with gray hours, infirmity, and privation."[3] Hazlitt, often as much of an emotionalist as Madame de Staël, agreed with the French critic that Ossian is a name never to be forgotten, that the Highland bard conveys better than any other poet "the sense of privation, the loss of all things, of friends, of good name, of country—he is even without God in the world."[4] This view is more fully developed by Nathan Drake. Having spoken of the relationship of Ossian and Malvina as "more lovely and more hallowed" than any "in the history of human affection," he declares that one's sympathy is based largely on what the poet says of himself. "We feel the highest degree of interest mixed with our pity" in the case of a mighty, primitive genius who has become blind and neglected in his old age; "our tears flow as his orb, more deeply interesting in its close than in its noonday splendour, seems sinking into darkness and the grave." For the calamities endured by Homer and Milton it is possible to feel true sorrow, but if any reader still thinks poorly of Ossian after noting the allusions to his blindness in his address to the sun, "it can only be said, that he has furnished ample proof of a most deplorable deficiency both of head and heart, of an insensibility indeed, to some of the best and noblest feelings of our common nature."[5] Thus again, as in the criticism of modern epics and of poems in general, attention was being focused on the author himself, and it is easy to see how sentimental judgments of Ossian as a man would slide over into sentimental judgments of his poetry.

Homer, nevertheless, was far more commonly cited as an example of the ideal bard. Though Romantic concepts of poetry (as spontaneous, emotive) directly promoted this view of him, the view itself was by no means new. It can be traced back to the writings of Herodotus, Aelian, Plato, and the long line of historians, rhetoricians, and Homeric critics from the time of Pisistratus on down. Often obscured since the Renaissance by moralistic and rationalistic interpretations of literature, it had even received occasional expression during the Age of Reason. But just before 1800, just at the moment when criticism was rapidly becoming emotionalistic of its own accord, along came the surprising and shocking theories of the German scholars, Heyne and Wolf. A man named Homer had never existed; the *Iliad* was originally a group of separate heroic ballads composed by a host of rhapsodists; the poem was eventually assembled by Pisistratus. Thus, in 1798 Charles J. Fox takes issue with Wolf, saying that he sees no reason to dissect Homer's poems and to assign the detached pieces to different ages. The *Edinburgh Review* in 1803 and the *Athenaeum* in 1807 summarize at some length the German arguments in favor of diversity of authorship, while in lectures delivered in 1812 Thomas Campbell discusses the evidence for and against the unity of Homer. Others who took up the matter in detail were R. Jamieson in the preface to his *Popular Heroic and Romantic Ballads* (1814), Charles Elton in *Specimens of the Classic Poets* (1814), T. J. Mathias in *Observations on the Writings and on the Character of Mr. Gray* (1815), and most important of all, Richard Payne Knight in *Prolegomena ad Homerum* (1816). In conversation, Coleridge, Wordsworth, and Southey discussed the German theories—how thoroughly it is impossible to say—and all three "leant to the Wolfian, or as my brother (Hartley Coleridge) called it, Wolfish and Heinous hypothesis."[6]

As we shall see later, belief in this hypothesis was often damaging to the reputation of Homer. But Englishmen usually appear to have rejected Wolf's idea of multiple authorship and to have accepted other ideas of his. The result was that real impetus was given to primitivistic appraisals of Homer, to the view that the *Iliad* and *Odyssey* were the genuine, sincere effusions of a child of nature rather than the lucubrations of a craftsman. Thus, Campbell reminds his readers of "the necessity of its being understood that in Homeric times a poet was a singer";[7] while William Trollope draws an interesting parallel between Homer, on the one hand, and such supposedly natural geniuses of the modern age as Burns and Bloomfield, on the other: their "untutored lays eclipse, with their beauty and simplicity, the laboured numbers of their predecessors."[8] John Sinclair, though clearly more impressed by Ossian than by Homer, declares that the Greek epics were "to be recited, and not read"; that, as Eustatius had said, "Homer breathed nothing but verse"; and that "the genuine effusions of his muse" were not recorded till long after his death.[9] Another critic, stressing the rhapsodic character of the *Iliad,* compares Homer to "those shapely human bodies, that grow up in the ruder stages of society, which have every exertion at command . . . but which, when unmoved by passion, spread in listless indolence."[10] Henry N. Coleridge refers to Homer as a "minstrel-bard" incapable of constructing a poem "with such a minute care for a beginning, a middle, and an end, as is said to be apparent in the *Iliad*"; the verse of this poem, he says later, "seems the musical efflux of a minstrel whose unpremeditated songs are borne of the breezelike tunings of a lyre."[11] And Drake sees in Demodocus a fairly accurate picture of Homer himself. The description of Alcinous' bard, he observes, "places Homer before us as he lived, and as he sung, and we dwell with rapture on the sketch, as exhibiting in the most pleasing light, the kind manners of that remote period, and the very affectionate respect which was paid to age and talent"; the description is "dear to every great and benevolent mind" since it shows us "genius, under adversity, fostered and protected by the sympathy of a whole people."[12]

To idealize Homer and Ossian was of course to idealize their epics. Convinced that both poets had been primitive bards, critics after 1800 did not try to extract ever-relevant moral lessons or deep allegorical meanings from the *Iliad* or from *Fingal.* Nor did they make more than a half-hearted expostulation with Wolf regarding the plan of the Homeric epic, for we will recall that formal unity no longer seemed as crucial a matter as it had in the Age of Pope. In the case of Ossian, stress was inclined to fall, on the contrary, upon one or two qualities that were also to be found in Dante and Milton, and upon several others that definitely were not. The old bard's "plain and artless expression,"

his treatment of the "sublime and tender passions," his pictur-
esque descriptions of the wild and rugged aspects of nature, of
customs and manners so unlike those prevailing in the modern
world—these were among the things that the Romantic period
valued so highly in Ossian and that it believed so deplorably
lacking in the urbane verse of Virgil and of Pope. It was typical
of the age that it could prize Milton as the true and eloquent voice
of Christianity and also betray a sentimental reverence for what-
ever in Ossian seemed to typify the remote, the primitive, and
the picturesque. For instance, Southey spoke delightedly about
the "melancholy obscurity" in the history of Ossian and his
heroes.[13] Campbell complained that science and philosophy have
destroyed the charms of ancient mythologies, regretting that
"even the pillars of Fingal's cave are expounded by the hard-
hearted mineralogist on principles of chemical fusion."[14] Charles
Butler said, perhaps with a note of wistfulness, that "the icicles
on Dian's temple are not more pure, more chaste" than the
women in Ossian;[15] and Brydges attributed the popularity of the
Scottish epic, especially among younger people, to the excep-
tional bravery of the heroes and the unsurpassable beauty of the
women.[16] More sentimental than most male critics, Anna Seward
called attention to "those original and pensive traits of description,
that sweetly delineate the lonely beauties of uncultivated and
mountainous country," the passages in which "often a single word
conveys the whole generous meaning to the heart of the reader,"
the purity of the moral code in Ossian, and the graceful and
dignified manners. Reading Ossian, she said, is " 'like the memory
of times that are past, pleasant and mournful to the soul.' "[17]
Equally sentimental, and certainly more naïve, Elizabeth Smith
wrote to a friend about the Scottish poet: "I really *love* his poems
beyond all others," beyond Homer's at times; "one of my greatest
reasons for admiring him is, that all his heroes are so *good*.
There is not one of them that would be guilty of a cruel action
for the world, nor would they insult over the dead." His descrip-
tions far exceed anything in Greek poetry, she added; "I love
your flowery meadows and murmuring streams; but I cannot
help preferring rude mountains, roaring torrents, and rocky

precipices."[18] Thus does her letter combine Romantic sensibility with a Byronic admiration for the awe-inspiring.

If critics could speak in this way of Ossian, it is not hard to imagine how they regarded the poetry of old Homer. True, one might prefer the wildness and color of the Oriental tale, or the pageantry and the spiritualized concepts of love and honor typical of the medieval romance and more recently of the historical novel; but no literary work revealed so clearly and so comprehensively as the Homeric epic the vigor and simplicity of primitive man. In an era that often thought of these qualities as superlative, that was often disillusioned with its own materialistic and artificial way of life, it was perhaps natural that Homer's poems should be relished for their vivid portraits of the ancient Greeks. "Reader, beautiful or brave!" exclaims John Wilson as he begins the second of several glowing discourses on the *Iliad*. "Lend us your ears, while again we seek to hold with you converse high about old Homer and the Heroic Age. These are mechanical times in which we live; those knew no machinery but of the gods." Later Wilson sharply contrasts as subjects for poetry the "repast of heroes" in Homer with the refined entertainments of Guildhall, entertainments which he says "cannot bear description—nothing more than a horseshoe table, however august the guests, lined with flunkies at a great city-feast."[19] In speaking of Homer, Campbell points to the "artlessness of his age and manners, which, though remote from savage monotony, yet exhibit nature still fresh, and free from conventional formalities"; and on another occasion he declares that the "unsophisticated traits of the human heart" give to the Greek epic "a charm that we should exchange with reluctance for the representation of a more intellectual state of society."[20] Wordsworth, though he refers to Homer rarely, says that he "was never weary of travelling over the scenes" through which the Greek poet led him;[21] while Keats, in his famous sonnet, appears to admire an elemental Homeric world wonderfully different from the poetic realms he had hitherto known. For Leigh Hunt, nothing could compare with the "passionate sincerity" of the poetry of Homer, Chaucer, and the early balladists, who "were not perplexed by a

heap of notions and opinions, or by doubts how emotion ought
to be expressed."[22] Consistently primitivistic is the attitude of
Elizabeth Smith. Charmed with *Werther,* she writes enthusias-
tically of the several Nestors she has seen among the countryfolk
around Patterdale.[23] But it is Hazlitt who gives one of the most
exuberant descriptions of the Homeric epic. "Homer's poetry," he
says, "is the heroic: it is full of life and action: it is bright as the
day, strong as a river." And again, "his poetry resembles the
root just sprung from the ground, rather than the full blown
flower. His muse is no 'babbling gossip of the air,' fluent and
redundant; but, like a stammerer, or a dumb person, that has just
found the use of speech, crowds many things together with eager
haste, with anxious pauses, and fond repetitions to prevent mis-
take."[24] Sparing no words, Hazlitt himself "crowds many things
together" in his effort to describe vigorously and vividly the vigor
and vividness of Homer's primitive art.

If the panoramic views of primitive life were highly admired,
so too were the personages that appeared in ancient heroic poetry.
But there is hardly a point of comparison between early eighteenth
and early nineteenth century treatments of epic heroes. Pope
had said of Homer that "nothing can be more exact than the Dis-
tinctions he has observ'd in the different degrees of Virtues and
Vices," and he had gone on to explain not only that a quality like
courage is personified by various Homeric heroes but also several
sub-species or kinds of courage.[25] After 1800 there was little of
such cool, abstract analysis. In this era which commonly attached
a good deal of importance to feeling—to emotion as a basic
cause and its communication one of the chief ends of art, to the
sympathy of the poet for his subject and the sympathy of the
reader for the poet and his poem—it is to be expected that emphasis
would fall upon the dramatic situations in which the epic charac-
ters found themselves. Many persons were highly sentimental
about the "sublime and tender passions," the pathos, of both the
Greek and Scottish epics. One is deeply impressed, says Brydges,
by the "affecting intercourse of Ossian and Malvina, of which
there is no parallel" in any other ancient writer;[26] and Drake
observes that the touching relationship of these two affords "ex-

cellent lessons of mutual kindness and charity."[27] The spiritualized love and the chivalric self-sacrifice of Ossian's characters charmed everyone who had any belief in the authenticity of the poems. In fact, *Fingal* seems to have been read and admired more as a romance than as an epic.

It was Homer, however, who generally appeared to be the true poet of sensibility; he was often said to have felt far more sympathy for his characters than did any other heroic poet. Shelley, for example, singled out for special praise the final books of the *Iliad,* which describe the "close of the whole bloody tale in tenderness and inexpiable sorrow."[28] According to Hartley Coleridge, speaking in almost direct contradiction to his father, "Homer is as capable of exciting the pathetic emotions as any writer that has ever lived; they are the only passions he ever does excite, though not the only passions he enacts."[29] Hartley, in fact, denies that Homer knew how to represent anger and the desire for vengeance—a view that no progressivist would have shared with him. "He had not the organs of pugnacity. Whatever bird he may have transmigrated into, it certainly was not a gamecock." There is, he concludes, more "military passion" in *Chevy Chase* than in the whole of the *Iliad.*[30] Samuel Rogers was in complete agreement: "in delicate touches Homer excels all poets. For instance, how beautiful is Andromache's saying, after Hector's death, that Astyanax has lost *his playfellow.*"[31] Generally it was the meeting of Achilles and the aged Priam which seems to have stirred these critics most. Thus, Butler finds as much real pathos in this scene as in the well-known interview between Jeannie Deans and Effie in Scott's novel;[32] and Campbell says that when Priam begs his subjects to let him go forth to "implore the pity of the destroyer, the struggle of his people to detain him, and the voice of his instinctive agony, surpass almost every thing in the pathos of poetry, and affect us more like an event passing before our eyes, than a scene of fictitious calamity." Waxing eloquent, Campbell adds that "never was the contrast of weakness and strength more fearful, than when he throws himself at the feet of Achilles, whilst his feeble perspicacity makes us tremble at every moment lest he should light up the inflammable temper of

Achilles, fluctuating between wrath and compassion."[33] Referring
to the moment when Achilles finally relents, Leigh Hunt says
that less emotional and imaginative poets than Homer would have
made no mention of Priam's "gray chin" or of Achilles "gently
pushing the old man aside." "O lovely and immortal privilege of
genius! that can stretch its hands out of the wastes of time, thou-
sands of years back, and touch our eyelids with tears."[34] Nor was
John Wilson less impressed than Hunt with this part of the
Iliad, for he wrote a long and flowery paraphrase of the famous
meeting, interspersing it with exclamations such as "how consola-
tory that address to the royal supplicant! and how dignified! . . .
and what a princely expression of profoundest sympathy,—'Come,
sit down beside me on this seat!' "[35] Also popular, however, was
Homer's account of the death and burial of Patroclus and of the
grief and anger which Achilles felt on the occasion. Often too,
critics were moved by the "lamentations of Hecuba" and par-
ticularly by the "heart-sick swoon" of Andromache.[36] "Look on
her," says Wilson, "the chosen of the Prince of Troy—the loveliest,
we ween—in her sorrow-shaded stateliness, of all the Trojan
dames whose garments sweep the ground—ere long, in the sack
of the city, to be sadly soiled with rueful dust."[37] Actually, the
sublimity of these scenes had impressed some of the Augustans
too, but the Augustans had spoken with far greater restraint.

On the whole, comparatively little was said about the pathos
of the *Odyssey.* Campbell refers to the "involuntary outbursts
of sensibility" in which Odysseus indulges when he hears De-
modocus narrating the exploits at Troy, while Drake observes
that "the grief of Ulysses, occasioned by his absence from home,
forms one of the prominent features of that well-drawn character,
and breathes indeed, throughout the whole of the *Odyssey,* by far
the most interesting epic poem which has ever been written, an
indescribable charm."[38] But it is perhaps not difficult to see why
critics were more interested in the episodes of the *Iliad,* and, in
fact, in the *Iliad* as a poem. As Shelley put it, the *Odyssey* is
"sweet"; it is charming. Physical dangers are encountered and
a wife endures gruelling trials, but in the end all works out
happily. To an age that clearly preferred Milton's Satan to his

Adam and that often thought of Shakespeare's tragedies as the highest kind of creative literature, the *Odyssey* was pleasant reading but not sufficiently moving or tear-inspiring.

It would be gross exaggeration, however, to suggest that Romantic criticism of the early epic was exclusively concerned with emotionalism and with particularity. For one thing, there was still a good deal of emphasis on the element of conscious artistry to be found, if not in the Scottish epics, at least in the poems of Homer. Like the primitivists of the eighteenth century, critics could think of Homer as highly spontaneous and yet as "conspicuous for art and regularity." Though less frequently than before, references were made to the judgment, the common sense, the knowledge, the consummate skill of the Greek bard, and even to the "fixed and exact laws of versification" which he had supposedly followed.[39] Peacock, whose *Four Ages* was in part a parody of contemporary opinion, speaks of Homer as knowing how to write, as composing epics in order to flatter kings and princes. In the "golden age of poetry," to which the *Iliad* belongs, "passion still has scope and play" but poetry is "more an art: it requires greater skill in numbers, greater command of language, more extensive and various knowledge" than in the primitive "age of iron"; and Homer, as one of the "greatest intellects" of the time, was in every respect a craftsman.[40] Moreover, as we have seen previously, the Romantic period was by no means averse to concepts of timelessness. Critics might be solidly opposed to the "rules," but some of them, at least, subscribed wholeheartedly to the Aristotelian idea of the universal, insisting that a great poem, in whatever period it is written, is one which depicts the basic traits of human nature. Others took the point of view that the simplicity and extroversion of uncivilized life had enabled the early bard, merely by copying what he saw before him, to represent an exceptionally clear and valuable picture of man as he really is—of man as a sentient and active rather than an introspective and contemplative being. For them, presumably, the primitive epic was the supreme type of literature. Still others —Shelley is of course a notable example—thought of Homer, and of Dante and Milton, as adumbrating in their own unique ways the eternal Idea partially reflected in the particular; or, more often, they discovered the Aristotelian universal in the early epic and at the same time the neo-Platonic or Christian ideal in the modern epic. However all this may be, Patrick Graham was not alone in suggesting that Ossian had exhibited "the feelings and passions of mankind,"[41] and many writers spoke of Homer's warmly sympathetic treatment of human nature in general. Campbell, who had said that one must always remember Homer was a "singer," commends the Greek poet for "shading off the forms of human character into high and life-like resemblances of nature."[42] Leigh Hunt, in declaring the epic the supreme species of poetry, praises Homer as the most "universal of poets;[43] and even Hazlitt, though he distinctly prefers the tragic drama to the epic, ascribes Homer's immortality to his having copied "the indestructible forms and everlasting impulses of nature, welling out from the bosom as from a perennial spring."[44] Thus, on occasion at least, Romantic critics could deviate from the customary procedure of judging an early epic on the basis of its individual characters, its subjective elements, and its emotive passages.

During the Age of Wordsworth there was one writer who stands out above all the others as a panegyrist of Homer. That writer was John Keble. Because his lectures were originally composed in Latin, Keble was not widely known as a literary critic until 1912 when an English translation was published; and there is a tendency even now to overlook or to minimize his contributions. Yet Keble's opinions have the distinction of being unique in one sense and typically Romantic in another. They were developed with thoroughness and care, and they were remarkably consistent. For these reasons, and also for the reason that Keble seems to anticipate certain aspects of later critical thinking, it would appear profitable to give him rather detailed consideration.

Keble's approach to literature is basically emotionalistic and psychological. He regards all men as being impelled, purely for the sake of sanity, to find occasional vents for their pent-up emotions; and the only effective way to achieve such release appears to be through poetry, which Keble, like Tolstoi later on, practically equates with self-expression. Poetry is thus found in fervent religious devotion, in eloquent speech, in heroic deeds, and of course in the composition of verse. Eventually confining his discussion to the last of these modes of self-expression, Keble revives the primitivist concept of poetry as the language of nature and then makes an important distinction between "primary" poetry, born of a sincere urge to seek for the "relief and solace of a burdened or over-wrought mind," and "secondary" poetry, which, like Dryden's, is concocted or deliberately fashioned without the aid of the emotions. One would expect Keble to come out at this point as an ardent exponent of the lyric, but he does not do so. Instead he suggests that even a long and intricate poem such as the epic can be "primary": "it is a mistake to dissociate utterly all deep feeling from laborious finish and deliberation."[45] A truly great heroic poem is inspired by "troubles which have clearly grown up with the character, silent and unnoticed, interpenetrating a man's whole life."[46]

At long last Keble begins to apply his theories to Homer. The Greek poet, he supposes, was unable to find civil or military employment and decided to become a rhapsodist so that "he might beguile his years" by singing of deeds which his contemporaries were performing and of other deeds done by the superhuman heroes of earlier times. Achilles became the poet's favorite: "you might safely say he would have wished, had he not been Homer, to be Achilles."[47] While the *Iliad* thus sublimated or purged the emotions of the bard in the vigor of his youth, the *Odyssey* presumably served as a "safety-valve" for the frustrated feelings of his mature years. Strife had sprung up "between desperate adventurers and men of means," and in the later poem Homer "places before us the picture of an age full of unrest, as seen by a veteran who loves and clings to the old order."[48] Odysseus now becomes his ideal in the determined struggle against "innovators" and upstarts like Antinous.

In his *Lectures* Keble says a great deal more about Homer. For instance, he argues at length against Wolf and possibly Coleridge that the Homeric poems are the work of one man and are unified masterpieces of art. But the signal feature of his criticism is the constant stress upon the "safety-valve" theory of poetry, a theory which he champions elsewhere in his writings, notably in a review of Lockhart's life of Scott. There he defines poetry as "the indirect expression in words, most appropriately in metrical words, of some overpowering emotion, or ruling taste, or feeling, the direct indulgence whereof is somehow repressed."[49] Clearly Keble was poles apart from the Homeric critics of Pope's time. If he did not transform he at least extended the usual primitivist concept of poetic creation, and he foreshadowed the concept sanctioned by the Freudians of more recent periods.

Homer and Ossian were thus favored by many writers after 1800. Both were praised as spontaneous singers; both were praised for their understanding of human passions and motives. There is, however, quite another side to the story. Basically, Romantic criticism was not conducive to really high respect for early heroic poetry. The many factors which were elevating other literary kinds above the epic, the frequent bifurcation of all literature and the tendency to magnify the importance of art belonging to the Christian epoch, the admiration for the idealism and readily apparent subjectivism of Dante and Milton—these prompted strong objections to the Homeric and Ossianic poems and even stronger ones to Virgil's *Aeneid*. Moreover, it would appear that the very criteria which were being utilized in favorable re-estimates of early epics were just as often being used as grounds for complaints. Assuming, for example, that emotionalism is essential in a poem, could isolated moments of pathos in Homer really be compared, quantitatively or qualitatively, with the pathos and subjectivity which seemed virtually to dominate so much of contemporary and of Renaissance literature?

Opposition to Ossian came almost entirely from England. Scots, Germans, Italians, and Frenchmen continued to prefer his epics even to a work like *Paradise Lost,* to relish his moods of melancholia, his gloomy descriptions of nature, and his portraiture of saintly women, of heroes more akin to medieval knights than primitive warriors. Actually, the poems contained little that could offend the taste of the period. And even in England disapproval was voiced principally by professed literary critics and the better poets rather than by the reading public at large. Summarizing the situation around 1810, a reviewer points out that while the literati unanimously scorn Ossian, "the vulgar at home and almost all classes of readers abroad . . . still continue to admire; and few of our classical poets have so sure and regular a sale, both in our own and in other languages" as Macpherson-Ossian.[50] Ever since the devastating attacks by Johnson and others, well-educated Englishmen had been inclined to question the authenticity of the Highland poems, and it is their skepticism in general, more than any impartial attempts at critical examination, which seems to have led to most of their scathing denunciations. Deriding the chauvinism of the Scots, R. P. Gillies says that "a sheaf of penny Punches is worth more in our market than would be the *editio princeps* of Ossian, richly bound in Russia and lettered in gold!"[51] Nor can there be any doubt about Wordsworth's opinion when he too exclaims: "All hail, Macpherson! hail to thee, Sire of Ossian! The Phantom was begotten by the snug embrace of an impudent Highlander upon a cloud of tradition."[52] One writer records that Wordsworth thought the Scottish epics "a disgusting imposture, the manners, and imagery, designated as false, and unreal, condemned in toto, yet to the blind Bard himself he had some relentings."[53] Equally outspoken is R. P. Knight. "Had a blind bard, or any other bard, presumed to utter such a rhapsody of bombast in the halls of shells, amid the savage warriors, to whom Ossian is supposed to have sung, he would have needed all the influence of royal birth, attributed to that fabulous personage, to restrain the audience from throwing their shells at his head, and hooting him out of their company as an impudent liar."[54] But Malcolm Laing is the critic—oddly enough he was a Scot—who launched the most systematic of all attacks on Ossian. In his *History of Scotland,* an elaborate four-volume work, he said that the Highland epics revealed "no accurate delineation of character, no observations on human nature, no research into human actions, no artful transitions, nor talents for narration or plot."[55] He ridiculed "those naked, sanguinary barbarians . . . residing promiscuously in wattled booths,"[56] Ossian's "savage society of refined atheists," and Fingal in particular as having "all the strength and bravery of Achilles, with the courtesy, sentiment, and high breeding of Sir Charles Grandison."[57] Surely all the opprobrium being heaped upon Ossian, like all the extravagant praise being bestowed upon him, could mean only one thing: that a half century after Macpherson's "discovery" the controversy was still a live one.

Antagonism towards Homer was far milder but was perhaps a good deal more persistent. Needless to say, the adverse criticism was basically the result of the major shifts in literary theory which we have already discussed. A more specific factor, however, was the speculation about Homeric origins that stemmed ultimately from eighteenth century conjectural studies of history and more directly from the writings of Wolf. Though the German hypotheses were often said to be absurd, and though they might prompt one to visualize the *Iliad* and *Odyssey* as highly emotionalistic and therefore highly "poetic," they also contained certain implications detrimental to the prestige of Homer. Could he be admired as a real person? Was he the great and original genius he had been supposed, a "blazing star," as Lord Kames had described him, generating light from within and illuminating a dark and barbaric age? Whether or not one believed implicitly in everything that Wolf had said, it was obviously hard to disregard some of his contentions. Wordsworth was not alone in believing that Homer had written the *Iliad* but not the *Odyssey*. Others questioned the very existence of the poet. The reality of Homer, Jamieson declared, "appears to us to be even more doubtful than that of Troy,"[58] and Coleridge said, in a rather off-hand manner, "of course there was a Homer, and twenty besides."[59] Since the Greek poet had been robbed of his very name, it is small wonder that a writer in the *Quarterly* notes rather wistfully, "the blind and venerable father of poesy . . . has sunk first to an itinerant rhapsodist, doling forth his unconnected ballads, till at length his very existence has been denied, his name reduced to an appellative either derived from the not unusual blindness of that wandering race, or from words which imply the stringing together of these separate poetic fragments."[60] Nor are comments lacking about Homer's supposed originality. Percival Stockdale declares that it has been a false "poetical creed" of the past three thousand years that the Greek epics were produced by force of untutored genius;[61] and Gilbert Wakefield holds that it is "irreconcilable at once to reason, to history, and experience" to assume that Homer had had no predecessors.[62] Jamieson says that the Greek bard drew his materials from earlier poets, from "different ages, nations, dialects, and tongues," and that in reality his epics are little more than a "methodized, corrected, and new-modelled anthology."[63] In an article in the *Quarterly*, John J. Blunt observes that the *Iliad* could not have been the first of its kind,[64] while according to Isaac Disraeli "it is probable that the Maeonian was not more original than his imitator the Mantuan."[65] Finally, a review attributed to Hazlitt contends that the fables of antiquity evolved over many centuries, and that there is nothing like "that artificial fabrication of a continued fiction which critics like Bossu have ascribed to Homer so gratuitously."[66]

In yet another way did Wolf's theories tarnish the glory of Homer: they threw suspicion upon the completeness and inner consistency of both his epics. While it is true that narrative, unified and well-rounded narrative, no longer seemed indispensable in higher types of poetry, it became an almost habitual practice during the Romantic period to point to passages in which Homer was presumed to have nodded and to look for possible expungings and interpolations of the text. William Taylor decided that inconsistencies in the fables proved Homer was "not the polished artist" people had supposed,[67] Henry Hallam said that "the *Iliad* wants completeness,"[68] and even Henry N. Coleridge, a Homeric zealot, could not detect the "exquisiteness of artifice" of which critics had so insistently spoken.[69] In one of his essays, De Quincey made facetious reference to a man who, by an amazing stroke of genius, had discovered that Ulysses had attended three "dinner parties" on the same evening.[70] And S. T. Coleridge declared that many books of the *Iliad* "might change places without any injury to the thread of the story. Indeed, I doubt the original existence of the *Iliad* as one poem."[71] Some critics, moreover, went so far as to suggest that there is no central theme in either of Homer's epics. For example, in his *Imaginary Conversations,* W. S. Landor had Southey accuse the poet of a "discontinuity of agency": while the *Iliad* at first proposes to treat the dire consequences of the wrath of Achilles, "these disasters are of brief continuance, and this anger terminates most prosperously."[72] It was also said that the announced subject is carried only as far as the twentieth book of the *Iliad,* or that the real subject is quite different from the announced one. According to Granville Penn, the action of this poem is supposed to illustrate "accomplishment of the divine will."[73] Trying to put an end to such postulations, another writer observed that "much of the difficulty has arisen from seeking in the *Iliad* a kind of technical unity, foreign to the character, and at variance with the object of the primitive epopee." The question is not, he explained, whether "the whole fable is strictly comprised within the brief proposition" but whether in stopping short of the actual end of the poem Homer "would have left a feeling of dissatisfaction in the mind."[74] On the whole, it is perhaps small wonder that some literary men began to be alarmed for Homer; for, as one of them protested, scholars and critics had tried to take from him "his best parts, his affecting episodes, his battles, his shield, or his games," had distributed them among "forgotten troubadours," and had "put, as it were, the very genius of Homer into commission."[75]

Often with no obvious ill intentions, the "separatists" and hunters of anomalies and inconsistencies were thus beginning to shake one's confidence in the artistry of Homer. But there was also a good deal of declared hostility towards him, hostility inspired more by current literary tastes and by concepts of progress than by the Wolfian hypotheses. In many different ways it was intimated that Homer's epics are simply too primitive to be denominated the finest poems ever written. The *Iliad* is merely a tale, said one critic; it is not a poem "veiling an arcanum of the sciences, physical and moral" as people had thought a century ago.[76] In ethical instruction, said others, it is "infinitely inferior to that which may be gained from the fables of Esop."[77] De

Quincey was by no means opposed to Homer, but he declared on one occasion that "if you insist on *my* telling *you* what is the moral of the 'Iliad,' I insist upon *your* telling *me* what is the moral of a rattlesnake or the moral of a Niagara."[78] Stockdale thought Pope's translation "infinitely finer and greater" than the original—more elegant, more pathetic, and more vigorous.[79] Sometimes it was observed that the Greek epics were too pedestrian, too much devoted to the recitation of mere facts. Thus, John Aikin objects to the elaborate description of palaces and dress in the "primitive" poetry of Homer;[80] and Wordsworth believes that while Homer's "customs, rules, and ceremonies" may have historical interest, "as Poetry, they are to me often barely tolerable and not for their own sakes, but for the evidence they give of a mind in a state of sincerity and simplicity."[81] There were also attacks on the warlike spirit of these epics: Boyd denounces Homer because he "lays whole nations in blood merely for his *glory*,"[82] while Cottle characterizes the *Iliad* as a poem in which "one human being ferociously mangles another."[83] In fact, most of the complaints seem to have concerned the Homeric heroes, the poet's representations of human nature. Anna Seward, we will recall, greatly preferred the dramatis personae of Shakespeare to the warriors of the Greek epic; and William Godwin summarized an attitude common in the Romantic period when he said that Homer's characters "will not bear the slightest comparison with the delineation of the same characters as they stand in Shakespear. . . . The dispositions of men perhaps had not been sufficiently unfolded in the very early period of intellectual refinement when Homer wrote . . . . Homer's characters are drawn with a laudable portion of variety and consistency; but his Achilles, his Ajax, and his Nestor are, each of them, rather a species than an individual, and can boast more of the propriety of abstraction, than of the vivacity of a moving scene of absolute life."[84]

It was Coleridge, however, who was most antipathetic towards Homer. Aside from aligning himself with Wolf and boasting that he could patch together an epic like the *Iliad* from Arthurian ballads,[85] he employed the Schlegelian distinction of Classical and Romantic for the purpose of showing how greatly modern literature surpassed the literature of the ancients. While ardently praising Dante and Milton, he deplores the finite quality of all pagan art, its inability to transcend ordinary reality. He agrees with Boyd that the Homeric epics are essentially Greek; "there is no subjectivity whatever" in them.[86] "You can not conceive for a moment any thing about the poet, as you call him, apart from that poem. Difference in men there was in degree, but not in kind; one man was, perhaps, a better poet than another; but he was a poet upon the same ground and with the same feelings as the rest."[87] And, like Godwin and Seward, Coleridge has little respect for the warriors in Homer. "Compare Nestor, Ajax, Achilles, &c., in the Troilus and Cressida of Shakespeare, with their namesakes in the Iliad. The old heroes seem all to have been at school ever since. I scarcely know a more striking instance of the strength and pregnancy of the Gothic mind."[88]

Thus far we have said little about Virgil. We have not said more for the simple reason that he was in a category by himself. He was anathematized or merely ignored by almost every critic in the Romantic period; he was less popular at that time than at any time before or since. True, there was respect for his pastorals, and Wordsworth admired the "language" of the *Aeneid* enough to begin translating the poem; but it was rare that Virgil was mentioned in the same breath with Homer and even more rare that he was named in lists of great poets, heroic or otherwise.

Why did Virgil's reputation as an epic poet sink so low at the beginning of the nineteenth century? Broadly speaking, the reason was that the *Aeneid* seemed to manifest the same supposedly unpraiseworthy traits as did the poetry of Pope and other English Augustans. It was highly imitative in form and content; it drew upon the past for its mythology, characters, and action; and it was composed by an urbane poet who knew scarcely anything of military life or of heroes. On the one hand, the *Aeneid* lacked the idealism and sincerity of Dante and Milton, and on the other the emotionalism and simplicity of Homer—precisely the qualities which were being most highly prized. It appeared to be unsatisfactory from every standpoint. More specifically, critics had an aversion for an unheroic hero like Aeneas, who had none of the integrity and spirit of Milton's Satan or of the firmness and defiance of Achilles. Charles Butler, for instance, says that the principal figure in Virgil's poem "is worse than insipid:—he disgusts by his fears, his shiverings, and his human sacrifices: and, in his interview with Helen, while Troy was on fire, he is below contempt."[89] Thomas Green observes that "Homer's second rate actors amuse and engage us infinitely more than Virgil's principal performers."[90] "Aeneas exhibits few traits which either conciliate our affection or command our respect: and after all the efforts which have been made to interest us in his favour, we dismiss him at last from our recollection with frigid indifference."[91] Even more scathing comments come from Charles Elton, an ardent lover of Greek literature. Aeneas, he says, "alternately excites our contempt and disgust. His piety has the air of cant; of bragging ostentation, and hypocrisy: it is the piety of a monk, hugging his images of saints, and counting his beads. It appears no where in his actions, except where it is wanted to excuse villainy. . . . The faultless character of Aeneas is in the mouth of every school-boy. It is every where but in the poem itself."[92] Nor were critics more merciful in speaking of Virgil's gods. One reviewer writes that they have become "toys and playthings in the hands of genius"; having seen them act their parts through most of the *Aeneid,* we know that "when the curtain falls, they will undress and go to supper."[93] Hartley Coleridge calls them "mere creatures of memory and tradition,"[94] while Elton refers to them as "unnatural and unnecessary, and therefore cold and insipid."[95] Samuel Rogers tells us that on the whole Southey "thought meanly of Virgil; so did Coleridge; and so, at one time, did Wordsworth."[96] In fact, no question could be more damning to any poet than the one which Coleridge asked: "If you take from Virgil his diction and metre, what do you leave him?"[97]

But it was John Keble, the ardent admirer of Homer, who had the most interesting and novel things to say about Virgil.

Applying his "safety-valve" theory once again, Keble decides that Virgil's one real passion was "rural peace," a religious life far from courts and cities, and that when he was writing on pastoral subjects he was a great, a "primary" poet. As for the *Aeneid,* Keble alleges that critics have been under a grave misapprehension for hundreds of years. "As soon as they read of heroes, wars, a burning city, household gods carried away in flight, fate leading the fugitives to Italy, the conquest of that country by war, and all the rest which goes to make up the apparatus of a poem in the great style, forthwith they proceed to imagine for themselves another Homer."[98] They fail to realize that the *Aeneid* was a mere tour de force or "secondary" work, that it was composed only to express the poet's gratitude because Augustus had spared him his farm at a time when land was being freely parcelled out among the soldiery. Keble says that nearly everything in Virgil's so-called epic "seems the outcome of a duty and a task rather than the spontaneous flow and impulse of the poet's inmost heart,"[99] the only successful parts being those in which he found an opportunity "to scent the breeze that blew from his country and his homestead."[100] It is no wonder, therefore, that so many people find Virgil's characters frigid and unreal, his gods ridiculous, and the plot loosely organized. "In fine, gentlemen, Virgil—if I interpret him aright—will withdraw from any claim to a primary rank in the proud hierarchy of Epic poets without regret, indeed, joyfully and gladly: for, to begin with, he has not drawn one single leading character—not even Aeneas himself—with any real zest; in the second place, he narrates action and affairs in such wise as to show that his main interest lay in recollections of well-loved regions and Nature's charms; lastly, he has plainly declared that all the world of affairs, and especially of military affairs, is alien to him, and that not without disgust does he engage in it."[101] Thus, after rivalling Homer for many centuries, Virgil was on every hand being disqualified as a competitor. Not a few people were beginning to wonder how Dante could have uttered the words, "Go with me and be my guide."

Many Romantic critics found much to delight them in the poetry of Homer and Ossian. They liked, even idealized, the vivid pictures of primitive manners and the descriptions of nature; they formed pleasing mental images of ancient bards performing before enraptured audiences of kings and beggars; and they waxed sentimental about the sublimely tragic things which had happened to the bards themselves and to the personages of whom they sang. In the case of Homer especially, they sometimes took the double point of view of the Scottish primitivists, finding conscious artistry not incompatible with spontaneous self-expression nor universality with abundant representation of the local and particular. But Romantic theory was so malleable and many-faceted that there was also frequent disapproval of pagan epics. If Ossian was sometimes said to be sublime and pathetic, disbelief in his authenticity often brought forth against him (i.e., Macpherson) accusations of inconsistency and bombast. If Homer was applauded for his emotionality, he was also criticized for his objectivity, or his pedestrianism, or his imperfect knowledge of human nature, or his sheer barbarism. And Virgil was of course attacked without mercy from every side.

What generalizations can we make about the prestige of the epic around 1800? It must be remembered, of course, that interest in ancient Greek civilization had never been keener, that scholars such as Heyne (at Göttingen), Wolf (at Halle), Hermann (at Leipzig), Boeckh (at Berlin), the brothers Schlegel, Porson (at Cambridge), and other Englishmen such as Gilbert Wakefield, Richard Payne Knight, and William Mitford were all intensively studying or lecturing or writing about the literature, as well as the language, art, and customs of the early Greeks. Naturally, a great deal of attention was being paid to Homer. In all the chief European countries, new editions of his poems appeared one after the other, and there was a steady stream of books and articles on Homeric mythology, Homeric society, Homeric prosody, Homeric geography, and of course on the authorship of the Homeric poems. But if the flourishing of classical scholarship did much to heighten interest in the *Iliad* and *Odyssey* and to sustain the reputation of those poems, if philological, textual, and historical study tended to bring about a fuller understanding of Homer, it must be acknowledged, on the other hand, that literary aesthetics in general was inclined to disparage not only the Greek epic but also the epic as a genre. The eighteenth century, we will recall, had usually put the epic and the tragic drama at the top of the hierarchy of poetic kinds because these two seemed to provide the most significant and valuable imitations of human action. However, few persons in the Romantic period really stressed this point of view or any modification of it. Emphasis in literary criticism had definitely shifted from external action and ethical purpose to the emotional origin, content, and effect of literature, from the mechanical integration of parts to the organic unity spontaneously achieved, from systems of rules imposed from without to the unique principles by which each work of art came into being. But though there was thus a new and substantial basis for valuing the Italian and English epic as never before and for rescuing Homer from the hands of the more extreme progressivists, even the most enthusiastic appraisals of heroic poems, to say nothing of the negative ones, were apparently serving to undermine the prestige of the epic. Let us consider from different points of vantage how this might be true.

First, the depreciation of plot and the purely formal elements led to a confusion of the genres and therefore to an uncertainty as to whether "epic" was really a useful term in criticism. It encouraged critics to classify as epics a vast multitude of poems that barely resembled the traditional heroic poems at all. Often, on the basis only of a thin thread of narrative—whether unified or not seemed immaterial—such different works as *Don Juan,* the *Nibelungenlied,* and the *Columbiad* were admitted into the more august company of the *Iliad* and *Paradise Lost.* The hitherto aristocratic genre of the epic, now that it included virtually every poem that was not eminently lyrical or dramatic, was almost certain not to be so highly esteemed.

In the next place, the growing emphasis upon emotion helped to subvert the reputation of the epic. If poetry was to be judged largely on the basis of the presence and the intensity of feeling, it meant that the epic had no distinctive virtues of its own, that it could be legitimately compared with poetry of every conceivable sort and compared, often, to its detriment. The frequent tendency to parallel Homer not with Milton or Virgil but with Chaucer or Shakespeare or Scott or Burns shows rather clearly how the heroic poet was now having to compete with poets who did not strictly belong to the heroic tradition at all. Again, if emotionality was to be considered an all-important criterion, was it not more notably present and more effectively displayed in literary types other than the epic? In whatever way one chose to argue, the answer appeared to be in the affirmative. The very length of the epic poem militated against it. One felt either that a work like *Paradise Lost* had an inherent element of artificiality and was unemotional (therefore pedestrian and "unpoetical") in parts, or that it maintained its emotional intensity for so long a time that the reader found himself exhausted and unresponsive. Clearly it would seem, as it did to Mill and Poe, that the lyric is better adapted as a vehicle for the expression of emotion— or more correctly, perhaps, of emotionalized thought. A. W. Schlegel spoke of the "equanimity" of most epic poetry and compared it unfavorably with the "more immediate and vehement" appeal of tragedy: an epic tends to recall things that are past, hence fails to stir one deeply; a drama appears to deal with things present, therefore has greater impact.[102] A rival of an altogether different kind was the novel. The character of the epic—a story in poetry or poetry in a story—made it seem rather an anomaly, while the novel, being prose rather than poetry, seemed a more legitimate form, a more proper vehicle for an extensive and complex imitation of life and for thorough analysis of human nature.

Finally, the way in which epic poems were dichotomized did much to undermine the reputation of the heroic tradition. Regardless of their historical perspective, critics in the English Romantic period were rarely true historical critics. Instead of simply considering Homer and Milton as the respective voices of their eras and honoring them as such, they separated the epic into early and modern (or Classical and Romantic) on the basis, largely, of the quality and degree of emotion and thought.

As we have seen, this meant approval of the one species or the other but not of both; Shelley, with his neo-Platonic approach, stands forth merely as a notable exception. If critics valued the blend of mind and feeling in Dante and Milton, they were almost certain to depreciate or brand the older epics either as too objective or too naïve. If they approved of the pathos of Homer and Ossian, of spontaneity without deep thought or idealism, of the revelation of primary human emotions in dramatic moments, then they were likely to attach considerably less worth to the spiritual aspirations and self-consciousness of Dante and Milton. To recast the familiar phrase somewhat, to divide, if not quite to conquer, was at least to threaten the reputation of the heroic tradition.

One final observation might be made. The word "tradition" usually suggests something more or less established, something handed down without radical alteration from one period to the next, something respected because of its antiquity. The eighteenth century accepted poetic theories grounded to a large extent on the practice of the classical epic poets; it imitated, often slavishly, both Homer and Virgil; it had a reasonably clear conception of an heroic tradition fixed in its purpose and in its principles. On the other hand, the Romantic period regarded change and growth as the dominant principles, and feeling instead of intellect as the prime mover, in life and in literature. Breaking away from the poetic theories of the past, critics were unable to define an epic with precision, to assign any specific set of rules for judging or formulae for creating or at times even any exact reasons for esteeming an epic per se. The confusion of the genres, ideas of progress, perpetual stress on emotion were among the major threats to the prestige of the epic as a type. The heroic tradition ceased, for the time being at least, to have peculiar virtues of its own, indeed almost ceased to exist as a recognizable tradition.

4   The Epic in an Epic Land: American Theory, 1812-1860

Is NOT AMERICA herself a great epic? Or, is it not her destiny to become one? After 1812, such questions were being asked in New York, Philadelphia, and Boston. Having emerged safely if not victoriously from the war with England, the young nation was growing aware of her vast natural resources and her promise as a commercial power, of her potential importance as a political force, of the possibilities of illimitable progress under her democratic form of government. She was also growing aware of a need, or at least of an irresistible desire, to lessen her cultural dependence upon Europe, to develop, among other things, a new literary tradition that would reflect the realities and the ideals of democracy. Needless to say, this spirit of self-reliance soon infiltrated not only American critical theory as a whole but also that part of it which is our present concern, American attitudes toward the epic. Homer, Milton, and the other heroic poets were often, though by no means always, re-estimated from the point of view characteristic of a young, a democratic, a self-assured but at times self-apologetic country.

To understand the attitude of the American Romantic, it is necessary to glance briefly at the critical estimates that had obtained in colonial days and in the period of the Revolution. The Puritans, as men of the Renaissance in recognizing the values of pagan poetry, conceived of the epic as a conscious work of art by which the author intended, perhaps primarily, to call attention to certain eternally valid ethical truths. The moral insight and purpose of Homer and Virgil were regarded as only slightly less admirable than those of the Holy Scriptures. However, in view of subsequent Romantic blasts at the classics, it is significant that the Puritans were occasionally perturbed not a little by the lessons that the ancients presumably taught. Thus, Cotton Mather declared that while the *Iliad* does bring out effectively "many points of morality" acceptable to a Christian, it also "set open the flood-gates for a prodigious inundation of wickedness to break in upon the world"; and he went on to express no surprise that Plato had banished Homer from the ideal commonwealth.[1]

→ The Age of Reason of course inherited this rather static and decidedly moralistic approach to the epic, but it paid a great deal more attention to the purely aesthetic aspects of Homer and Virgil, to the sublimity of passages, the architectonic skill displayed by the poems, the striking beauty of images and descriptive details—in short, to whatever appeared to give immediate pleasure to the reader. Jefferson is at once typical and atypical. He is like other critics in admiring the grandeur of Milton, in dwelling with delight upon the technique of Homeric versification, and especially in emphasizing the lasting didactic value of the *Iliad*. But in some ways he goes beyond the urbane literati of London and, one suspects, beyond the average well-educated American of the period. At least for a time his admiration of Ossian was boundless: "I am not ashamed to own," he remarked in 1773, "that I think this rude bard of the north the greatest poet that has ever existed."[2] And he made Homeric poetry a highly meaningful and a lifelong concern. Year in and year out, no matter how busy with practical affairs, he took the time to jot down in his commonplace book the gems of wisdom that he had unearthed in Homer. Moreover, he tried to apply to contemporary problems the lessons which the Greek epics had taught him. According to a recent scholar, Karl Lehmann, Jefferson felt that the behavior of Homeric heroes was a guide to the actions of the Indians and that the impulsiveness of Achilles and his peers was clearly mirrored in the conduct of the politicians in Washington.[3]

Neo-classical, or at least traditional, opinion of the epic continued to flourish long after the new nation was established, in fact throughout the entire Romantic period. Conservative atti-

tudes are of course evident in any age and in any country, for
there are always people constitutionally opposed to ideas that
have not been put to the test of time. But one of the things that
helped to perpetuate older points of view in America was the
general use, in schools and colleges, of Hugh Blair's middle-of-
the-road *Lectures on Rhetoric and the Belles-Lettres.* Between
1785 and 1854 some 75 editions of this work, abridged and un-
abridged, were published in America. Far more important was a
reaction against the militant clamoring of chauvinists to disavow
earlier literature and critical standards. "One of the foolish whims
of this age," declared a writer in the *North American Review,*
"is to deride a love of the old. Those who are absurd enough to
do so, forget, or perhaps never knew, that there lies deep in the
human heart, an inextinguishable reverence for the past. . . . The
past is sacred."[4] Similarly, H. B. Wallace complained about "a
school of criticism, very limitary and insular in its sympathies,"
which would "consign Homer himself to neglect" and "push
Horace and Virgil quite out of the line of poets."[5] Possibly a third
significant factor was the great American dream that someday a
poet would come along who would compose an epic of the classical
sort in celebration of the fabulous history of the new land. In
1797 Freneau opined that "perhaps no other event in the history
of man, as a subject of epic poetry, has equal claim on the exer-
tion and animation of genius, with the emancipation of the
western world. . . . If the genius of such authors as Homer and
Virgil could aggrandize events, even in those limited times, . . .
how much the more should this sublime incident of our times, the
AMERICAN REVOLUTION, awaken genius, and enable it to
transmit to posterity . . . this STORY OF FAME, this *real Revolu-
tion.*"[6] And it was not until the years before the Civil War that
poets gave up trying to be a Homer or a Virgil and that all
critics were agreed that an American *Iliad* was out of the question.

Whatever the reasons, the concept of the epic as an historical
narrative in verse, as an imitation of men in action, as a con-
sciously contrived type of art in which form and content seemed
to be separable, appeared in American critical essays long after
Romantic theory began to prevail. Hardly a neo-classicist in

many respects, Legaré praised Homer because "his is true *epic* poetry—it not only has an *action,* but it is full of action."[7] Lowell was a great admirer of Dante, a hater of rules and imitation, and at times an organicist, but he could speak favorably of Homer's "consummate art, the last achievement of poets and the invariable characteristic of the greatest among them,"[8] of the "noble reserve and self-restraint" of the classical epic,[9] and of the universality, "the perennial beneath the deciduous" which had made the Homeric poems immortal.[10] Especially given to traditional views was the *North American Review.* In 1824 it declared in the fashion of the preceding century that Homer is a great teacher of virtue, that he has influenced the conduct of poets, critics, and artists since time immemorial;[11] in 1833, opposing the hypotheses of Wolf, it observed that the impeccable unity of action in the *Iliad* "is the principal source of that interest which this wonderful poem uniformly excites";[12] and as late as 1842, after making some preliminary comments on the Greek epic, it attacked the "long, very long poems" of Southey because of their discontinuity of action: "the reader, whose epic tastes have been formed in the classical school, is puzzled and confounded by these varieties. . . . The separate Books, or Cantos, are in fact separate poems."[13] Nor, finally, should one overlook the traditionalism of critics and translators like C. C. Felton whose education was almost wholly classical.[14]

Though older opinion thus continued to subsist, it soon showed marked symptoms of debilitation. Even before the turn of the nineteenth century, neo-classicism was beginning to yield, as a matter of course, to the same critical forces that were exerting themselves in England, in Germany, and less often in France. By 1830, if not before, American critics had generally discarded the "rules," the view that external form is the proper basis for classifying poetry, and the Aristotelian concept of mimesis. They had adopted instead the historicism of Madame de Staël, or the impressionism of Hazlitt, or the organicism and "classical-romantic" distinctions of the Schlegels and Coleridge. Moreover, because of the desire of Americans to think for themselves, the disintegration of the neo-Aristotelian approach was eventually all the more complete in this country. Classicism and classical literature were automatically associated, in many people's minds, with the derivative culture of the colonial period, and Aristotle seemed a major obstacle preventing the free expression in poetry of American interpretations of experience. Hence the belief in the progressive development of literature, the notion that spontaneity is a basic requisite in poetical composition, that self-revelation and individualism are to be expected from a poet—in fact, most of the salient views of the Romantics—found the American climate particularly congenial. As we shall see, however, this climate was hardly suitable for the heroic tradition, for the epic as a poetic type and for some of the major epic poems written in the past.

What is an epic? Now that emphasis had shifted away from action or plot, Americans were becoming as vague as the English about the matter of definition. In 1789 Timothy Dwight seems to have anticipated the dilemma in which critics were soon to find themselves. "The word epic," he says, "signifies merely narrative, and according to its plain meaning, every narrative poem is epic. But the phrase epic poem has been appropriated to such narrative poems, as concerned a dignified subject, were written in an elevated style, and contained noble images, and interesting sentiments. In this sense, also, the poems referred to (Milton's and Tasso's) are as truly epic, as any hitherto written. But if an epic poem must be exactly like the Iliad, Odyssey, or Aeneid, or if it must rehearse the actions of a warrior, Paradise Lost will be excluded from the number."[15] To settle the problem, Dwight proceeds a moment later to express a view which no American had as yet expressed. "Most poems are of such a nature as to blend and harmonize, in several characteristics, with the kinds bordering on them; and can be no more exactly limited or separated than the hues of the rainbow."[16] With him later critics were in substantial agreement. They implied that the term "epic" could rightly be applied to any story in verse, ancient or modern, long or relatively short, historical or purely imaginary; and they sometimes went so far as to suggest that an epic is any poem in which the "grand manner" predominates. Perhaps the most extreme attitude was that which Emerson took. In his critical writings, the Concord

poet repeatedly speaks of "epics"; over and over again he declares that "Homer's is the only Epic."[17] But he has no formalistic concept of genre whatsoever. Using the term in as broad a fashion as Shelley, he seems to associate it with any poetry that is original, that arises "out of the wants and deeds of the age as well as the writer,"[18] or that, in a more general way, expresses what he calls "the spirit of humanity,"[19] the sense of the oneness in all and the "allness" in the one. Certainly nothing could be more diametrically opposed to the usual neo-classical view, or for that matter to the historical views of many Romantics, than Emerson's notion that "one master could so easily be conceived as writing all the books of the world. They are all alike."[20] Presumably he meant "all the great books," for he had little sympathy for the imitativeness of the *Aeneid* and the erudition displayed by *Paradise Lost*.

Just how ambiguous "epic" was now becoming is evident in the generous and even gratuitous application of the term to poems that have barely anything in common. As in England, *Madoc*, the *Kalevala*, the *Lay of the Last Minstrel*, the *Song of Roland*, *Don Juan*, the *Heimskringla*, and sometimes Wordsworth's *Excursion* were all classed as epics. George Bancroft observed that "there are not wanting critics, who persuade themselves that Homer hardly deserves higher esteem than the poets of love and the singers of the Nibelungs";[21] while Prescott, in applauding the *Cid* as a primitive epic, said that the poem had "a moral elevation not inferior, a tone of courtesy and generous gallantry altogether unknown, to the heroes of the *Iliad*."[22] But Americans were ready to extend the genre to include still other literary works. Though Lowell was alone in remarking about Chaucer that "here was a truly great epic poet without knowing it,"[23] many critics acclaimed the poetic narratives of Dwight and Barlow as bonafide epics, and with some hesitation even *Hiawatha* and *Moby Dick*. Usually, however, they employed a degree of caution. Thus, Jones Very suggests that *Paradise Lost* is "epic" in form but "tragic in spirit";[24] while Legaré opines of both *Paradise Lost* and the *Divine Comedy* that they are "more remarkable for Lyrical (and sometimes for dramatic) than for epic beauties—for splendid details, than an interesting whole—for prophetic raptures bursting forth at intervals."[25] Lowell says that Dante's subject is "essentially lyrical" but that his handling of it is "epic";[26] and another writer spends much too long a time confusing himself and his readers by speculating whether *Hermann und Dorothea* is a "pastoral epic" or an "epic idyll."[27] All in all, it is perhaps not very surprising that Longfellow observed, in his conservative way, that "epic" is a term "of late so much abused."[28]

Despite the fact that the world now appeared to be full of heroic-lyrical-dramatic poems, of primitive epics and hybrid epics that should share in the glory of the purer ones, American critics were generally agreed that all of the so-called heroic poems did have a single characteristic in common—a sequence or group of events, physical or mental. And, year by year after the War of 1812, many of these critics became increasingly skeptical about the value of the genre as a whole. Over and over again, and far oftener than Englishmen, Americans remarked upon the obsolescence of heroic poetry. Perhaps one reason was the obvious failure of the new nation, with all her great promise, to produce a single epic poet of real importance. In the early 1820's Giovanni Grassi was quoted by a reviewer as saying that many Americans seemed to think that Barlow's *Columbiad* was superior to the *Iliad* and the *Aeneid;*[29] but many years later Timrod averred that if Barlow's "ponderous production could be crushed into a space no bigger than that occupied by an epigram, not a drop of genuine poetry could be forced from it."[30] Another critic observed that "since Barlow's unfortunate essay," with its "Sahara-like dryness and platitude," the epic had seldom been attempted by American poets,[31] and still another that early in the century "we were busy growing a literature. We watered so freely, and sheltered so carefully, as to make a soil too damp and shaded for any thing but mushrooms"; critics "wondered a little why no oaks came up, and ended by voting the mushroom an oak, an American variety." Changing his metaphors, the same writer adds that "Joel Barlow made the lowest bid for the construction of our epos, got the contract, and delivered in due season the *Columbiad,* concerning which we can only regret that it had not been entitled to a still higher praise of nationality by being written in one of the

proposed new languages."[32] Certainly one can say that the creation
of third-rate epic poems did nothing at all to forward the cause of
heroic poetry in America.

There were, however, far more basic reasons for the decline
of interest in the epic. For one thing, people often seemed to feel
that the heroic poems of some hundreds or many hundreds of
years ago could occupy no significant place in the rapidly changing
modern world: fundamental attitudes towards religion, towards
politics, towards art, towards life itself, had altered so profoundly
that even the greatest of heroic poems now seemed outmoded.
Though Englishmen were well aware of these changes, and hence
were inclined to depreciate the epic, the phenomenal developments
so close at hand in America—the conquest of the West and the
rapid growth of cities—appear to have made critics on this side
of the Atlantic even more vocal about such matters. Echoes of
the Schlegels and Coleridge can of course be detected in the
many Romantic encomiums on Dante and Milton, particularly in
those of Longfellow, Channing, and Lowell. But not even the
relative modernity of *Paradise Lost* and the *Divine Comedy*
obviated the assumption that all the famous epics were becom-
ing antiquated. More than the English with their strong sense
of tradition, Americans were inclined to think in terms of the
present moment and of a future that seemed to offer so much
to men everywhere. One writer says that the epic is obsolete
because of "the change of manners, philosophy, and taste";[33]
another that the *Iliad* is largely a "curiosity as a literary monu-
ment, and cannot fairly be brought into comparison with any
production of a civilized age."[34] In part this seemed owing to
scientific discovery. Mythologies appeared to be ridiculous, fit
only for highly credulous ages. "Jove is to be sought for in the
Magnetic Telegraph, Mercury pilfering a pocket, Neptune is a
steamer, . . . Mars 'covers nine acres' in the shape of Flying Artil-
lery now engaged in the Mexican war; Vulcan forges not the
wonderful shield of Achilles, worth a library in itself, but fires up
a steam boiler."[35] Usually, however, critics emphasized the mental
and spiritual progress that mankind was presumably making.
Optimistically, Jones Very holds that the advance of the human

mind has "unfolded a new form of the heroic character, one which finds no paradise, nay, no heaven for itself in the creations of Milton, and for which the frowns of Dante's hell have no terror."[36] Legaré mentions, though he rejects, an idea then current that the "increase of the 'materials of thought'" has been so rapid that "Shakespeare and Milton must, ere long, cease to be talked of as unrivalled";[37] while Edward Everett, one of the more extreme progressivists, predicts a poet to come whose work will easily equal if not surpass *Paradise Lost*. "A continued progress in the intellect is consistent with all that we know of the laws that govern it," and one of the greatest bards of all time will arrive on the scene "when knowledge shall be universally diffused, society enlightened, elevated, and equalized."[38] Another critic justified his wholehearted admiration for contemporary writers on the ground that "the stronger our hope in the future, the more intense is, and ought to be, the interest of a healthful mind in the present, and what ever tends to unfold, disentangle, or illuminate that puzzling, but most precious, present."[39] One reason that Poe cared little for epics of whatever period was that, as a perfectibilitarian, he looked forward to a time when man and his poetry would both be vastly improved; "then will the word *Man* be changed to that of *Angel*."[40] Finally, a reviewer boldly directs his fire at Homer, the entire heroic tradition, and indeed at all poets in the past, because of their foolish delight in war; "the world has gradually become better informed and more enlightened—other occupations beside the military have been introduced into society, and other views are generally entertained of war by judicious men."[41] One need not comment on the accuracy of this statement.

A belief in the worldwide progress of the human mind, of science,[42] of politics, of poetry in general—this was certainly an important factor in making the epic seem outmoded to many, though hardly all, American critics. Another factor closely related to it, and one which radically differentiates the American from the English attitude towards the epic, was the conviction that the people of the New World were particularly unable to find solace or interest or profit in the masterpieces of heroic poetry and were in no position to write epics even if they so desired. According to Parke Godwin, "a man who has his fields to clear, his house to build, his shoes and clothing to make, his ways of access to his neighbors to open, and above all, his government and social order to invent and institute,—in short, who has to provide by dint of the severest toil for the most immediate and pressing wants of his existence, is not the man who constructs epics, or amuses his fancy with the invention of dramas or tales. His epics, and dramas, and romances he finds in his work."[43] In 1824 Bryant remarked sadly that nobody "cares a fig" for poetry, presumably including the epic; they are all "occupied with politics, railroads, and steamboats."[44] In 1848 the *Literary World* said that "success—business success—is in an American community the inexorable touchstone of merit in every undertaking. And if a man should publish another *Paradise Lost* in numbers, which would not sell, he would lose among us in personal respectability, for throwing himself away on an empty enterprise. 'That Milton (quoth a shrewd spirit from Wall Street), that John Milton was a smartish man, but he showed a great want of practical sense, in giving so much time to a book which it seems, after all, the public did not want.' "[45] And the same magazine expressed considerable surprise that William Munford had successfully translated an epic, Homer's *Iliad,* in an age and country "both languishing beneath the Upas-like shadow of the tree of Mammon, with no possible hope of remuneration for his labor, and with little reasonable hope even of a barren fame, except from the judicious few—so few, alas!"[46]

But critics more commonly pointed out that the epic is peculiarly alien to a democratic land. As the spirit of nationalism mounted up after the War of 1812, as Americans and Englishmen drew up their battle-lines over the bluntly asked question "Who reads an American book?", people in this country declared again and again that the chief heroic poems had been written in nations in which a hierarchy of social classes prevailed, and that in glorifying the deeds of princes and leaders they were essentially aristocratic. James Hillhouse, though he holds out great hope for the poetry of a republic, affirms that "the well-ordered government, the quiet, moral, intelligent community, where tranquillity flourishes under the shadow of the law, where one happy neighborhood represents every other, offers nothing to the Epic or Tragic Muse."[47] Grimké down in Charleston stirred angry retorts from Simms when his fervor for Protestantism and Americanism led him to launch a scathing attack on the classics. "What, though my country may never produce a Homer or a Virgil?" Grimké asked, rather petulantly. "Yet have we already brought forth men, greater and better, wiser and more valuable than the Poet, the Painter, the Statuary, and the Architect; . . . each citizen, free, educated, happy, is to America a pearl above all price."[48] An unusual patriotic twist is evident in Edward Everett's remark that it would seem to him "degenerate and ungrateful" in an American to "hang with passion upon the traces of Homer and Virgil" and to regard coldly the poetic geniuses of "that other native country, which holds the ashes of his forefathers."[49] Emerson, despite his profound respect for both Homer and Milton, could say that "America is a poem in our eyes" for the great poet of the future to sing, and that "Milton is too literary, and Homer too literal and historical" to qualify as his rivals.[50] "The world has no such landscape, the aeons of history no such hour, the future no equal second opportunity. Now let poets sing!"[51] A reviewer was happy to find that the Indian legends of *Hiawatha* had not been "wrought into an epic" simply because "other countries and times have loved epics";[52] while Lowell suggests, though from no feeling of patriotism, that there can be no "democratic epos"; democracy is "too abstract" an influence on the poet, who, if he were a true genius, would "certainly look for his ideal somewhere outside of the life that lay immediately about him."[53] Finally, and obviously, there is Whitman. As a critic of heroic poetry, he appears to have shifted his views repeatedly. At one time he speaks of the European epic and the whole European literary tradition as essential for the great American literature to come; the New World considers foreign epics and plays "as indispensable studies, influences, records, comparisons," and the ideal American poet must absorb the best that he can find in Homer and Milton, and of course in Shakespeare too.[54] But so great is Whitman's concern for democratic

poetry, so fearful is he that it will be shackled by European tra-
ditions, that he says, on another occasion, that the poems from
across the Atlantic "are poisonous to the idea of the pride and
dignity of the common people." "Ye were, in your atmospheres,
grown not for America, but rather for her foes, the feudal and the
old, while our genius is democratic and modern." Homer becomes
the voice of the "god-descended dynastic houses" of Greece, and
there is scant praise for either him or Milton in Whitman's remark
that the "true poems" will not deal with "the glorification of the
butcheries and wars of the past, nor any fight between Deity on
one side and somebody else on the other."[55]

De Tocqueville once observed that democracy "gives men a sort
of instinctive distaste for what is ancient,"[56] and even Emerson,
probably in an unguarded moment, asked a question we would
scarcely expect from him: "Whoever found, of all the generations
of the readers of Homer—where is the madcap?—that his conduct
in life was ruled or biassed one moment after merry boyhood by
the blind bard's genius?"[57] On every side, in short, the epic was
being challenged, and often for reasons that would never have
occurred to a European critic at that time. The fantastic outlook
for science, the realities and especially the ideals of democracy,
the perpetual concern for the immediate and the practical—these
were giving Americans a unique perspective on the epic and were
tending to lessen their esteem for what appeared to be an exotic
and essentially primitive genre. But it must not be forgotten
that much of the disapprobation sprang from the new critical
attitudes of the age as a whole rather than from any peculiarly
American ways of looking at things. As we saw earlier, critics
in this country were as vague as critics in England regarding the
definition of "epic"; everywhere there was a tendency to con-
fuse the genres, to treat poems as unique, organic entities, to
recognize how obviously external form is determined by his-
torical circumstance rather than by some inexorable, universal
law. And the same can perhaps be said about the way in which
American critics elevated other literary types above the epic: it
was more characteristically Romantic than specifically American.
Nevertheless, even in their comparisons of epics with novels, or

lyrics, or dramas, writers in this country did not merely parrot European points of view. They had something original to add or a modification to make, and they were certainly a good deal less restrained than Englishmen in expressing their opinions.

In England one usually implied that the lyric is superior to the epic; in America one usually said so without hesitation. Even John Stuart Mill was not nearly as explicit as Poe. "A poem must intensely excite," declared Poe. "Excitement is its province, its essentiality. Its value is in the ratio of its (elevating) excitement." But *Paradise Lost* is so lengthy that after a time readers "are wearied": platitudinous passages follow highly emotional ones in rapid sequence "until the poem (which, properly considered, is but a succession of brief poems) having been brought to an end, we discover that the sums of our pleasure and of displeasure have been nearly equal." As for the *Iliad,* Poe averred that since poetry, to be intense, "must eschew narrative," Homer's epic "is based on a primitive sense of Art"; at least it "is *not* the highest type."[58] But Poe's view, though justly famous, does little more than epitomize what many Americans were saying. W. A. Jones concludes some statements in praise of epics and dramas by making what seems like an obvious about-face: "Brevity," he remarks, "is the essence . . . of passion and imagination." "Few, very few, great, long poems survive a very limited period; and even the classic national epics . . . are by no means perfect throughout. In the grandest of epics, *Paradise Lost,* how much there is one could willingly let die."[59] Obviously Jones was not thinking of the epic as essentially an imitation of human action or even as a narrative of interior events but rather as a vehicle for the expression of the poet's own emotions. Compared to the ballad and the song, it seemed to him "strained and elaborate."[60] A somewhat similar view was held by Timrod. Though he does not depreciate the epic, he says that the sonnet is highly valuable and eminently lyrical, a form for the exuberant poet rather than the skilled craftsman. "Brief as the sonnet is, the whole power of a poet has sometimes been exemplified within its narrow bounds, as completely as within the compass of an epic."[61] "Power," one assumes, is here equivalent to forceful and sublime self-expression, though admittedly Timrod may have in mind the matter of architectonic ability as well. Likewise, a reviewer observes that "a simple ballad may please us as truly as the *Paradise Lost*"—in short, many have as great an emotional impact.[62] And finally, there is a too-often-neglected discussion of lyric and epic in the writings of Henry Tuckermann, a discussion that is almost as interesting and novel as Poe's. Men, he says, are now more democratic, more nearly equal in education, than ever before. Since "literature is so common a luxury," the poet must "distill his roses and touch his harp at graceful intervals." "Fifty pages of blank verse are too formidable to be adventured, and the mere sight of half a dozen cantos of heroics provokes a yawn." Holding that the epic is perhaps "buried in the grave of nationality," Tuckermann observes that the lyric has come to the fore because "it is indissolubly entwined with individual destiny," and because it is so well adapted "to our own busy and unimaginative country." Read by children in schoolbooks, sung by maidens at the piano, quoted by lecturers at assemblies, lyrics have done much to promote good taste and virtue in America. One may esteem the "men-of-war of literature —the Iliads and Divine Comedies—" but a "series of external events, however well described in stately verse, are now deemed less entertaining than a single incident or emotion freshly portrayed from a living mind."[63] Tuckermann's point of view can hardly be called European.

Comparisons of the epic with the drama were at least as numerous in America as in England. Margaret Fuller, Oliver Wendell Holmes, and W. H. Hudson thought of tragedy as "the highest reach of poetical art," well above the epic, for the reasons usually assigned in the Romantic period: it was direct in its appeal to the spectator's emotions and it displayed plainly the innermost springs of human action. But a few American estimates strike one as rather less stereotyped. Emerson, though he never ceased to call Homer's the only true epics, once said that in his opinion "the unpopular and austere muse that casts human life into a high tragedy" is superior to "the art of the epic poet, which condescends more to common humanity, and approaches the ballad. Man is nine parts fool for one part wise, and therefore Homer and Chaucer more read than *Antigone, Hamlet,* or *Comus."*[64] His view appears all the more unusual and interesting when we remember that those who admired the lyric did so because it seemed simple and direct, and "human" rather than esoteric. Nor did Emerson's opinion concur with that of De Tocqueville: "the love of the drama is, of all literary tastes, that which is most natural to democratic nations"; hence in America "the number of authors and of spectators, as well as of theatrical representations, is constantly increasing."[65] And it is equally at variance with that of C. K. Newcomb, who, as an advocate of the drama, was happy to find how much ordinary folk could enjoy *Hamlet.* At a performance of the play in the 1860's, he observed "shopmen, stockbrokers, lawyers, apprentices, news-boys, sailors, loafers, scholars, & hod-carriers" listening intently "to a problem which all the ingenuity & mythology of Greece & Egypt had not presented to their schoolmen & kings."[66] The prevailing opinion was, in brief, that tragedy is for the many and the epic for the few.

When English Romantics praised the novel at the expense of the epic, they usually did so with a degree of hesitation and restraint. One has the feeling that their instinctive likes and dislikes tended to be at odds with their critical judgment, with their rational, perhaps traditional, sense of values; that they had reached no decision as yet as to the proper place of the novel among the literary genres. But the same can hardly be said of many Romantic writers in America. For decades the works of Scott enjoyed a tremendous vogue, and if people had abandoned hope for a great American epic, they could at least point with unabashed pride to the achievements of Cooper, Hawthorne, and Melville, in the field of prose fiction. In short, the Romantic period came at a later date in America than in England, and by the end of it the novel had not only become strongly entrenched and universally acclaimed but had even begun to undermine the reputation of poetry in general. As early as 1817 Lydia Child admitted that she enjoyed a first-rate novel "better than any other reading"; and the chief reason she gave was that "the need of being entertained grows upon people in general as the sad experiences of life multiply."[67] In a less melodramatic fashion, another writer says that "we have no more epics in these days; or if they are born, they are consigned to an early grave. . . . It is impossible that poetry, constrained as it is by metre, should give us the completeness of a prose picture." A moment later he adds that "we may, without much exposure to error, venture to predict, that poetry has seen its best days, and must be content henceforth to retreat behind sober, simple, manly, and energetic prose."[68] Parke Godwin observes that the novel is not "confined to a narrow list of time-consecrated themes";[69] the *North American Review* that it "may be viewed as forming the real modern epic,"[70] and again that it "is one of the most effective, if not most perfect forms of composition, through which a comprehensive mind can communicate itself to the world."[71] In 1844 E. P. Whipple wrote that "from being the weak companion of the laziest hours of the laziest people, the novel, under the impulse it received from Scott, became the illustrator of history, the mirror and satirist of manners, the vehicle of controverted opinions. . . . In its delineations of character and its romantic and heroical incidents, it took the place of the drama and the epic."[72] At about the same time John Neal made some remarks which put one in mind of Poe's discussion of the lyric and the epic. Lauding prose fiction to the skies, he asks: "Could you possibly hold out to read any poem by the greatest poet that ever lived which should contain as many words as one of the Waverley novels? It would be above five or six times as long as *Paradise Lost*. If it were the best of poetry would you not get the sooner tired of it? Assuredly. In the confusion of such a beautiful and confounding exhibition of power and brightness your senses would lose all their activity."[73] Neal did not of course foresee that a day was to come when many readers would find Scott's novels at least as wearisome as any of the great epics. Finally, there is an interesting statement in a review of Irving's work on Columbus, a statement which shows how fundamentally the whole critical outlook had changed in the hundred years following the death of Pope. "A polished and civilized age may well be supposed to prefer, especially in a long composition, the delicate melody of flowing prose, setting forth a spirited and elegant picture of actual life, to the 'specious wonders' of Olympus or fairy land, expressed in artificial measures, strains and subjects that seem more naturally adapted to a yet unformed, than to a mature and perfect taste. Hence a fine history and a fine novel may perhaps with propriety be viewed as the greater and lesser epic (to use the technical terms) of a cultivated period, when verse is better reserved for short poems accompanied by music."[74] Though this reviewer seems to have forgotten that the English Augustans were "polished" enough and yet could admire Homer, one will note how he elevates both the novel and the lyric well above the epic poem.

Was American criticism completely antagonistic towards heroic poetry? Certainly the evidence given thus far would seem to necessitate an answer in the affirmative; certainly no other conclusion could be reached if one were to judge solely by the way in which American writers alluded to the epic as a type, to the various factors that had made it less interesting or pertinent than other literary types. But as it was indicated earlier, Romantic theory everywhere was tending to minimize the importance of external structure per se and to stress other things instead. One view was that a poem is a unique organism in which form is (or should be) so thoroughly fused with content that it is futile to compare any two poems with respect to their form alone. As Whipple said in one of his essays, "A tree, growing by virtue of inward properties, has, we all feel, an independent existence, and is itself its own apology and defence. So with a true poem, instinct with vitality. To judge it simply on its agreement or disagreement with the form of other poems, is about as wise as to flout the willow because it is not the oak."[75] Another view was that a poem is unique in many ways but that comparison is both possible and valuable: it may be made partly on the basis of structure and partly on the degree of emotion present or the manner in which ordinary reality is transcended. Usually espousing this latter opinion, many American writers kept in mind some formalistic conception of the epic as a genre and at the same time proceeded to dichotomize heroic poetry into Classical and Romantic or ancient and modern or pagan and Christian. Generally speaking, their estimates were not dissimilar to those of the

English and German Romantics; approval of more recent epics meant little enthusiasm for earlier ones, and of course vice versa. On the other hand, it is again obvious that Americans did not merely echo the Schlegels, Coleridge, or Hazlitt. Their emphases were often different, in fact sometimes radically different.

Behind most of the praise of the modern epic was the belief that literature and human society as a whole have advanced together. It was repeatedly asserted that "the progress of mankind in self-knowledge, or at least in the habit of self-reflection and introspection, and the increase with time of the mind's disposition to direct its thoughts to the field of contemplation, rather than to that of action, is strikingly exemplified in the history of poetical literature."[76] For the progressivist, the Greek epic was a narrative of physical action and therefore too primitive; the Christian epic was a subjective account of mental events, of religious feelings and aspirations, and therefore of infinitely more interest to modern man. Because this point of view was so popular in Romantic America, one would naturally look for a good deal of highly enthusiastic and original criticism of Dante's *Divine Comedy*. But there was actually rather little. The first well-rounded commentary on Dante was written by John Chipman Gray for the March, 1819, issue of the *North American Review,* and the first American translation of any sizeable portion of the *Divine Comedy,* one made by Thomas W. Parsons, was not published until as late as 1843. Though Longfellow lectured on the poem in the 1830's, his own translation appeared after the Civil War; and though Lowell made frequent references to Dante in his letters during the 1840's and 1850's, his important criticism of the Italian poet dates from an article in the *North American Review* in 1872. Thoreau and Whitman barely mentioned Dante; Emerson said little more, and then it was partly to quarrel with "what is almost a national quality, the inwardness or 'subjectiveness.' "[77] Even Longfellow, as one of the first Americans to teach the *Divine Comedy* to a group of students, could remark in 1847: "Finished the *Inferno* with my class; and am not sorry. Painful tragedy, called by its author comedy!" He added, it is true, that the poem is "full of wonderful pathos, horror, and never ending

surprise."[78] In the minor critical writings of the period one
finds some expression of admiration, but the many brief com-
ments on Dante's idealism, or his amazing personality, or his
ability to create vivid scenes, are drawn almost entirely from the
English essayists, and they reveal only a passing acquaintance with
the *Purgatorio* or the *Paradiso*. Whatever the reasons may be—
whether, among other things, the difficulty of Dante's allegory,
their own ignorance of Italian, and the cultural time lag between
the Old and New World—American critics did not really begin
to consider the *Divine Comedy* an especially important epic poem
until the Romantic period was virtually at an end.

But there can be no question at all about the popularity of
Paradise Lost. Long eulogized by the Puritan colonists as a reli-
gious poet, then by the neo-classicists for his sublimity and for
the significance of the fable he had chosen, Milton was often
regarded in nineteenth-century America as second only to Shake-
speare. Between 1787 and 1851 over sixty editions of his poems
were published in this country; throughout that period *Paradise
Lost* was used as a text in the schools of New England; and
the influence of the poem upon American verse became at times
almost excessive. In literary criticism, since Lowell's "Milton"
did not come until 1872, the most notable and highly appreciative
essay on *Paradise Lost* was of course the one by the Unitarian
clergyman, William Ellery Channing. Channing could not find a
defect in this English epic, and largely, one suspects, because his
outlook was much more ministerial than aesthetic. Poetry has
the "same tendency and aim with Christianity," he declares; it is
a divine art, "a breathing or expression of that principle or senti-
ment, which is deepest and sublimest in human nature; we mean,
of that thirst or aspiration, to which no mind is wholly a stranger,
for something purer and lovelier, something more powerful, lofty,
and thrilling than ordinary and real life affords." Milton is great
because he satisfies the soul in its "struggling against the bounds
of its earthly prison-house."[79] Nor is there in Channing any of
the extraordinary delight in Satanism which some of the English
critics expressed. Though he may have admired the rebel angel
of *Paradise Lost,* he was careful to point out that "many a virtuous

man has borrowed new strength from the force, constancy and dauntless courage of evil agents," and that one's interest actually fastens, "in this and like cases, on what is not evil."[80] Moreover, Channing differs from so many of the English Romantics in calling Milton's epic "always healthful, and bright, and vigorous"; at least "we find nowhere in his writings that whining sensibility and exaggeration of morbid feeling, which makes so much of modern poetry effeminating."[81]

Channing made other interesting remarks about the human personages in *Paradise Lost* and about Milton as a sincere and dedicated Christian. All of these remarks have some degree, some tinge of novelty. The same is not true, however, about most American criticism in praise of Milton. Whittier is content to think of the English poet as "another Prometheus on his rock" and to by-pass *Paradise Lost;*[82] Prescott calls him a reformer and a Puritan whose blindness opened to him "more glorious and spiritualized conceptions of heaven";[83] while the *North American Review* spoke respectfully but rather too broadly of the "moral sublimity," the devoutness, the manliness of Milton, and the "sacredness" of his theme. In fact, almost everyone seemed readier to comment upon the noble character of the man than upon his epic, to generalize about the Christian virtues exemplified by his life than to attempt a critical exegesis of *Paradise Lost.* "His character," said Legaré, "is as grand as his epic";[84] "the man is paramount to the poet," a reviewer declared;[85] while the *Literary World* went further than either when it proclaimed, "Yes, it is less as a poet than as a man, that we reverence Milton."[86] On the relatively few occasions when attention was directed at *Paradise Lost* itself, there was no praise of the epic specifically as a work of art, no effort to say something new and incisive about its aesthetic value; one merely declared that the poem was otherworldly or sublime or, most often, inspirational to true Christians. Indeed, Milton's epic, like *The Pilgrim's Progress,* seems to have been popular rather largely as a kind of adjunct to the Bible.

There was, however, an undercurrent of opinion which tended to offset some of this blind and often uncritical admiration for

Paradise Lost. Writers objected to Milton's egocentrism, to his "manner," to his lack of "impetuosity and animation," to his giving "earthly form and language" to the Supreme Being, and to the erudition which appeared to have been foisted upon the poem. Though he calls Milton a "hero," Whitman observes that "with all his grandeur, this poet certainly wants some endearing and softening accompaniments";[87] and another critic says that in *Paradise Lost* there is no reflection at all "of this wicked but interesting world, with its pursuits and passions, its weaknesses, its tears and agonies, its hopes and fears." There is "moral grandeur," to be sure, but "there is something cold, and as it were, desolate in this feeling."[88] These were of course traditional complaints, for they are to be found in earlier European writings as well. But now and again an American critic seems to have come to his own conclusions. Poe's attitude, which we have already discussed, was original in the main. So too was Emerson's. The Concord critic never wrote about Homer or Milton in any detail, yet his pithy remarks about them, when taken collectively, seem to suggest a definite preference for the Grecian. On one occasion, Emerson makes the primitivistic statement that early bards had been able to "chant more impressively" than "cultivated poets"; the heroic age was a time when "the spiritual nature unfolded in strict unity with the body," when courage, self-command, and justice were among the prevailing virtues. Therefore the poetry of that age had "native force" and a "volatile principle."[89] Such a view would hardly appear to favor the modern epic. Elsewhere in his writings Emerson declares that the few great names in history are those of Homer, Phidias, Jesus, and Shakespeare;[90] and we can perhaps deduce his honest opinion of the English poet from his constantly reiterated statement that "Homer's is the only Epic." In fact, his opinion becomes fairly obvious when he says that "Milton was too learned, though I hate to say it,"[91] and when he confessed to a journalist that he had "read much" from Milton's prose works but had "rather avoided" *Paradise Lost.*[92] The most unusual of American views, however, was that of Harriet Beecher Stowe. Unlike Coleridge and the many, many critics who thought of *Paradise Lost* as an outstanding example of "romantic" art, she all but condemns Milton because he was too "Grecian," too much of an imitator of the Homeric epic. His love for the classics, she explains, accounts for the fact that one cannot find in his heroic poem "that wreathed involution of smiles and tears, of solemn earnestness and quaint conceits; those sudden up-rushings of grand and magnificent sentiment, like the flame-pointed arches of cathedrals; those ranges of fancy, half goblin, half human; those complications of dizzy magnificence with fairy lightness; those streamings of many-colored light"—any of the very best characteristics of Shakespearean drama.[93]

There was one striking feature of Miltonic criticism in Romantic America: a perpetual concern for what we might denominate "moral effect." Well aware that Milton had lavished a great deal of attention upon his Satan, had made him, wittingly or not, the protagonist of his epic, critics were always reluctant to speak of the rebel angel with unbounded admiration; they were torn between moral and aesthetic considerations. This was true of Channing, as we have already seen. And it was equally true of W. B. O. Peabody. In discussing *Paradise Lost,* Peabody refers to the popular view that the traits of Satan "are too fearfully sublime to be regarded with the horror and aversion which they ought naturally to inspire. He is indeed invested with many sublime attributes,—the fierce energy, unbroken by despair; the uncon-querable will, which not even the thunders of the Almighty can bend: but these qualities, though they may fill us with wonder and awe, are not attractive. His tenderness is only the bitterness of remorse, without end and hopeless; his self-devotion is only the result of wild ambition."[94] Legaré speaks of the "preposterous vauntings and menaces of the devil against the Omnipotent" as being like "the swaggering insolence of a slave behind his master's back";[95] while Parke Godwin, in refusing to compare Satan with Prometheus, says that in Milton's protagonist "we see the demigod, fierce, defiant, unconquerable, wage a proud strife with the Omni-potent; but while we pity his fancied wrongs and sympathize with his ambition, the nature of the combat forbids us to applaud his courage, and the exhibition of his envy, falsehood, and revenge destroys our admiration." Prometheus, on the other hand, is "an

Innocent One exposed to the oppressions of evil; . . . a spirit full of godlike fortitude and hope, warring with the gods."[96] Some years later H. N. Hudson, the Shakespearean critic, said that "my own feelings have somehow been so steeped in the foolish old doctrine or faith which holds obedience to be a cardinal virtue, that they have never sided with Satan in that controversy" with God.[97] Americans of the early nineteenth century took little delight in Byronism or Satanism of any kind.

After 1812 a good deal was thus said both for and against the "modern" or "romantic" epic. Dante's star was still far down on the horizon. Milton's was perhaps at its zenith despite the fact that so much criticism of *Paradise Lost* seems perfunctory and derivative. But what did critics think of the pagan epic? Remembering that neo-classical principles did not completely lose their hold during the first half of the nineteenth century, what can we say about the overall effect of American progressivism, republicanism, moralism and religionism upon the critical attitude towards Homer and Virgil? Also, what seemed to be the dominant feeling with regard to Ossian? These are questions it is now time to consider more specifically than heretofore.

American views about two of these poets, Ossian and Virgil, do not require detailed discussion. Up until the War of 1812, magazines debated the authenticity of Ossian, and a string of "translations" and imitations appeared in print. Afterwards, though the Scottish epics continued to influence a number of our leading poets (notably Whitman), they received rather scanty notice in critical essays and reviews. Emerson made scattered references to them, Whitman of course many more. Longfellow as a youth went about the house "declaiming the windy and misty utterances" of the Caledonian bard;[98] Thoreau, so Lowell said, cited similes from Ossian as proof "of the superiority of the old poetry to the new";[99] and Margaret Fuller described a misty night on a hillside in Scotland when "such apparitions as visited Ossian" appeared to float in the air around her.[100] As in England, however, comment was largely discouraged by the increasing skepticism about the genuineness of the epics. A reviewer summed up the situation in 1836 when he said that Ossian had seemed to earlier readers "like a voice from the depths of the ages, uttering the lofty inspirations of chivalry, breathing the softest notes of love, and pealing like a trumpet-call above the roar of battle." Then, as people became convinced that the poems were essentially forgeries, "all these impressions vanished, like the wreaths of morning mist; the sound was full of sublimity so long as it was mistaken for the distant thunder, but became almost ludicrous, when it was believed to proceed from the rattling of the wagon on the pavement."[101]

As for Virgil, Americans, like Englishmen, were in general agreement that the *Aeneid* was an execrable poem. Lowell once called all Roman poetry "a half-hardy exotic," and he said that he was far more deeply impressed when he stood on the *Sasso di Dante* than by the tomb of Virgil. Preferring "romantic" to classical" verse, Grimké appended this note to a Phi Beta Kappa oration he delivered in Connecticut in 1830: "I would certainly rather know by heart, Campbell's lovely and spotless poem, *Gertrude of Wyoming,* than the fourth Book of the *Aeneid,*" in which the passionate love of Dido is portrayed; and a few sentences later he added that the shipwreck of the *Ariel* in Cooper's novel "far excels the storm in the first Book of the *Aeneid.*"[102] A. H. Everett sounds remarkably like Coleridge when he rates Virgil's epic only slightly higher than the *Henriade,* says that the poem "fails in attracting any interest," and finally decides that "its great merit is the charm of the language."[103] Nearly every critic, reacting to the extreme idolization of Virgil in the preceding century, argued or intimated that the Roman's imitativeness, his insincerity, his lack of spontaneity, and his ignorance of heroic manners were quite sufficient grounds for relegating him to the third or fourth rank of epic poets.

Towards Homer, however, many American writers were favorably disposed. Retaining and applying traditional criteria, some of them characterized the Greek epics as highly original imitations of men in action, as incomparable sources of what Bryant termed "direct lessons of wisdom."[104] But the majority took a more or less primitivistic point of view. There is Emerson, for example. Though he often adopted a strictly monistic approach to poetry, emphasizing the essentially unitary nature of all great poems, he sometimes shifted to an approach that was very largely historical. A presumption of change and variability certainly underlies his assertion that "Homer, who in spite of Pope and all the learned uproar of centuries, has really the true fire and is good for simple minds, is the true and adequate germ of Greece, and occupies that place as history which nothing can supply."[105] His evaluation of the ancient poet, and of literature past and present, becomes rather obvious when he says that "in antiquity, nature towered above all man had done: it sunk the personal importance of man. The bard taught as the minister preaches, and felt an impertinence in introducing self. Now man has grown bigger, a commercial, political, canalling, writing animal. Philosophy inverts itself, and poetry grows egotistical."[106] At other times, speaking in direct opposition to Coleridge and the admirers of subjectivism, Emerson praised the union of the physical and the spiritual as found in Homer, the combination of "the energy of manhood with the engaging unconsciousness of childhood" as displayed in his heroes.[107] With regard to the Greeks, he asks: "Whether they had an equivalent for our organized *morale?* Whether we have lost by Civilization any force, by Christianity any virtue?" And his answer is that "machinery encumbers. Homer is to us nothing personal, merely the representative of his time. I believe that to be his sincerest use and worth."[108] Nor was Emerson the only critic to rebel against the complexity and subjectivism of modern times. A reviewer declares that "especially in this day, when there is so much morbid sentimentalism, and false, obtrusive spirituality, is it well to go back to old Homer and Chaucer."[109] George Bancroft says that Homeric scenes "are hopeful as on the morning of a battle, when the war horse is prancing, and the hero exulting as a strong man before a race"; in the poems of Goethe, on the other hand, one finds "men driven to despair and suicide by hopeless desire, women languishing from a passion, which their own innocence condemns; persons of delicate sensibility brooding over unreal pains."[110]

But it was of course Thoreau who most earnestly took issue with the tendencies of the day. Primitivistic to the core, Thoreau withdrew from a world of steam-engines and taxes to pursue what he regarded as a Homeric mode of living. And in his mind daily experiences, even the most inconsequential incidents, found their counterpart in the Greek epics. A mosquito at dawn sang "Homer's requiem," its "own wrath and wanderings";[111] a "fire-eyed Agamemnon" was to be seen "at town meetings and elections, as well here as in Troy neighborhood";[112] Thoreau is visited by a simple, natural "Homeric or Paphlagonian" woodcutter "who had supped on a woodchuck" and had heard of the Greek poet;[113] and out in his garden "the beans saw me come to their rescue armed with a hoe, and thin the ranks of their enemies, filling up the trenches with weedy dead. Many a lusty crest-waving Hector, that towered a whole foot above his crowding comrades, fell before my weapon and rolled in the dust."[114] Again and again Thoreau said that when Homer spoke "it is as if nature spoke. He presents to us the simplest pictures of human life, so the child can understand them, and the man must not think twice to appreciate his naturalness."[115]

Thoreau was indeed exceptional. In contrast to him, most Americans were trying to overcome a primitive way of life rather than to encourage it, to speed up rather than to retard the proverbial wheels of progress. And as staunch Christians many of them had little sympathy for paganism. Primitivistic idealization of Homer as a bard, and lachrymatory appreciations of the Priam-Achilles or Hector-Andromache episodes are conspicuously absent from American critical writings; there is nothing whatsoever to compare with Leigh Hunt's exclamatory "O lovely and immortal privilege of genius! that can stretch its hand out . . . and touch our eyelids with tears," or with similar ejaculations by Nathan Drake and Hazlitt. Instead, we perpetually encounter references to the barbarism of Homer, to the unmitigated spirit of vengeance in the Greeks and their uncontrollable love of fighting. Whittier announces that "the brawny butcher work of men whose wits, like those of Ajax, lie in their sinews, and who are 'yoked like draught oxen and made to plough up the wars,' is no realization of my ideal of true courage";[116] and Simms calls the Homeric heroes "neither more nor less than highwaymen and pirates" who bear a resemblance to "the hunter of the American forest, the dark, fierce barbarian, Choctaw or Cherokee."[117] Speaking more generally, and rather like Cottle in England, a reviewer declares that "the poets are a race of imitators, and it had been correctly observed before, that it is quite impossible to say how much mischief the works of Homer alone may have done the world by encouraging a taste and fondness for military scenes": even the popular Walter Scott is cited as an example of this infectiousness.[118] Longfellow, though he admired the *Iliad,* could not help jotting down in his journal, "Rather heavy, all this fighting";[119] while Legaré is revolted by some of the scenes in Homer: the heroes pursue a victim, then "butcher him in cold blood, cut off his head and set it upon a pole, drag his body at their chariot wheels, and cast it forth to be devoured by the dogs and the fowls of the air."[120] Such comments were of course far from original, for they had appeared even in some of the neo-classical essays of the eighteenth century. But there is often a uniqueness of tone in these later appraisals, an indication of a Puritan, or at least of a highly religious or moralistic, point of view. Bryant, though in the midst of translating Homer, explained in a letter that "I believe the gods behave more shamefully in the *Iliad* than in the other poems, and their conduct is so detestable that I am sometimes half tempted to give up them and Homer together."[121] Parke Godwin emphasizes the despicableness of "the wrangling, squabbling, concupiscent, and, very often dirty gods of Greece" in contrast to the glorious conception of the Supreme Being in the Gospels.[122] E. P. Whipple observes that "the practice of revenge" as depicted in Homer has always been "denounced by moralists" and "forbidden by Christianity."[123] And the *Literary World* speaks derisively of the many Americans who, in raising their children, "are mindful to keep all dangerous matter at a proper distance, in the hope of thus developing a nice, steady, trafficking piece of humanity, adapted to the age, . . . a member of the common council, a vestry man, and, probably, referee in difficult matters": among these parents "it is a favorite idea to banish the sturdy, dashing, generous old Greek from the library of the young student, and, in his stead, leave Upham on Peace, Pollock's

Course of Time, and Luther, a poem, together with Festus, and other works of a safe or progressive tendency."[124]

There was thus an endless number of remarks about individual heroic poets, ancient and "modern"—remarks pro and con, incisive and superficial. However, one essay in particular would seem to deserve our close attention, Jones Very's unimaginatively entitled but rather provocative "Epic Poetry." Though its basic premises and conclusions are by no means original, it has the distinction of being the most elaborate expression, in England or America, of the Schlegelian and Coleridgean attitude towards the heroic poem; it sets forth with unusual clarity some of the principal reasons why Romantic critics on both sides of the Atlantic were tempted, and were sometimes induced, to relegate the epic to an inferior station among the literary genres.

Ignoring the patriotic songs and ballads of primitive peoples, Very traces the rise of heroic poetry to Homer and his immediate predecessors. The *Iliad,* he says, is the "true model" of the epic; it was composed at a time when all poetry automatically portrayed external action, when there was a "heroic greatness to war which cannot now be seen in it."[125] "Man viewed himself with reference to the world; not as in the present day, the world in reference to himself"—and it was this outlook on things which gave the *Iliad* an "epic interest" not to be found in modern literature.[126] After defending Aristotle's "great principles" as ever-relevant, Very proceeds to the later heroic poets. He visualizes them as struggling against terrific odds, for "the wonder and interest of the world" had been transferred "to the mind, whose thought is action."[127] The *Aeneid* becomes "a lunar reflection of the *Iliad.*" Ariosto idly indulges in "dreams," Tasso has modest success because he is born in the only age in which "the heroic Christian character" can be displayed in outward action, and Dante, realizing that the era of the true epic is past, turns to a form which is essentially dramatic.[128] Since Very thinks that the Christian world favors tragedy rather than the epic, that it demands "a more spiritual representation of the mind's action," one expects him to find serious faults in *Paradise Lost.* He does not do so, however. He praises it, instead, as a kind of epic-tragedy ("the epic form it has taken seems but the drapery of another interest"[129]), and he says that it is the only Christian epic with "great epic interest."[130] The poem has the "materiality" of Dante as well as "the spirituality of the present day";[131] its subject, the fall of man, is the only one which could have been treated with success in the seventeenth century. But it seems obvious to Very that the era of the epic came to an end with Milton, and in arguing the matter he reveals himself as a confirmed progressivist who cares rather little for "true" heroic poetry. "To sigh that we cannot have another Homeric poem is like weeping for the feeble days of childhood";[132] and again, "purely objective poetry" like Homer's "is the most perfect, and possesses the most interest, only in the childhood of the human mind."[133] Great poets will arise in the future, he assumes; but they will compose dramas and lyrics rather than epics: they will choose poetic types in which they can exhibit the conflicts they feel within rather than those present in the physical world around them.

On the whole, it seems quite apparent that the prestige of the epic was ebbing away during the Romantic period, and that its decline closely paralleled that of neo-classicism in general. Argue as we may, we cannot escape the conclusion that almost every new trend in criticism was militating in favor of other literary forms. True, pathos could be found in some epic poems, but it was usually confined to an episode here and there; true, the heroic poet expressed his own ideas and feelings, but he did so only from time to time, and in a work like the *Iliad,* it seemed doubtful whether he did so at all; true, poetry might conceivably attain high levels as an art even before society itself had made substantial progress, but history appeared to demonstrate that new genres evolve from older ones as changes occur in man's conception of himself and of the external world, and that as a result older ones like the epic tend to become outmoded with the passage of time. Such basic considerations were of course in the minds of critics everywhere. But American critics had additional reasons to regard epic poetry in a rather unfavorable light. Though some were conservative enough to adhere to traditional theories of literature and to long-accepted standards, others were fully prepared to break with the past, to pander to the transient tastes of the present, of the democratic majority; to subscribe to ideas of scientific and intellectual progress and to recommend literature which would properly reflect these ideas; to base their estimations of literary worth on some notion of equalitarianism or of individuality and unusualness; and to resort to the moralistic approach of Puritan or another kind of Protestant religionism. Collectively, these emphases made the poetry of Homer, Virgil, and Ossian—in fact, all pagan verse—seem largely obsolete, reflective of ideals long since superseded by more enlightened ideals. And though the prestige of Dante and Milton was high, it was scarcely unassailable; the habitual treatment of *Paradise Lost* as a religious work rather than eminently as a work of art was at last to lead to a frontal attack on Milton soon after the middle of the nineteenth century.

Though the climate of opinion everywhere was thus forbidding for the epic, there was an occasional ray of sunshine. The primitivism of Thoreau in America and of lesser figures like Drake in England provided an historical basis for admiring Homer and to some extent Ossian. There was also an admittedly sluggish undercurrent of Aristotelianism, with its stress on the depictions of universal human nature in the classical epic; the divorce of Romantic from Classical and the provision of new reasons for especially esteeming Dante and Milton; the monism of Shelley and Emerson and the notion that all great epics, like all great poetry in general, objectify the same transcendent reality. More important, there was the organicism of Coleridge, Emerson, and many others, a concept of poetry which, when operant in practical criticism, counteracted the proclivity to fragment a work of art and to value it on some such narrow basis as its historical place, its emotionalism, or its "beauties." Because of its great complexity and length, an epic poem seemed to fare better among critics who regarded it as a totality rather than as an agglomeration of diverse elements. Nevertheless, viewing all these rays of sunshine, one reaches the immediate conclusion that none of the approaches was able to award any distinctive virtues to the epic, to discover any merits that were peculiarly its own; and that most of them were inclined, in a rather futile way, to pit one heroic poet against another or a heroic poet against some other kind of poet.

How are we today to regard Romantic interpretations of the epic? Do these interpretations really seem legitimate, seem superior to those of the Age of Reason? Undoubtedly they represent a swinging of the pendulum, a reaction against a type of criticism which had become mired in rules and prescriptions, in meticulous logicality, in a largely pointless disassembly of literary works. Undoubtedly there was crying need to recognize more fully that poetry springs from emotion as well as rational thought, is affective as well as intellective; that biographical study has its rightful place in the exegesis of literature; that circumstances of time and place may not only appreciably mould a poem like the *Iliad* but may also overlay it with a thick residue of manners and customs which now require thorough explanation. However, one cannot avoid feeling that so many critical emphases after 1800, while respectable enough in theory, were pursued too far in practice and did unnecessary damage to the prestige of the epic. The historical approach often led to a confusion of history and literature, to extreme and mistaken notions about their relationship; undue attention was paid to what the neo-classicist would have considered the "dress" of a poem. Encouraged by the historical approach, primitivism fostered many quite wild opinions about the Ossianic epics, completely blinding some critics to their modernity; it also brought about a conception of Homer which, in view of the art presiding in his poems, hardly seems in keeping with the truth of things. Progressivism, on the other hand, tended to obscure the time-proven fact that human nature is always essentially the same, that Odysseus is a good deal more than an Ithacan prince of long ago. In narrow fashion, it gave undeserved stress to the Christian view of life (Boyd, Everett), to the desirability of introspection on the part of the poet (Coleridge, Hazlitt), to literary vogues of the moment (Tuckerman and many re-viewers), and in America in particular, to poetry that reflected nationalistic aspirations or prevailing social and political attitudes (Whitman). Progressivism was of course inherent in many Romantic attempts to substitute the distinction of Classical and Romantic for the older formalistic distinction of the various genres. But the counterbalancing of "subjective" and "objective," of "internal" and "external," at best a rule-of-thumb procedure, again led to excessive depreciation of many heroic poems and a blindness to their central purposes and values. There was too strong an inclination in applied criticism to mistake change for progress, to elevate emotionalistic and reflective poems above poems of action and suspense, contemporary ones above less recent ones like *Paradise Lost* or the *Divine Comedy*. Nor can one speak highly of the way in which theorists utilized biographical data. Perhaps it is impossible to examine a work of art adequately without considering the artist at all, but too regularly in the Romantic period the study and estimation of personality was transmuted into an evaluation of the poem itself. For instance, how one appraised *Paradise Lost* was often dependent on whether one regarded Milton as forbiddingly austere and inhuman, as shockingly unorthodox in his attitude towards marriage, or as a valiant Prometheus steadfastly resisting the tyranny of kings and bishops, a champion of freedom and democracy. Just how far afield critics could go in using this approach is evident in the writings of Drake. Drake eulogized *Fingal*, the *Iliad*, and *Paradise Lost* not so much because of any inherent greatness in those poems but because of the sufferings their authors had endured. And there was of course impressionism. Neither Hazlitt nor Hunt nor Wilson had any intention of disparaging the epic, yet their uninhibited response to poetry amounted to and perhaps encouraged the repudiation of all objective standards, a total obscuration of the values on which the prestige of an epic, if prestige there is to be, must finally depend.

Organicism alone promised well for heroic poetry. At least it was not tangential, concerned with matters of a peripheral or irrelevant nature; at least it represented a real attempt to see a poem in its wholeness. But if this approach was advocated repeatedly, it was put into actual practice only rarely. It was overshadowed by approaches of an emotionalistic, historical, biographical, or impressionistic sort. In brief, whatever the obvious drawbacks of neo-classicism, a basically Aristotelian point of view had tended, and in a few critical writings was still tending, to do greater justice to the epic poem than any of the points of view more commonly adopted after 1800. There is possibly little wonder that a day was to come, much later in the century, when a writer here and there was to plead for greater centrality in criticism as a whole and in epic criticism in particular.

5   The Pendulum Begins to Swing: Early Victorian Estimates: 1832-1880

In some respects the Victorian era up to 1880 was a second "Romantic" era. From the Age of Wordsworth it inherited, almost as a matter of course, the historical-biographical approach to literature, the propensity not merely to explicate the backgrounds of a work of art but to make them an important basis for critical judgment. It continued the earlier practice of bifurcating literary history into "classical" and "romantic," of challenging the neo-Aristotelian systems of rules on the ground that they were dogmatic and arbitrary, of stressing emotionalism rather than architectonics or ethical purpose as the salient criterion of greatness in poetry. At the same time, in reacting to the positivism of Comte and to an ever-increasing accentuation upon utilitarianism as a measure of worth, it sought to perpetuate or refurbish the neo-Platonist concepts of beauty and the Christian idealism that had underlain the critical pronouncements of earlier writers.

Because of this continuity in literary opinion, we can hardly look for any precipitous abandonment of "Romantic" definitions and estimates of the epic as a genre. Some Victorian critics, implying that "epic" is synonymous with "narrative," held that either of these terms could rightly be applied to any versified tale, ancient or modern, long or short, well organized or loosely constructed, to the *Nibelungenlied* or Tennyson's *Idylls* as properly as to *Paradise Lost*. Others, placing a special premium on emotionalism in poetry, associated "epic" with Homer and spoke derogatorily of the *Iliad* as a consciously contrived and therefore artificial composition, as an altogether archaic type of poem. Still

others, disregarding completely the matter of external form, agreed
with Shelley that an epic is a poem which adumbrates eternal
truth and beauty through the guise of the local and particular.
Thus John Addington Symonds, though scarcely a neo-Platonist
at heart, describes Shelley's definition as "remarkable," as contra-
dicting all previous definitions, and as awarding special distinction
to Homer, Dante, and Milton because they "have summed up
the experience and expressed the spirit of great eras of civilisation,
and have formed the education of succeeding centuries."[1] Often
too there was concurrence with earlier Romantic opinion as to
the lowly position of the heroic poem among the several literary
kinds. While John Stuart Mill once praised the epic because it
seemed to contain all the elements of poetry, he more frequently
intimated a preference for the lyric: "I do not think that epos
qua epos, that is *qua* narrative, is poetry, nor that the drama
qua drama is so; . . . I think Homer and Aeschylus poets
only by virtue of that in them which might as well be lyrical."[2]
On another occasion he suggested that the lyric is "more eminently
and peculiarly poetry than any other, it is the poetry most natural
to a really poetic temperament."[3] Edward Dowden, agreeing
with Coleridge and the Schlegels that the drama is supreme, com-
plained that "the calm, somewhat historical progress of the epic
seems wanting in the entire full presence of life, the immediate
vitality of dramatic art."[4] And there were of course innumerable
critics who argued for the novel in the fashion of the Romantics.
John Conington, for example, frankly acknowledged in his trans-
lation of the *Aeneid* that a modern rather prefers characterization
to plot, and he went on to assert that "prose fiction combines the
depths of tragedy with the breadth of epic poetry."[5] Not without
interest too is the comment of a writer in *Blackwood's* in 1851:
recent decades have brought "a revolution of taste in favour of
the lyric, and at the expense of the epic poet"; moreover, the
public has become so impatient with narrative verse that "if
you have a long story to tell, by all means tell it in prose."[6]

The period after 1832 significantly altered the general intellec-
tual milieu. In some respects it was also one that proved to be
peculiarly inimical to the epic and to other early forms of litera-

ture. For the major writers of prose fiction, for instance, heroic poems were little more than historical curiosities, idle tales that cast no light upon the grave problems of the contemporary world. Neither Thackeray nor Dickens displayed any interest whatsoever in Homer or Virgil or Milton: Thackeray was too much concerned with Victorian snobbery or with the creation of modern heroes who are anything but heroic, while Dickens was too pre-occupied with his crusade against social injustice. Among the scientists and utilitarian philosophers, moreover, there was an unmistakable antagonism not only towards the epic but towards every kind of verse; Bentham's idea that "all poetry is misrepresentation," at best providing momentary amusement, won the wholehearted approval of Victorian positivists, of every "practical-minded" person. Reminding one of so many ingenuous readers today, Charles Darwin wrote in his autobiography that he found Homer, Virgil, Milton, and poets in general intolerably boring; Shakespearean drama seemed so dull that "it nauseated me." But he went on to remark that novels "have been for years a wonderful relief and pleasure to me. . . . I like all if moderately good, and if they do not end unhappily—against which a law ought to be passed."[7] Only slightly less extreme was the opinion of Herbert Spencer. After suggesting that "Prometheus Unbound" was the only poem he ever truly enjoyed, Spencer frankly owned that he had particularly developed "an indifference to epic poetry." His feeling was "due in part to the unchanging form of the vehicle and in part to the inadequately varied character of the matter: narratives, incidents, adventures—often of substantially similar kinds. So great was his desire for amusement and novelty that after the first few pages of the *Iliad* Spencer decided he "would rather give a large sum than read to the end."[8]

On the whole, however, despite strong forces working against the epic, the Victorian period seems to have restored to the epic a good deal of the prestige that it had lost during the Age of Wordsworth. After 1832 most of the leading men-of-letters were professed anti-Romantics. Convinced that literary criticism, like society itself, was on the verge of chaos, they declared that earlier theorists had gone too far in repudiating eighteenth century opinion, that their evaluations had become peripheral, prejudiced, erratic, and eccentric, or as one writer puts it, "spasmodic and sensational." Rightly enough, one believes, many Victorians were inclined to think that the Romantics had done well to discredit certain features of neo-classicism but that they had made the serious mistake of eradicating the virtues with the vices; they had behaved like Jack in Swift's *Tale of a Tub,* ripping asunder a valuable fabric in the process of removing superfluous lace and ruffles. Hence writers in Tennyson's time became intent on bringing literary criticism back to what seemed to be its proper course, on giving due emphasis again to clarity, restraint, style, unity of plot, and centrality. And as eighteenth century theory became renascent, modifications of neo-classical definitions and estimates of the epic began to appear more and more frequently in Victorian criticism. Rejecting the vague concept of "classical" and "romantic," a concept that had usually militated in favor of all Christian art, Thomas Arnold made external form a basis for re-classifying poetry into some eleven kinds, including epic, dramatic, heroic, narrative, and didactic; and he proceeded to give the epic poem the honored place at the top of the hierarchy, observing as he did so that "its essential principles were laid down by Aristotle in the *Poetics,* more than two thousand years ago, and they have not varied since."[9] For Thomas Arnold, for his illustrious son, for many of their contemporaries, "epic" did not merely denote "narrative" or a poetic unveiling of Beauty or a composition which synthesized the life-philosophy of an era, nor did comparisons of Homer and Shakespeare, on some such basis as emotionalism, seem either the obligation or privilege of the true critic. In theory if not always in practice, the epic was treated as relatively fixed in its nature, as an organic representation of men in action, as a poem whose delineations of mankind would never cease to delight and to instruct. Critics did not usually separate poetry into as many as eleven kinds; in fact, the vast majority were not at all explicit about the matter of classification. But their literary estimates were certainly more Augustan than Romantic when they denounced the lyric for exhibiting mere moods and isolated feelings, when they spoke of the epic as revealing character more clearly than did the drama, when they objected to Milton's plot and the peculiarities of his spiritual ideas, when they spoke again and again of the impeccable structure of the *Iliad,* and when in praising epic poetry, they called novels abominable because "the life which they represent is not worth representing," because they "make a merit of weak man's nothingness."[10]

If we overlook the critical opinions of the novelists and scientists, we can see from this broad survey that two important and quite opposite attitudes towards the epic existed side by side during the Victorian period. One had originated in classical antiquity and had become dominant in England around 1700; the other, if indeed it is distillable into a single attitude, had evolved around 1750 and had become ascendant in the Age of Wordsworth. This does not mean, however, that Victorian criticism of epic poetry was entirely derivative or that our present task is merely one of distinguishing between points of view that were already commonplace in literary theory. A juxtaposition or clash of older ideas is bound to modify those ideas or to produce essentially new ones, and after 1832, when critical, religious, and scientific opinions became almost inextricably entwined, it was inevitable that evaluations of epic poetry were to assume a high degree of originality. To see how truly this was the case, we have only to turn, as we shall now do, to Victorian analyses of the principal heroic poets, both ancient and modern. Since Homer and Virgil were restored to a portion of their birthright while Ossian, on the other hand, was almost completely forgotten, since what was said of the *Iliad* and *Aeneid* to some extent determined what was said of the heroic poems of the Christian era, it seems most logical to begin with the Victorian appraisals of the classical epic.

Had a Homer ever existed? If so, had he been an inspired primitive bard or a skilled artist? In short, had Wolf been right or wrong? The answers which Victorians gave to these perennial questions have more than an antiquarian interest, for they actually serve as a kind of touchstone to the critical proclivities and moods of the time. According to William Smith, an historian writing in the 1850's, no literary theorist of the day was immune to the insidious hypotheses of Wolf and the other so-called "separatists": "even those who were the most opposed to his views have had their own opinions to some extent modified by the arguments which he brought forward, and no one has been able to establish the old doctrine in its original integrity."[11] Though one is impelled to take Smith's statement *cum grano salis,* the Victorians were certainly more excited about the German theories than the Romantics had been, and not a few of them came to regard the traditional "unitarian" view as completely unrealistic. Basing his argument largely on the anthropological evidence supplied by the Greek epics, F. A. Paley went so far as to say that "our Homer," Homeric poetry as it now exists, would appear to belong to a time as late as that of Plato;[12] while a reviewer in *Blackwood's,* after observing that Wolf's endeavor to explain Homer seemed to earlier Englishmen "pretty much as profane as to explain the world without God," gives the German full credit for having discovered, "with a keen glance, and a grand comprehensiveness, the minstrel character of the POPULAR EPOS."[13] On the other hand, Thomas Keightley, a critic and biographer of Milton, shows us how damaging the separatist theories could be to the prestige of Homer when he refuses to include the Greek poet on a list of the world's chief figures in literature: "Our omission of Homer may cause surprise; but much of the fame of Homer is merely traditional, and arose when he was regarded as the sole author of the poems that go under his name." For Keightley the *Iliad* is of course "a composite and not an organic whole," a poetic anomaly or agglomeration of episodes in verse rather than an integrated work of art.[14] Considerably better known but somewhat along the same lines were the speculations of George Grote, whose history of Greece first appeared in 1846 and was still being reprinted after 1900. Grote endeavors to seem impartial in his judgments: he opposes Lachmann's view (Kleinlieder-Theorie) that at least sixteen poets were contributors to the *Iliad,* and he censures the supposition that all passages betokening real artistry are "decidedly post-Homeric." He is bold enough, however, to parallel the *Iliad* to the *Sagenpoesie* of other primitive peoples, and to assent to the German notion that at least two poets composed the Greek epics, that the tale of Troy is divisible into an *Achilleis* and an *Iliad* proper, and that the whole poem as we have it is to be admired for its primitive simplicity and picturesqueness rather than for its structure or its ethical insight. In "Homer," Grote says, one cannot detect "any ulterior function beyond that of the inspired organ of the Muse, and the nameless, but eloquent, herald of lost adventures out of the darkness of the past."[15]

Of all the champions of Wolf in Victorian Britain, Thomas Carlyle was clearly the most important. Lecturing in the 1830's on the history of literature, he declared that the *Iliad* is comprised of what he calls "ballad delineations" of historical events and that "one may cut out two or three books without making any alteration in its unity."[16] But as a confirmed separatist—Clough once reported that Carlyle "thinks anyone mad" who believes in the unity of Homer—he judges the Greek epic in ways that are, to say the least, both unexpected and inconsistent. On the one hand he could laud Homer as "a Voice coming to us from the Land of Melody";[17] he could speak of the *Iliad* as a poem that "sings itself" and that sets forth "the impressions of a primeval mind";[18] and on one occasion he went so far as to draw the typical organicist parallel between the growth and self-realization of the oak tree and of the Homeric poem. "This all-producing earth knows not the symmetry of the oak which springs from it. It is all beautiful, not a branch is out of its place, all is symmetry there; but the earth has itself no conception of it, and produced it solely by the virtue that was in itself. So is the case with Homer."[19] On the other hand, Carlyle seems to revert to the usual progressivist and separatist point of view when he refers to the artificial way in which Homer portrays his various heroes. "There is not at all the sort of style in which Shakespeare draws his characters; there is simply the cunning man; the great-headed, coarse, stupid man; the proud man; but there is nothing so remarkable but that any one else could have drawn the same characters for the purpose of piecing them into the Iliad." He is reminded of Italian comedy with its stereotyped dramatis personae, its harlequin and its doctor.[20] What view, then, did Carlyle really take? Was the *Iliad,* and presumably the *Odyssey* as well, an organic entity, an organic expression of the collective mind of a people, or was it an artificial patchwork from which one may cut out two or three books without violating its unity? It would be hard to decide.

If he retains any idea at all of Homer as an actual person, the separatist is inclined to conceive of him in either of two ways. He will visualize Homer as a mere barbarian, as a rhapsodist without any clear understanding of art as art, without any real knowledge of why men behave as they do; or as a great primitive bard "rapt into paroxysm and enthusiasm," expressing uninhibitedly the most intense emotions of all humankind. Though both conceptions were extremely common in the Romantic period, they were not so much in evidence after 1832. In the first place, there was a strong reaction against the progressivist interpretation of literary history, against the notion that the earlier the poem the less meaning and value it will have for the modern world. No longer, therefore, were critics inclined to assail the warlike spirit of Homer, to call his heroes and gods disgusting, to say that his attitude towards life was puerile and unenlightened; Edward Fitzgerald was one of the few to treat the Greek poet with any degree of superciliousness, and even then he was willing to admit that his opinions might be mistaken.[21] In the second place, there also seems to have been something of a reaction against the Wertherian primitivism of the Romantic period. Fully aware that Homer had lived in an early era, that he was a bard to whom the art of writing was unknown, most Victorians nevertheless refused to think of him as the poet of true sensibility or to express lachrymose sympathy for Priam and Andromache. They did not repeat the romanticists' rhapsodies over the "lovely and immortal" power of genius to "touch our eyelids with tears" as Leigh Hunt had done.[22] If one was in a sentimental mood, one was likely to turn to some latter-day novels, not to Ossian and certainly not to Homer.

That there was little support for separatism or for the pro-

gressivist and primitivist estimates admirably attuned to it around
1800 becomes apparent if we turn for a moment to the caustic
comments that were now being made about Wolf and his fol-
lowers. Never before had the Germans been subjected to so much
indignation. William Mure, usually hailed as the great champion
of Homer in Victorian England, spoke of the separatists as in-
dulging in a "tasteless course of hypercritical subtlety," and he
asked the skeptics why Homer could not have composed both
the *Iliad* and the *Odyssey* if it was generally agreed, as it seemed
to be, that a single author had written plays so dissimilar as
Macbeth and the *Merry Wives of Windsor*.[23] Reviewers in the
Quarterly were far more violent in their language. In 1850 one
of them declared that among the Germans "eccentricity has long
been the standard substitute for genius. Accordingly they worked
each after his fashion for nearly fifty years with most pertinaceous
alacrity—one cutting and slashing—another pruning and paring
—score upon score mumbling and nibbling."[24] In another issue
a writer damns Lachmann's "imbecile deductions," his "micro-
criticism," his "crazy theories like a Neapolitan gig on a *festa*."[25]
Nor did *Blackwood's* hesitate to join in the chorus of anathemas
when it railed at the Germans as "those charlatans, impostors,
knaves, idiots, heretics, schismatics, atheists."[26] The Homeric
scholar J. S. Blackie was not particularly given to the launching
of imprecations, but in his chief work, *Homer and the Iliad,* he
described the separatists as lawyers, "supersubtle, curious, cap-
tious, and impracticable. They are like men, if we may imagine
such, with microscopic eyes, who see the mites crawling so
gigantically through the mass, that they lose all stomach for the
cheese."[27] It is, in fact, with some feeling of relief that one comes
across the rather flippant verses by Elizabeth Barrett Browning:

> *Wolf's an atheist,*
> *And if the Iliad fell out as he says,*
> *By mere fortuitous concourse of old songs*
> *We'll guess as much too for the universe.*[28]

British patriotism, the extremism of Continental scholars, a reaction to the relativism and subjectivity of the Romantics, a compulsion to re-examine all critical theories and standards in the light of common sense and reason, a return to traditionalism and the opinion of the ages, a general re-discovery of the glory that was Greece, a less prejudiced attitude towards the thought and the ideals of the eighteenth century—these are some of the factors responsible for the revival, in certain quarters at least, of a more or less classical conception of Homer. There was certainly no tendency to follow the English Augustans blindly, to regard a conscious moral purpose as the mainspring of the Homeric epic, or to dissect the *Iliad* into such infinitesimal fragments that the character of the whole became obscured. Nor was there any propensity to codify the principles on which the Greek poems had been constructed, or to proclaim, as some of Pope's contemporaries had done, that all epics must contain twenty-four books and that the first book must have no more than a specified number of similes. Such arbitrary rules, said J. C. and A. W. Hare, are about as applicable even to the Homeric poems as "the rules of carpet-making are to the side of a hill in its vernal glory."[29] But Victorian critics had one important thing in common with earlier neo-classicists: a real if imperfect awareness of the artistic greatness of the Greek epic. Though Conington thought of Homer as an unlettered bard, he described him as the only early poet "who has attained the grace and finish of a literary period";[30] the *Quarterly* went out of its way to praise the "skill of Homer," "that rarely erring instinct which forbade him to forget his whole in running after its details";[31] and E. L. Bulwer attributed to the Greek epic a form "so symmetrical that the acutest ingenuity" of the ancients could not discover what Wolf believed he had discovered.[32] W. E. Gladstone, one of the staunchest of the unitarians, observes that "the plot of the *Iliad* is one of the most consummate works known to literature";[33] again, in praising the "close mutual relation of parts" and the "solidity, balance, and measure" of Homer's poetry, he calls the *Iliad* "a product of the nicest and most consummate constructive art."[34] Similarly, Blackie epitomizes Homer as "the epic artist": "if anywhere among human compositions we have a grand imaginative plan, and a gradually consistent execution of that plan, we have them here" in Greek heroic poetry.[35] In part because of the comprehensiveness and unity of the Homeric plot, in part because of Homer's grand manner, Blackie goes on to denounce earlier Romantic parallelisms of Walter Scott's lays and of the *Iliad:* the lays "differ from an epic as a pipe does from a trumpet;[36] and he reproves Carlyle and others for daring to compare the Greek epics with the *Nibelungenlied,* a poem that "has lived now for more than half a century a life beyond the Rhine, rather of erudite resuscitation than of continued powerful popular influence."[37] Finally, William Mure finds in Homer not only a well-integrated plot but also "perspicuity of style, richness of imagery, harmony of numbers," three qualities which the eighteenth century had admired and had described in precisely the same phraseology.[38]

But greater emphasis upon excellence of structure and technique hardly accounts for the resurgence of Homer's prestige after 1832. More important by far was the return to the old belief that both the Greek epics are unrivalled sources for the study of human nature and are not mere historical curiosities as Coleridge and so many Romantics had stigmatized them. Pointing out that biological evolution is an imperceptible process, one Homeric critic found a measure of solace in the fact that "so long ago men were so very like what men are now."[39] William Morris bravely declared that "Homer is no more out of date than Browning."[40] George Meredith observed that all the Homeric characters "are distinct, painted without effort, but with the sharp outline of life";[41] Mure that "the same deep knowledge of human nature" is discoverable in both the *Iliad* and *Odyssey;*[42] Blackie that Homer draws "real pictures of healthy human life," of "lusty-bodied" men who "never torture their brains with incalculable theories";[43] and James A. Froude that one is continually unearthing in the Greek epics "some little trait of humanity which in form as well as spirit is really identical with our own experience."[44] In a similar vein Gladstone proclaimed that through Homer "we are introduced to man in every relation of which he is capable. . . . The study of him is not a mere matter of literary

criticism, but is a full study of life in every one of its depart-
ments."[45] And a writer in *Blackwood's* spoke highly of Homer's
"natural man," of his "true men" and "true women."[46]

Naturally, this general shift to a new—more correctly, to a
traditional—point of view encouraged a re-estimation of the
various characters upon whom Homer centers his attention. Rather
neglected by theorists around 1800, Nausicäa again becomes the
ideal maiden she had seemed to Joseph Warton and to Rousseau;
Helen is transformed from a calloused voluptuary into an attrac-
tive and dignified matron, and old Laertes is described by one
author as "a calm, kind father of the nineteenth century."[47] But
the most pronounced change of all occurred in the conception of
Achilles. No longer a vengeful homicide or a bestial maniac, as
Romantics had often called him, Achilles emerges as a pattern of
the true hero. Mure speaks of him as "ideal," as "surpassing in
the splendour of his attributes, any living example of humanity."[48]
Walter Bagehot says that the valiant trio of later times—Sieg-
fried, Charlemagne, and Arthur—"are but attempts at an Achil-
les."[49] And Gladstone, though he considers the son of Peleus too
violent on certain occasions, points out that "any degree of self-
government is a wonder, when exercised over such volcanic
forces"; "the scope of this character is like the sweep of an organ
over the whole gamut, from the lowest bass to the highest
treble."[50] Moreover, in re-appraising the personages of the Homer-
ic epics, critics were by no means as confident as earlier Romantics
that the Achilles, Helen, and Troilus of the drama are superior
to Homer's. The women of the *Iliad* and *Odyssey,* one writer
says, are not "the wax-dolls of the Greek tragedians, miscalled
heroines," but "true women such as one meets with any day, with
all their lovely weaknesses."[51] Nor were Shakespeare's Greeks
generally to be preferred. In *Troilus and Cressida,* a reviewer de-
clares, "we see perhaps one of the lowest and latest pictures of
mere mediaeval Homerism. The sun of ancient criticism had
set"; and "we scarcely find one single living trait of the Father
of all Bards preserved."[52] Similarly, the Hare brothers aver that
Coleridge "has seldom been less happy in his criticisms than in
his remarks on the Greek chiefs" as depicted by Homer and

Shakespeare, and that Hazlitt was not "less wide of the mark when he held that the English dramatist 'seems to have known them as well as if he had been a spy sent into their camp.' The Homeric heroes are not mere graceful outlines: they are every whit as substantial, living flesh and blood as Shakespeare's."[53]

After 1832, many critics thus regarded the Greek epics as immortal poems concerned with men in action, primarily with men doing but also with men feeling and thinking; and if one notes the frequent use of the adjective "constructive," it is apparent that they were inclined, like the English Augustans, to dissever form from content. But does this utilization of a "classical" approach imply that a large segment of Victorian criticism was non-historical, that it neglected the principles of growth and change in literature, that as far as Homeric theory was concerned, only the separatists and certain "Romantics" paid heed to the time and place in which the Greek epics were composed? Obviously, the day when one made no more than passing reference to the backgrounds of an author, to the "religion, country, genius of his age," lay almost two centuries in the past; and no Victorian critic was able to blink the fact that early literature remains largely unintelligible unless its locus in history is examined with care. Hence even those who adhered closely to classical standards were prepared to discuss the distinction between *Volksepos* and *Kunstepos,* or Homer's possible role as a bard, or the historical relationship of the epic and the drama, or the extrovertive character of all early poetry; and especially after Schliemann's archeological discoveries at Mycenae in the 1870's, they debated whether the tale of Troy was merely a nature-myth pertaining to "the struggle of the earth with the seasons" or whether Homer was a historian of real events, "the greatest chronicler that ever lived."[54] Books treating the backgrounds of the Greek epic flowed from the press in an ever-swelling stream. Among the most ambitious of these was Gladstone's *Homer and the Homeric Age* (1858), a work extending to some sixteen hundred pages and so fraught with infinitesimal details about ancient gods, geography, rituals, and the like, that a search for critical estimates becomes a painful and almost frustrating experience. One thing, however, can certainly be said in favor of Victorians like Gladstone. If they were excessively concerned with backgrounds of literature, if they were usually antiquarians rather than critics, at least they were more successful than the Romantics had been in distinguishing between what Matthew Arnold called the "real" estimate and the "historical" estimate. Homer was presumed to have been a very early poet, but one did not therefore become either a primitivist or a progressivist.

This does not mean to say that most Homeric criticism after 1832 was entirely objective. No large body of literary theory is free from the "personal" estimate, and especially in the past two centuries, from the "historical" estimate as well. Thus however strongly they insisted upon classical standards, Victorians esteemed the Greek epic, to some extent at least, as a commentary on the present and as a mirror of their own particular interests or philosophies of life. Those who were perturbed by the materialism of the day and by the apparent dissolution of religious faith were able to discover in Homer an interpretation of human existence that was almost Christian, one that earlier Romantics had associated with Dante or Milton but never with Homer. Referring to the Greek poet, William Mure says that "one so familiar with the passions and foibles of human nature could not fail to be deeply sensible of its vanity. . . . Homer's lively sense of this standard truth, with the importance he attached to it, is evinced by the prominence given to it throughout both poems."[55] Gladstone goes much further than Mure. In the world of Homer, he says, we find "the taint of sin at work, but far, as yet, from its perfect work"; "here first we see our kind set to work out for itself, under the lights which common life and experience supplied, the deep problem of his destiny." The "controversies of materialism" were unknown to man in that early time; "human life had an aspect mostly sad: but the universe, as to its general constitution, was still in tune."[56] In his memoirs John Churton Collins reports that Froude "spoke very sadly and bitterly of human life and said that Shakespeare's and Homer's attitude was, Poor Devils, why be hard on them, they have so many miseries";[57] while Froude himself, in his *Short Studies on Great Subjects,* finds self-forgetfulness and religious faith the true basis of Hector's greatness. Hector "knows that there is a special providence in the fall of a sparrow, and defies augury. To do his duty is the only omen for which Hector cares."[58] J. A. Symonds, after observing that a modern tends to minimize the sadness inherent in the Greek *Weltansicht,* asks whether any reader of the *Iliad* "has not felt that the glory of Achilles, coruscating like a star new-washed in ocean waves, detaches itself from a background of impenetrable gloom." Just as the story of this hero "involves a dreary insight into the end of merely human activity," so the story of Odysseus is for Symonds, as perhaps for Tennyson, one that illustrates "the troubles of our pilgrimage through life."[59] Likewise, John Ruskin asks one to consider whether "there is any sadder image of human fate than the great Homeric story": Achilles, at once tender and cruel, first loses his mistress and then his dearest friend. "Yea— even for his dead friend, this Achilles, though goddess-born, and goddess-taught, gives up his kingdom, his country, and his life— casts alike the innocent and guilty, with himself, into one gulf of slaughter, and dies at last by the hand of the basest of his adversaries. Is not this a mystery of life?"[60]

But Symonds was perfectly right: many critics did not find their own sadness at heart, their own sense of the tragic reflected in the poems of Homer. Like Mme. Dacier, Joseph Warton, Rousseau, and the nineteenth-century Romantics before them, they often glorified the Age of Homer as a golden age, as one that knew none of the problems and woes of the present. Writing to Browning about the Greek epics, Julia Wedgwood asked in rather typical Victorian fashion: "Ah, that morning twilight that is stolen from us, shall we ever find it again?—our evening twilight is something different, though it may have its own force too. How beautiful it was with the deep Heavens and the dim earth, now it is the heavens that are dim, and the earth so obtrusive."[61] Browning probably disagreed with Miss Wedgwood: though he once made a vague reference to "that far-away carelessness of common hopes and fears" in the Greek epic, he was too much of a modern, of a realist and a progressivist, to nourish any illusions about the felicities of primitive life or to sympathize with Homeric conceptions of

morality and religion.[62] William Morris, on the other hand, would
have been almost as happy as Thoreau to have lived in the time
of Homer rather than in the nineteenth century. But while it was
the vigorous existence of embattled warriors at Troy which mainly
fascinated the man of Concord, it was the wanderings of Odysseus
that appealed to Morris, the character of the Greek chieftain as
revealed through his trying experiences—his simple dignity, his
heroic determination to conquer both internal and external forces
of evil, his "open-heartedness" and his never-abating loyalty to
Penelope. In translating the *Odyssey,* Morris must have dwelt
with a real sense of pleasure upon the "beauty of life" in ancient
Ithaca, upon Homer's descriptions of the palatial households of
Alcinous, Menelaus, and the son of Laertes himself—households
so unlike the "foolish rabbit-warrens" of well-to-do Victorians;
he must also have noted with delight that Odysseus was enough
of a craftsman to build his own raft and to construct a most
elaborate bed.[63] Similarly, J. S. Blackie observed that no menial
task was beneath the dignity of a Homeric chieftain, whereas a
nineteenth century gentleman would hardly think of doing any-
thing with his own hands: we have "printing machines, and wash-
ing machines, and calculating machines, and rotatory hair-brush-
ing machines; and by and by we shall have preaching machines
and lecturing machines."[64]

What impressed critics most deeply, however, was the vast
difference between Homeric poetry as poetry and the kind of
verse that was being written in modern times. Unlike so many
theorists around 1800, they did not summarily dismiss the *Iliad*
as too "classical" and objective, then crusade for all "romantic"
and reflective verse; instead, it was usually the "romantic" verse
that they dismissed. Homer "teems with life, like a morning in
spring," the Hare brothers observed; but if a reader turns to a
modern poem he will find that "first one thing was described and
reflected upon; and then something else was described and re-
flected upon; and then . . . some third thing was treated in the
same way. The power of infusing life and exhibiting action is
wanting."[65] J. S. Blackie, asserting that Homer is a "plain man
with plain men" and hardly the type to attend the "aesthetical

tea-parties" of the Victorians, admits with a tone of sarcasm that "those who love to soar in the aërial balloon with Percy Bysshe Shelley, or to wrestle with the darkest social problems of the day under the leadership of the authoress of 'Aurora Leigh,' will not be apt to consider the wrath of a Thessalian captain, or the wanderings of a world-wise Ithacan laird among savages and giants 3000 years ago, subjects of very hopeful significance for the lofty Muse, by whom they love to be inspired."[66] Likewise, J. C. Shairp declares that "all contemporary literature" is concerned with "describing and probing human feelings and motives with an analysis so searching, that all manly impulse withers before it, and single-hearted straightforwardness becomes a thing impossible." Against this modern tendency, "so weakening, so morbidly self-conscious, so unhealthily introspective, what more effective antidote, than the bracing atmosphere of Homer, and Shakespeare, and Scott?"[67]

Did the Greek and Roman classics have an important place in a scientific age? Many Victorians were positive that they did not, that ancient literature had no real meaning for a utilitarian and democratic society, that it was imperative to add biology and physics and geology to university curricula even if, as a result, all classical studies had to be abandoned. "It is physical science only," said T. H. Huxley, "that makes intelligence and moral energy stronger than brute force."[68] For the moment, however, opinion seemed to be weighted against the Huxleys and the Spencers and the common citizenry who put all their faith in the study of empirical fact. Interest in the Greeks and Romans was mounting rather than waning; interest in classical poetry in general, and in the classical epic in particular, was becoming conspicuously more intense than it had been for more than a hundred years. Even if we overlook the critical views of Matthew Arnold—we shall turn to them in due time—it is patent that the majority of critics were intent on restoring to Homer the prestige which he had lost at the start of the century. Between 1860 and 1890 there were above a dozen attempts, most of them futile, to provide better English translations of the Greek epics—translations into prose, into couplets, into blank verse, into hexameters, into ballad meter, and into Spenserian stanzas. Nor is it without significance that around 1850 Oxford University first began to give examinations covering some twelve books of Homer in the original.[69]

But a still more unmistakable sign of a new appreciation of the classics, hence of the classical epic, was the gradual reappearance of Virgil's name on lists of the "best poets." In Wordsworth's day, we will recall, critics could hardly find language opprobrious enough to express their distaste for the *Aeneid*. Keble denominated the poem a mere tour de force, Coleridge declared peremptorily that its only assets were its diction and meter, and everyone railed at Aeneas as a coward, a reprobate, a degenerate, and a dissimulator (Aeneas, said Landor, "is more fitted to invade a hencoop than to win a kingdom or a woman").[70] Now, after 1832, though this Romantic attitude remained prevalent, something like a reaction was beginning to take place, imperceptibly at first, more noticeably as time went on. There was a growing tendency, at any rate, to say a few things in favor of the *Aeneid,* to compare it in certain respects to the *Iliad* or to other epics, and once in a while even to show genuine enthusiasm for the poem.

Victorian attacks on Virgil differed little from earlier Romantic attacks. Always strongly opposed to classical conceptions of art, and especially to the notion that a good poet fashions or constructs, Carlyle believed that Virgil had failed because of "that fatal consciousness, that knowledge that he is writing an epic; the plot, the style, all is vitiated by that one fault."[71] The Roman could be "a great poet when he did not observe himself," but as far as the *Aeneid* is concerned, we must "conclude that he was, properly speaking, not an Epic poet."[72] Like so many nineteenth century critics, Gladstone objected to Virgil's lack of sincerity, to his "spirit of courtierlike adulation";[73] while Julia Wedgwood confessed that she could "just put up with Virgil's semi-demi belief in the old mythology."[74] As in the Age of Wordsworth, however, the loudest complaints were lodged against the personages who took part in the action of the poem. Macaulay, writing home from India in 1834, said that he had done a prodigious amount of reading during his voyage but that he had not enjoyed the *Aeneid* because of its "want of human character."[75] Carlyle could see nothing heroic in Aeneas' complete inactivity during a storm at sea, in his sitting still and groaning aloud "Was ever mortal so unfortunate as I am? chased from port to port by the persecuting Deities who give me no respite!"[76] George Brimley accused Virgil's hero of "sneaking off without even saying Good-bye" to Dido,[77] while Gladstone declared that "when he appears in arms we are tempted to ask, 'Son of Venus, what business have you here?' "[78]

It is apparent, nevertheless, that views like these were becoming rather less fashinoable, that what was happening in the criticism of Homer was also happening in the criticism of Virgil. In the year 1877, W. Y. Sellar published his *Roman Poets of the Augustan Age: Virgil,* a work containing the most eloquent but also the sanest plea for the *Aeneid* to be made during the entire nineteenth century. Discussing the reputation of the classics since the death of Pope, Sellar points out that "Roman literature is more in harmony with eras of established order, of adherence to custom, of distinct but limited insight into the outward world and into human life, than to eras of expansive energy, of speculative change, of vague striving to attain some new ideal of duty or happiness." Hence none of the chief Romantics—Goethe, Schiller, Byron, Scott, Shelley, and Keats—"were at all indebted, in thought, sentiment, or expression" to Virgil and the other Roman poets.[79] Even in his own day Sellar detects a hostility to the Augustan epic, a preference for Homer and for all literature belonging to "times of nascent and immature civilisation";[80] but he is happy to find that criticism of Virgil "is much more favourable than it was some thirty years ago."[81] Though he does not explain this change of attitude, the reason for it is perhaps implicit in Sellar's own evaluation of the *Aeneid.* Granting that the poem has a "tameness . . . in point of human interest" and a deficiency "in spontaneous invention," that it "produces the impression rather of careful construction than of organic growth," he nevertheless refuses to make psychological insight or sheer emotionalism or originality the touchstone of important art: Sellar is far from being a "Romantic" critic. At times his position is that of the historical relativist: the *Aeneid* is a "literary epic," an "epic of national fortunes," and it must be understood as such. The structure of the poem "implies powers of combinations, of arranging great masses of materials, of concentration of the mind on a single object, more analogous to those which produced the vast historical work of Livy and 'The Decline and Fall' of Gibbon, than to the spontaneity, the *naïveté,* the rapidity of conception and utterance, and that immediate sympathy between poet and people" which characterize the primitive epic.[82] In view of the time and place in which the *Aeneid* was written, the poem was all that it was intended to be, all that it logically could be; hence one has no right to complain about its imitativeness or its conscious artistry. Elsewhere Sellar argues in neo-classical fashion that the poem "is full of pathetic situations and stirring incidents which move our human compassion or kindle our sympathies with heroic action";[83] he finds the characters far from "common or mean," as the Romantics had branded them.[84] And finally, he points to the special values of the *Aeneid* for a Victorian reader. No longer is it a meaningless and ridiculous story about heroes that are not heroic and gods that are not godlike but once again, as in earlier eras, a powerful and inspiring religious poem. One would almost think that Sellar was confusing Virgil with Dante when he speaks of the Roman as a "Christian" in "his firm faith in Divine Providence, in his conviction of the spiritual essence in man and of its independence of and superiority to the body, in his belief that the future state of the soul depends on the deeds done in the body, in his sense of sin and purification for sin, in the value which he attaches to purity and sanctity of life."[85] And still wider is the gulf between Sellar and the early Romantics when he observes that "if poetry ever exercises a healing and reconciling influence on life, the deep and tranquil charm of Virgil may prove some antidote to the excitement, the restlessness, the unsettlement of opinion in the present day."[86]

Two other critics joined Sellar in a re-appraisal of Virgil:

F. W. H. Myers in an important article in the *Fortnightly Review* for February, 1879, and J. C. Shairp in a book, *Aspects of Poetry* (1881). Admitting that Aeneas is "ill-fitted to fill the leading *rôle* in a poem of action," and that an excessively passionate nature like Dido's "will now repel as much as it attracts us,"[87] Myers proceeds to build up a case for the *Aeneid* which is rather different from that of Sellar. In Victorian fashion he characterizes the hero of the Roman epic as a man perpetually conscious of his destiny and his duty, he lauds the calm dignity and the verbal splendor of the poem, and he speaks sympathetically of "the abiding sadness," the "indefinable melancholy," the *"Welt-Schmerz"* of Virgil's own soul.[88] The "modern air" of Virgilian poetry "is in great measure the result of the constantly-felt pressure of this obscure home-sickness—this infinite desire; finding vent sometimes in such appeals as forestall the sighs of Christian saints in the passion of high hopes half withdrawn, when the Divinity is shrouded and afar—oftener perceptible only in that accent of brooding sorrow which mourns over the fate of men."[89]

The third member of this triumvirate, J. C. Shairp, has even more striking things to say. Having acknowledged that "the poetry of an age in many ways so akin to our own as Virgil's was, is apt to pall on our taste, and to meet with scanty justice,"[90] Shairp launches into a plea for the Roman poet that is almost as eloquent and is certainly as earnest as Sellar's. Virgil abhorred military life and battles, he agrees with John Keble; moreover, "heroic portraiture was not in his way."[91] But must one then arrive at Keble's conclusion that the *Aeneid* is a total failure? Shairp's answer is an emphatic "no." If not a great military epic, the poem is something far better, "a great religious epic."[92] It reflects the lonely, "devout soul" of its author, "a vein of thought and sentiment more devout, more humane, more akin to the Christian" than we find in any other classical poet.[93] Though the Augustan age was skeptical, even irreligious, Virgil clung tenaciously to the old beliefs, conceiving that "to eradicate these would be to tear up some of the deepest roots of his spiritual life";[94] he somehow "maintained within himself a sense of poetry, faith, and devoutness" at a time when these things were being scorned.[95]

Gentleness, "natural piety," patience, fortitude, and manly endurance; "the mellow, if somewhat sad, wisdom that comes from a world's experience, the human-hearted sympathy that . . . feels the full pathos of the human story, and yet is not without some consoling hope"—these are the great virtues of the Roman poet, virtues that have made the *Aeneid* the immortal poem that it is.[96]

Sellar, Myers, and Shairp were not the only Victorians to acclaim Virgil. Challenging a common Romantic opinion, *Blackwood's* in 1845 asked a question that had not been asked for a long time: "Is Virgil other than a great poet because he owes debts, even in one of the two finest books of the *Aeneid,* to his gifted predecessors?" And the magazine followed up this question with another: "Is he not rather . . . to be commended, like one who, having inherited from different lines of ancestry several precious stones . . . should set them in one rich necklace, and enhance their value many times by engraving each with a clear-cut and nobly-shaped intaglio?"[97] John Conington also rejected the old notion that Virgil was a mere plagiarist: "he is an artist, an Italian antiquary, a Roman of the Augustan period, speaking to the average educated intelligence of his own day; he is anything rather than what modern admirers of Homer would wish him to be, a hierophant of 'the inner Homeric world,' an expounder of primitive history, philosophy, policy, and religion,'" as contained in the Greek epics.[98] Henry Nettleship called Virgil one of the half-dozen great poets whose "scope and grandeur" placed him "beyond any special human interest";[99] Stopford Brooke described him as "imperial and universal";[100] and Tennyson, the Virgil of the Victorian era, addressed the Roman as "Thou majestic in thy sadness at the doubtful doom of human kind," and again, as "Wielder of the stateliest measure ever moulded by the lips of man."[101] Even Blackie, one of Homer's greatest admirers in the nineteenth century, declared that "the author of the *Aeneid* may claim comparison with the best writers of lofty narrative poetry, and will fairly be deemed to have surpassed most";[102] while John Ruskin, though he preferred other poets, at least gave some credit to the Roman when he spoke of himself as "a man who is at one in every point and tone of thought with Dante and Virgil,

and who is discontented precisely as they are."[103] Generally, how-
ever, critics acclaimed the pathos of the *Aeneid*—the pathos which
earlier Romantics had construed as bathos. Writing to E. B. Cowell
in 1869, Edward Fitzgerald reported that he had "been visiting
dear old Virgil" again; Horace, he said, "never made my eyes
as wet as Virgil does."[104] A reviewer called attention to Virgil's
"tenderness" and "his exquisite pathos";[105] Sir Archibald Alison
to "the inimitable pathos" of the *Aeneid*,[106] and James Lonsdale
to the "tenderness" which is "more striking as contrasted with
the stern Roman character, and with the stately majesty of the
verse; the poet never becomes affected or sentimental."[107] Con-
ington, referring to the Roman poet's "modern" treatment of
the character of Turnus, pays special tribute to "the profound
human interest with which Virgil's dramatic power leads him to
invest a person for whom no minstrel of the heroic age would
have claimed a tear."[108]

Was the pendulum really swinging? Everything would seem
to suggest that it was, that the classical epic was regaining much
of the prestige which it had lost at the turn of the nineteenth
century. No longer were critics quite so prone to equate "poeti-
cal" with "lyrical," to demand above all else the intense and
the ineffable, the supramundane and the intangible, the highly
suggestive and the highly unusual. Reacting to Romantic re-
action, many of the literary theorists whom we have just consid-
ered were convinced that time is the supreme test of art and that
the consensus of aesthetic opinion, from classical antiquity to
the present, is more likely to be reliable than the judgments of
any one era or of any one person. By no means did these critics
underestimate the importance of the lyric, or for that matter of
the drama and the novel, but neither did they depreciate the long
narrative poem, the epic as defined by Aristotle. Homer was not
regarded as a barbarian singing of the vengeful deeds of other
barbarians, or as an unimpassioned and therefore unpoetical his-
torian, or even as a rhapsodist whom one could admire for his
occasional displays of pathos. Throughout Victorian criticism

there is the assumption that the Greek epics were composed by one man, by an eminently civilized man who had pondered long and deeply on the meaning of life and who had considered the Trojan War not as a mere series of battles but as a conflict of basic human forces and moral issues. This man was a skilled poet, moreover. With great deliberation he had dove-tailed and welded the manifold elements of his story, the facts and the fictions, into an unimpeachable whole. For Virgil, on the other hand, Victorian critics had far less respect: not a single writer after 1832 said or even intimated that the *Aeneid* was a close rival of the *Iliad*. But more and more often there was a tendency to revert to traditional opinion, to draw attention to the artistry of the poem, its superb meter and style, to speak of the pathos of certain episodes, and to minimize the importance of the love story which the Romantics had found so shocking and to stress instead the god-given mission that Aeneas was intent on performing. Virgil himself, called a sycophant and hypocrite by critics around 1800, was now becoming a symbol of indomitable courage, a worthy guide for Dante and all believers, a man of sincere faith but a man saddened, like numerous Victorians, by the skepticism and worldliness of the age.

From what has been said thus far, it would almost seem as if the Age of Tennyson were another Classical Age. The mounting prestige of Homer and Virgil, the re-affirmation of Aristotelian standards and of time-honored estimates, and, conversely, the notable absence of radical progressivism and sentimental primitivism, would certainly appear to point to some such conclusion. We must remember, however, that at no juncture in the past two or three centuries has criticism been essentially homogeneous. Victorian theory, like Romantic theory, was many-sided or composite. It lacked a discernible core, a basic premise or a group of integrable premises. Even within the writings of a single author there is frequent evidence of contending points of view, of incompatible criteria upon which literary judgments were formed.

Hence, in turning now to Victorian appraisals of heroic poets other than Homer and Virgil—chiefly to appraisals of Dante and Milton but also of many lesser figures—we shall encounter a complex of critical views traceable ultimately to a dozen different sources. Some opinions are not unlike those we have already discussed; others indicate the influence of the neo-Platonists or of Longinus, or of nineteenth century theorists such as the Schlegels, Goethe, Coleridge, Tieck, Hegel and Taine.

Minor heroic poetry caused relatively little stir after 1832. On the whole, critics seem to have felt that rather too much attention had already been paid to primitive epics, ballad-epics, and so-called "romantic" epics, that the sheer exuberance of these poems could hardly atone for their lack of ethical import and form, for their digressiveness and general extravagance—in short, that there was a real need to return to the sanity of the traditional classical approach. Hence poems like the *Cid,* the *Song of Roland,* the *Kalevala,* and the *Ramayana,* though given a respectable place in histories of literature, had no perceptible impact upon theoretical or practical criticism. The *Nibelungenlied* was usually neglected: Blackie, we will recall, rebuked Carlyle for finding in it "the glowing imagery" and the "fierce bursting energy" of Homer.[109] Despite the fact that Conybeare and Kemble had drawn attention to *Beowulf* during the 1820's and 1830's, philologians and historians were the only ones who displayed an abiding interest in this Anglo-Saxon epic. Ossian, attacked and zealously defended at the start of the century, was execrated by almost every Victorian critic. Blackie, for instance, spoke of the "vein of over-refined, almost sickly, sentiment" in *Fingal;*[110] Macaulay declared that the Scottish poems "are utterly worthless, . . . a chaos of words which present no image";[111] while Mrs. Browning, indignant that one of her correspondents, H. S. Boyd, had committed the unpardonable sin of praising the Highland poems more than Homer's, could not refrain from exclaiming, "What! Ossian superior as a poet to Homer! Mr. Boyd saying so!"[112] "Ossian," she remarked in another letter, "has wrapt you in a cloud, a fog, a true Scotch mist. You have caught cold in the critical faculty, perhaps."[113] Moreover, Victorians showed scant enthusiasm even for the somewhat more regular epics of Ariosto and Tasso. Macaulay, for example, branded the *Orlando* "extravagant";[114] Gladstone, always loyal to Homer, objected to the "irrelevant interpolation, incongruous mixture, and divided interests" of the *Gierusalemme;*[115] and Fitzgerald admitted that he "never cared . . . for *any* chivalric Epic; neither Tasso, nor Spenser, nor even Ariosto, whose Epic has a sort of Ballad-humour in it."[116] Obviously, many of the rivals of Homer and Virgil were rapidly losing ground.

Homer and Virgil did have at least one formidable rival, nevertheless. Familiar to a mere handful of English readers around 1800, Dante became an idol of almost every Victorian who had any pretension at all to a taste for literature. His reputation soared as high as that of Homer; it threatened to equal that of Shakespeare. Carlyle called Dante not only one of the greatest poets but also one of the greatest men that the world had ever known, while Macaulay made the rather extravagant claim that "very few people have ever had their minds more thoroughly penetrated with the spirit of any great work than mine is with that of the *Divine Comedy*."[117] So irreproachable did the Italian poet now seem that critics, journalists, scholars, and ordinary citizenry were either stunned or outraged by the theory which Gabriele Rossetti proposed in the late 1820's, namely, that Dante, as a member of an occult society, had written the *Divine Comedy* specifically as an anti-Christian attack on the Church and on the secular government of his time.[118] "Because much is clearly allegorical, Signor Rossetti will allow nothing to be merely literal," the *Edinburgh Review* complained in 1832; "to say the truth, the elasticity of our author's system is such, that, in the hands of so bold and enterprising a discoverer as himself, it is difficult to say what may not be brought within the range of its comprehension."[119] And translations of the *Divine Comedy* appeared in ever increasing numbers: John Carlyle, Mrs. C. H. Ramsay, C. B. Cayley, E. O'Donnell, Ichabod Wright, and Patrick Bannerman were among the many scholars who tried to improve upon the earlier work of Boyd and Cary.

It is not difficult to account for the phenomenal popularity of Dante around the middle of the nineteenth century. As we suggested earlier, there was no single basic standard in Victorian criticism; literary theory as a whole was diversified enough to accord nearly equal places to poems as radically different as the *Divine Comedy* and the *Iliad,* to the Christian epic as an allegorical narrative of spiritual experience, of the vacillation of man's feelings regarding his present life and the life-to-come, as well as to the pagan epic as a historical-mythical narrative of experience in this world, of human behavior under the stress of war, of mundane hopes and fears. Moreover, in modern times the *Divine Comedy* has tended to mean all things to all men. Since it is perhaps the most complex of long poems, since it contains not merely religious but also historical, scientific, philosophical, and purely autobiographical matter as well, it was bound to excite the interest of Victorian critics for one or more of a number of reasons. This does not mean that Dante criticism was usually original. In fact, there was such a monotonous reiteration of some points of view, such a plethora of opinions derived from earlier theorists, that it seems fitting to confine ourselves to a few influential estimates.

Throughout the nineteenth century, critics alluded to or quoted from Macaulay's appraisals of Dante, usually the one included in his essay on Milton (1825), less often the one that appeared in *Knight's Quarterly Magazine* a year earlier. Yet there is nothing really world-shaking about either of these appraisals. If we do not permit ourselves to be deceived by Macaulay's rhetoric and concentrate upon what he actually has to say, we discover a number of fairly superficial generalizations rather than a penetrating and balanced analysis of the *Divine Comedy* as a work of art. The earlier discussion opens with trite remarks on Dante's contributions to Italian culture, on his reputation as a poet, on his "turbid and melancholy spirit" and the sincerity of his religious faith.[120] Next come several paragraphs about the "power" of the poem, "the strong belief with which the story seems to be told" ("in this respect, the only books which approach to its excellence are *Gulliver's Travels* and *Robinson Crusoe*") and the "air of reality" produced by the imagery and descriptive details.[121]

Macaulay then declares that Dante was unlike many eminent English poets, as well as "the herd of blue-stocking ladies and sonnetteering gentlemen," in passing over the beauties of nature and fixing his eye instead upon "the sterner and darker passions" of mankind.[122] Finally, after briefly commenting on Dante's use of ancient mythology, he concludes the essay with observations on the style of the Italian poet ("there is probably no writer equally concise"[123]) and on some of the latter-day translations of the *Divine Comedy*. In the second essay, on the other hand, Macaulay makes rather tangential and sometimes challengeable comparisons of Dante and Milton. Their careers are described as parallel (both "had been unfortunate in ambition and in love"[124]), but "the character of Milton was peculiarly distinguished by loftiness of spirit: that of Dante by intensity of feeling."[125] As for their poetry, Macaulay's only concern is the imagery and descriptive detail in the two epics: Milton is properly "mysterious and picturesque" in his portrayal of supernatural beings; Dante "is picturesque to the exclusion of all mystery": his angels "are good men with wings," his evil spirits "spiteful ugly executioners."[126] But nowhere in either of his discussions of the Italian poet does Macaulay come to grips with large poetic elements or with fundamental aesthetic matters. He says nothing at all about the structure and the conduct of the narrative or about the blending of thought and image or even about the essential "meaning" or significance of the whole.

Some fifteen years after Macaulay wrote these essays, Thomas Carlyle presented in his lectures an altogether different estimate of Dante. Influenced by Tieck, Fichte, and other German thinkers, he was not content merely to point to the externalities and more obvious features of the *Divine Comedy* or, like so many Victorians, to explicate historical setting and esoteric allusions. Instead, he tried to penetrate to the innermost principle of the poem, to account for and exhibit it as a totality, as the end-product of a growth that began in the soul of a poet intent on discovering "the mystery of the Universe" behind all outward appearance. All men, according to Carlyle, "have some touches of the Universal," some intimation of its reality; but a "vates-poet" like Dante "is a man sent hither to make it more impressively known to us."[127] Having glimpsed Beauty in its essence and sensed the *"melody* that lies hidden in it,"[128] he bursts forth at length into what Tieck called "a mystic unfathomable Song,"[129] a song-poem that has "true inward symmetry" and that addresses itself to the soul of all mankind. By no means does Carlyle imply, however, that a poem like the *Divine Comedy* somehow fashioned itself, that it can be regarded as an entity more or less separable from the poet and the era in which he lived. Despite its essential universality, Dante's epic is still "the soul of Dante,"[130] a manifestation of the man himself and of his particular turn of mind, a product of his deep insight and incisive thought and complete sincerity. It is also the soul of Christianity of the Middle Ages, for it reveals "the Divine Idea" through the local and temporal, through the religious and philosophic beliefs of a specific period of history. Backgrounds, in fact, were of such paramount importance to Carlyle that as time went on he tended more and more to find "poetry" not in poems but in the lives of great men.[131]

Because of the tenuousness of transcendentalism, the Dante criticism of Carlyle had rather less impact than that of another theorist, R. W. Church. In his essay "Dante" (1850), Church endeavored to reach the ordinary reader of the day by making what might be called a "common sense approach" to the *Divine Comedy,* by avoiding the pitfalls of pedantry and keeping the poem as a whole under constant surveillance. He admits that Dante's epic seems obscure and lawless, harsh and incongruous, but unlike most Victorian critics, he observes that "no one has ever come to the end of the *Commedia* without feeling that if it has given him a new view and specimen of the wildness and unaccountable waywardness of the human mind, it has also added, as few other books have, to his knowledge of its feelings, its capabilities, and its grasp."[132] It has this effect upon readers because it is more than a mere theological poem: it is a "Story of a Life," "an *epos* of the soul, placed for its trial in a fearful and wonderful world, with relations to time and matter, history and nature, good and evil, the beautiful, the intelligible, and the mysterious, sin and grace, the infinite and the eternal."[133] Always mindful of the complexities in Dante, of the possibility of becoming utterly confused, Church suggests that one should not look for the homogeneous allegory of a Bunyan or a Spenser, that the allusions are "not so obscure but that every man's experience who has thought over and felt the mystery of our present life, may supply the commentary," that it is quite enough if the three beasts of the forest "carry with them distinct and special impressions of evil."[134] On the other hand, one is to realize that nothing in the *Divine Comedy* is really out of place. When Dante referred to persons whose very names are unfamiliar to us, it was because "he felt, what the modern world feels so keenly, that wonderful histories are latent in the inconspicuous paths of life, in the fugitive incidents of the hour": "there may be grades of greatness but nothing insignificant."[135] When he turned aside to describe external nature, the beauty of the dawn, of shooting-stars, of fireflies, and the light of the flame, of the water, of the fractured emerald, it was because these things were a part of the life of man. Again and again in his essay, Church reiterates the organicist view that "all is in character with the absorbed and serious earnestness which pervades the poem,"[136] that "episode and digression share in the solemnity of the general order."[137] The greatness of Dante's poem "is not in its details—to be made or marred by them. It is the greatness of a comprehensive and vast conception, sustaining without failure the trial of its long and hazardous execution, and fulfilling at its close the hope and promise of its beginning."[138]

The most outstanding of all Victorian estimates of the *Divine Comedy* was the one made by John Addington Symonds. In his *Introduction to the Study of Dante* (1872), Symonds argues like Church that critics have viewed the Italian epic in too narrow a fashion, that they have been obsessed with the idea of finding some single political, religious, or ethical purpose underlying the poem. Actually, he says, the *Divine Comedy* is "the voice and ultimate of articulation of a whole aeon of human culture . . . , the *logos,* the *verbum caro factum,* of the spirit of the Middle Ages." For this reason "its vast and complex organism must remain in part at least an undecipherable puzzle. Works of art, like works of animate nature, are, in the last resort, beyond the reach of critical or chemical analysis. We can observe, investigate, describe, admire them. But we cannot, and their authors cannot, by the aid of test-tubes or alembics, solve the problem of their vital principle."[139] Having this organicist view, Symonds goes on to show why one should not concentrate, as earlier Romantics had done, upon the *Inferno* alone: all three parts contribute, each in its own way, to a well-integrated and complete "epic of Man, considered as a moral being."[140] But to us today one of the most interesting sections of the *Study of Dante* is that in which Symonds discusses the poet's compression of thought, his use of myth to express conceptions otherwise inexpressible, and his employment of "type and symbol because he cannot speak in plainer language."[141] Four kinds of symbolism are attributed to Dante: "he either makes an arbitrary selection of natural objects to designate spiritual things; or he uses material metaphors . . . to signify the qualities of immaterial existences; or, again, he appeals immediately to the understanding, by taking some concrete person, animal, or object as the typical similitude of his thought; or, finally, he describes a pageant, in which long series of events are pictorially presented through the eye to the imagination."[142]

The oppressive materialism of the age, disapproval of utility as a measure of value, skepticism about the principle of progress, unsettlement of religious belief by the theory of biological evolution were factors prompting disillusioned Victorians to turn to the *Divine Comedy*. Christina Rossetti admired the Italian poet's invulnerable faith; Browning his strength of character and his perseverance. Gladstone thought of him as an exemplar and guide, as a mainstay for the heart and for the intellect. People read Dante, talked about Dante, and wrote about Dante. But the quantity of mere critical remarks was infinitely greater than the quantity of elaborative criticism. Not even John Ruskin, of whom Charles Eliot Norton said that "no other great English writer has shown such familiarity with the 'Divine Comedy,' "[143] had anything very comprehensive to say about

Dante's epic; his observations, abundant enough to fill an average-sized volume, were widely scattered, often desultory, usually concerned with single images or details. The four critics whom we have just discussed—Macaulay, Carlyle, Church, and Symonds—were therefore exceptional: they were, relatively speaking, both thorough and explicit. Three of the four, all but Macaulay, at least tried to see the *Divine Comedy* as an organic whole rather than as a collocation of detachable parts, to eschew the common practice of merely annotating or commenting at random and instead to determine why the poem was still vital after five hundred years.

If the prestige of the *Divine Comedy* was soaring as never before, what did Victorian litterateurs think of the other great Christian epic, *Paradise Lost?* Did they approve of the poem, as the Romantics had done, because it testified to the fortitude, the spotless integrity, and the earnest faith of its author? Could they derive assurance and comfort from the way in which it justified God's ways? Were they convinced that its fame would be immortal? Again it must be said that there is no sharp line of demarcation between Romantic theory and Victorian theory, that many of the estimates common in the Age of Wordsworth seem to have persisted throughout the entire nineteenth century. Hence we find, after 1832, a constant recurrence to the long-standing notion that *Paradise Lost* is one of the most universal of poems, is a supreme example of art that must endure. David Masson described it as "an epic of the whole human species,—an epic of our entire planet, or indeed of the entire astronomical universe."[144] "What story mightier or more full of meaning can there ever be?" he asked.[145] Stopford Brooke says that it is "worthy to exercise command over the heart and intellect of all ages,"[146] while Blackie sounds much like Coleridge when he declares that "Milton stands on the book of Genesis, the faith of universal Christendom, and a type of theological thought far older than the Protestant Puritans with whom he was accidentally connected."[147] There was the traditional emphasis upon the grandeur of Milton's theme and plan: "the design of every other mighty epic looks tame when compared to it," Edwin Hood remarked.[148] There was the same stress on Milton's loftiness of conception and of language: "Where in the poetry of the ancient world shall we find anything which approaches the richness and beauty, still less the sublimity, of the most triumphant passages in *Paradise Lost?*"[149] There was the same talk about the personality of Milton as glimpsed through his poem: "Into whatever he wrote," observed Masson, "he was sure to put as much of *himself* as possible."[150] And finally there were the customary discussions of the characters in the epic. Blackie finds a "depth of human interest" in Milton;[151] Masson describes Milton's Devil as sublime, admirable, intellectual, and noble, Goethe's as impetuous, mean, and shallow-minded;[152] and Hood reminds us strongly of Hazlitt, Hunt, or Drake when he says with respect to Satan: "Do what we will, we cannot but pity; care and woe sit upon that blasted brow, that figure smitten in its pride— faded, wan; . . . an oak, scorched in its manhood; a stately column left to solitude and loneliness by the flame, before Time had touched it with his finger."[153]

By all odds the most famous of these "Romantic" appraisals was that by Macaulay. Appearing in 1825, Macaulay's essay on Milton really belongs to the Age of Wordsworth with respect both to the date of publication and to the critical ideas it contains. There is the familiar argument that poetry flourishes best in rude ages—children and all "uncultivated minds" are presumed to be the most highly imaginative; and that it is to the great glory of Milton that he managed to compose immortal verse in spite of the fact that he lived in "an enlightened and literary society."[154] In Macaulay's all-too-brief treatment of *Paradise Lost*—he was more interested in Milton the man than in Milton the poet—there is also the common tendency of the Romantic critic to single out for discussion not the rationale or nature of the work as a whole but a particular and supposedly isolable quality of the poetry as poetry. He concentrates upon Milton's power to suggest, upon the "extreme remoteness of the associations" which he calls up, upon the "magical influence" of his verse. While Homer's poetry "sets the images in so clear a light, that it is impossible to be blind to them," that of Milton "sketches, and leaves others to fill up the outline." "It acts like an incantation. Its merit lies less in its obvious meaning than in its occult power. There would seem, at first sight, to be no more in his words than in other words. But they are words of enchantment."[155] And nowhere does Macaulay find this suggestiveness better exemplified than in Milton's muster-rolls of names. One name "transports us back to a remote period of history. Another places us among the novel scenes and manners of a distant region. A third evokes all the dear classical recollections of childhood, the schoolroom, the dog-eared Virgil, the holiday, and the prize."[156]

But in spite of all such adulation from Macaulay and the others, one thing is clear: *Paradise Lost* was no longer on secure ground. A storm was brewing. Romantic idolatry of Milton was giving way to Victorian depreciation. The epic that had once been called the best or the next-to-best in the world was slowly but surely being relegated to a third place, and there was danger that it might someday be stationed even lower. Why should this be so? Why should one Christian epic, that of Dante, achieve a higher and higher reputation, while another Christian epic, that of Milton, was beginning to lose a good deal of its prestige? What grave defects in the English poem had finally come to light?

The main reason for this strange state of affairs was the "discovery" that the claims of Coleridge had been fantastic: that *Paradise Lost* does not at all epitomize the Christian faith or serve (to quote from Coleridge) as "the basis of all religion, and the true occasion of all philosophy whatsoever." On the one hand, the intense interest of Victorians in all matters pertaining to religion led to closer study of the ideology of *Paradise Lost* and this study, in turn, led to greater stress on the Puritan elements in Milton: David Masson not only made free use of the term "Puritan" but employed it in a way that might easily seem to connote "narrowly sectarian" or "dogmatic" or "perverse." On the other hand, following the unearthing of Milton's *Christian Doctrine* in 1823, critics and scholars began to compare the theological concepts in Milton's prose with those in

Paradise Lost: the English poet was variously identified as an Arian, a Manichaean, and even as an Athanasian. No matter what creed was ascribed to him, however, the complaints were both frequent and vociferous. Bagehot proclaimed that the "orthodoxy of Milton is quite as questionable as his accuracy,"[157] that the poet "was not conscious of the effect his teaching would produce in an age like this, when skepticism is in the air, and when it is not possible to help looking coolly on his delineations."[158] John Sterling observed that "some of our most admired religious authorities have declared that the Rev. Mr. Pollok's *Course of Time* is superior to *Paradise Lost*" and that all that can be credited to Milton is the "dignity of his character."[159] Carlyle said that the poet was "too sectarian" and "polemical,"[160] Edward Dowden that "Milton's dogmatic idealism must now remain remote to me after Shakespeare,"[161] William Morris that "I hope I shall escape Boycotting at the hands of my countrymen" for not ranking the English poet among the immortals, "but the union in his works of cold classicalism with Puritanism (the two things which I hate most in the world) repels me so that I *cannot* read him."[162] Some critics went even further, suggesting that the religious concepts of *Paradise Lost* are inacceptable to all faiths and sects. J. R. Seeley asserted that Milton's pictures of the spiritual world "do not adapt themselves to any existing belief or sympathies," that his "Greek angels" are "not such as either Catholics or Protestants have ever believed in," that the poem "expresses no one's mind but the author's."[163] And John Ruskin, who admired Dante so intensely, suggested that Milton's story of the fall of the rebel angels is "evidently unbelievable to himself"; the rest of the poem, he added, is merely "a picturesque drama, in which every artifice of invention is visibly and consciously employed, not a single fact being, for an instant, conceived as tenable by any living faith."[164]

Criticism such as this was bound to ramify in all directions. Seeley said that the "whole form" of *Paradise Lost* is "outlandish,"[165] Thomas Arnold that the plot is too episodical,[166] a reviewer that the very purpose of the poem is obsolete: "We do not now compose long narratives to 'justify the ways of God to man.' The more orthodox we are, the more we shrink from it. . . . Our most celebrated defences of established tenets are in the style of Butler, not in that of Milton."[167] Objections were raised to the characters in the poem. Satanism apparently had no attraction for Blackie when he called Milton's rebel chief "a liar, a coward, and an eaves-dropper";[168] Bagehot pointed out that Adam, Eve, Satan, and all the others were "simple" when compared to the dramatis personae of *Hamlet*.[169] And there was a chorus of remonstrances about the personality of Milton as gleaned from his epic. Though he admired the poem because of its sublimity, Tennyson said "I feel certain that Milton after Death shot up into some grim Archangel."[170] The Hare brothers observed that "he wants the gentleness of Christian love,"[171] Seeley that he has "no tenderness like Dante's,"[172] and Carlyle that "he is conscious of writing an epic, and of being the great man he is."[173]

But one totally new fault was being found. An age that had seen geology develop into a recognized science, that had become intensely excited about biological mutation, heredity and environment, could hardly fail to examine and sift the basic "facts" of *Paradise Lost*. If Milton's heterodoxy seemed deplorable on the one hand, his concepts of the universe and of the genesis of life seemed just as deplorable on the other. Dowden spoke of Milton's astronomical system as "symbolically" though not scientifically "true,"[174] but in discussing the cosmologies of recent centuries he suggested that "to trace one's ancestry to Adam is to confess oneself a *parvenu;* our cousin the gorilla has a longer family tree to boast. Six thousand years!—why, a fox could hardly trim his tail and become a dog in so brief a period."[175] Thomas Keightley opined that to transport oneself back to the seventeenth century and to view the universe through Milton's eyes "is a difficult operation; and few therefore will ever attain to the height of the pleasure which *Paradise Lost* must have yielded to persons of taste and poetic feeling at the time of its first appearance."[176] David Masson, though he praises highly Milton's "great English mind" and his lofty imagination, intimated that the "power" of his epic might well be lessening.

"The Ptolemaism of Milton's astronomical scheme would alone put the poem somewhat in conflict with the educated modern conceptions of physical Nature. . . . The *primum mobile* has been for ever burst; and into the Chaos supposed to be beyond it the imagination has voyaged out and still out, finding no Chaos, and no signs of shore or boundary, but only the same ocean of transpicuous space."[177] But it was of course Thomas Huxley who really set the stage for future attacks on *Paradise Lost*. Lecturing in New York in 1876, Huxley declared open war on the poem because it stated so precisely that "the present order of things . . . had a sudden origin" in the not very distant past. "I believe it is largely to the influence of that remarkable work, combined with the daily teachings to which we have all listened in our childhood, that this hypothesis owes its general wide diffusion as one of the current beliefs of English-speaking people."[178] Reviewing Milton's account of the creation of the world, Huxley took the poet to task for making a serious error with regard to the evolution of life: geology disproves the notion that birds antedated terrestrial animals.[179]

There was thus an irremediable conflict in Victorian opinion of Milton. On the one hand, he was admired in the way that so many Romantics had admired him—as a man of strong convictions, of dauntless courage and resolution, of profound spiritual faith. His epic seemed to be an epic of "the entire universe," sublime in its conceptions, suggestive in its imagery, inspiring in its sincere attempt to justify God's ways. On the other hand, Milton appeared to be an austere, vindictive, sophistic theologian: he was an egocentric Puritan, or something worse. As for *Paradise Lost,* the religious ideas in the poem were thought to be narrow, outmoded, or eccentric; the cosmology was false, even ridiculous; Adam, Eve, and Satan were academicians rather than living, breathing characters; and the poet's supposed power of suggestion was, in reality, only a sign of vagueness, of an imagination that could not properly embody its abstract conceptions. On only one point did every critic concur: that Milton's style is, in the words of Bagehot, "the best specimen of pure style" in the whole realm of literature.[180]

There are reasons why we have said nothing up to now regarding Matthew Arnold. No other Victorian equalled him in stature as a critic. No other Victorian enables us to see so perspicuously some of the eminent differences between epic theory before and after 1832. No other Victorian did as much to shape epic theory at the end of the century. Certainly Arnold would seem to deserve rather special consideration.

To combat the centrifugal tendencies of latter-day criticism was of course one of Arnold's important missions. The earlier Romantics and most of his own contemporaries appeared to him prejudiced, whimsical, and provincial, too ready to judge a work of art by some segment rather than the whole, too prone to overrate it because of its historical importance. Urging above all else a greater centrality in literary estimation, he turned to many of the primary tenets and principles of classicism—to the traditionalistic concept of the genres (epic, drama, lyric, and so on, with the epic at the top of the hierarchy), to the equally traditionalistic concepts of poetry as an imitation of men in action, of universality as achieved through such imitation and through an appeal to the "great primary human affections." He emphasized the role of the poet in interpreting the "physiognomy and movement of the outward world" in all its natural magic and the "ideas and laws of the inward world of man's moral and spiritual nature."[181] He stressed the need for a premeditated plan, for careful construction, for proper proportion, and for the perfection of style.

Such a view of literature naturally meant the glorification of the classical epic. Arnold had little to say about Virgil: the "elegance" of the Roman poet, he once remarked, is what "makes one return to his poems again and again, long after one thinks one has done with them."[182] But Homer became almost an idol; he was acclaimed as the greatest poet the world had ever known—far greater than Virgil and Milton, somewhat greater than Dante and even Shakespeare. Homer was one of the "abounding fountains of truth, whose criticism of life is a source of illumination and joy to the whole human race for ever."[183] Homer derived his superiority to all other poets "from his application, under the conditions immutably fixed by the laws of poetic beauty and poetic truth, from his application, I say, to his subject, . . . of the ideas 'On man, on nature, and on human life,' which he has acquired for himself."[184] Homer was always ethical but he was never didactic. More often quoted than any other passage in Arnold's discussions of poetry is one which occurs in his "On Translating Homer" (1861). A person who endeavors to turn the Greek epics into his own language "should above all be penetrated by a sense of four qualities of his author;—that he is eminently rapid; that he is eminently plain and direct, both in the evolution of his thought and in the expression of it, that is, both in his syntax and in his words; that he is eminently plain and direct in the substance of his thought, that is, in his matter and ideas; and, finally that he is eminently noble."[185] A summary of this sort was intended not only to establish the consistency of matter and of manner in Homer—hence to establish his supreme artistry—but also to negate all separatist, all primitivist and progressivist theory as well. On the one hand, Arnold objected strenuously to attempts to compare the *Iliad* with the *Nibelungenlied* or with Scott's lays, to the assertions of translators like F. W. Newman that the Greek poet was really little more than a balladist, "direct, popular, forcible, quaint, flowing, garrulous, abounding with formulas, redundant in particles and affirmatory interjections."[186] On the other hand, he was persuaded of the folly of Wolf and his disciples. "The grand source from which conviction, as we read the *Iliad,* keeps pressing in upon us, that there is one poet of the *Iliad,* one Homer—is precisely this nobleness of the poet, this grand manner; we feel that the analogy drawn from other joint compositions does not hold good here, because those works do not bear, like the *Iliad,* the magic stamp of a master."[187]

Arnold's estimates of Homer are too familiar to detain us longer. Rather less widely known, however, are his opinions of the Christian epic, most of them representative of points of view current at the time. Like Symonds, Arnold placed Dante on his list of immortal poets because the *Divine Comedy* seemed to him "a criticism of life" that is "permanently acceptable to mankind."[188] Milton, on the other hand, did not appear on that list. True, his epic was called a "poetical classic," highly admirable for its "grand manner," its "flawless perfection" of rhythm and diction,[189] its sincerity and seriousness, and its "Celtic passion of revolt" as exemplified in the character of Satan.[190] But there seemed to Arnold to be some grave limitations both to the poem and to its author. Having denounced Addison and Macaulay as critics of Milton—the one for insisting that Milton ought to be admired whether the reader felt inclined to do so or not, the other for panegyrizing instead of criticizing him—Arnold proceeded to give implicit support to the arguments of Scherer: that while *Paradise Lost* can be an effective poem only if one takes the story of the Fall literally, even highly religious people now assume that story to be a myth; that Milton's epic is wearisome because of its didacticism, its sermonizing, its "almost burlesque" solution of the problem of evil, and its lack of solidity in general.[191] Arnold not only agreed with Scherer that "power both of diction and rhythm" is the worthiest feature of the poem but also ventured his own personal opinion that "if there is a defect which, above all others, is signal in Milton, which injures him even intellectually, which limits him as a poet, it is the defect common to him with the whole Puritan party to which he belonged,—the fatal defect of *temper*. He and they may have a thousand merits, but they are *unamiable*."[192] In his criticism of epic poetry, in his views on Homer and Virgil and Dante and Milton, it would seem, therefore, that Arnold was not far apart from many of the leading theorists of his day. If he influenced them, it is also probable that they influenced him.

Romantic criticism in England and in America had been largely antagonistic towards epic poetry. It had confused the genres hopelessly, it had rendered the definition of "epic" next to impossible, it had unearthed no values in heroic poetry which were peculiarly its own. It had often overrated the lyric exuberance of passages in poems and underrated the ethical worth and the form of the poem as a whole. It had often focused upon the personal, the intense, the sentimental, and the dramatic at the expense of the objective, the intellective, the pathetic, and the deliberate. It had often attached undue significance to the primitive or the modern or the Christian or the "romantic," and it had just as often neglected the permanent, the central, and the "classical." It had often favored Dante and Milton because of their religious idealism or their sheer emotionalism and individuality, and just as often opposed Virgil as a plagiarist and Homer as a barbarian. Certainly as far as epic theory is concerned, Arnold did not err in his estimate of the Romantics.

Was Victorian criticism of the epic superior to the Romantic? Did it have no inherent deficiencies, no tendency to be peripheral or tangential? To reiterate once again, Romantic approaches to literature were not abandoned after 1832. They have not been abandoned even yet. From the Age of Wordsworth to the present, some critics have been too prone to assume that the epic is outmoded, that it lacks real import, that it is "poetic" only at intervals, that "true poetry" is discoverable only in the lyrical moment, in the intensity and eloquence of an isolated passage, phrase, image, word, or possibly even of the hiatus between words. Also, there were after 1832, as there are yet current, two questionable assumptions regarding the merit of the genres: on the one hand that dramatic poetry is superior to epic poetry by virtue of its higher degree of instantaneous impact, on the other that prose fiction generally transcends all poetry because it approaches closer to the "real" by projecting ordinary persons into ordinary situations or by concerning itself with psychological subtleties and empirical fact. But one has additional reasons to quarrel with the Victorians. In the first place, the "personal" estimate was too much in evidence. Ironically enough, English Protestants could admire the *Divine Comedy,* an Italian epic, an epic written by an ardent exponent of Catholicism, but they were ready, in many cases, to censure *Paradise Lost* on the unsubtantial ground that its author had been an unorthodox Protestant and a somber and dogmatic person. Had there been no biographical data about Milton, had his prose writings not been extant, it is conceivable that the Victorian attitude towards *Paradise Lost* would have been rather different. In the second place, a single feature of a poem was too frequently the basis for judgments of the whole. Though it is to Macaulay's credit that he called attention to Milton's power of suggestion, one cannot properly assume that this power accounts for the greatness of the English epic. Nor is style an adequate criterion. Many Victorians were disposed to stress the excellence of the Virgilian style or of the Miltonic style as if it were something isolable from a poem, and even Arnold lost his usual perspective when he began to analyze the "grand manner" of Homer and Milton: surely poetic greatness cannot be detected in a single verse or group of words. In the third place, there is the fact that the Victorians were excessively concerned with the backgrounds of literature. Though the exegesis and elucidation of works of art is commendable, preoccupation with the poetic environment is surely to be deplored if it tends, as it did in Tennyson's day, to obscure aesthetic values or to divert attention from them. Generally speaking, Victorian men-of-letters were far too content to make mere critical remarks, to annotate or explicate, to probe for some coherent system of allegory in Dante and to conjecture about the basis of historical fact in the Homeric poems or about the way in which those poems had been composed. Their approach was almost consistently antiquarian. Moreover, one cannot thoroughly condone the use of this approach when it becomes, as it often did, a basis for literary judgments. In constructing in his mind a kind of Homeric dreamworld, a beautiful and heroic world without breadlines, riots, or sooty grime, Morris was certainly not recognizing the essential value of Homer's poems; nor, in finding the *Aeneid* a mirror of Victorian disillusionment, was Froude in any way establishing the true worth of Virgil. Perhaps this propensity is inevitable in every age. Perhaps men will always tend to value literature insofar as it serves as a commentary on or an escape from the problems of their era. In the long run, however, such estimates are bound to count for very little; they are not in any sense "real" estimates.

Notwithstanding blemishes of this kind,[193] Victorian criticism of the epic definitely marks a turn in the right direction. It succeeded in re-establishing some more or less precise meaning to the term "epic," in making rather clearer the distinction between the art-epic and the folk-epic, in differentiating between the aesthetic value of Homer or Virgil or Dante and the purely historical value of primitive heroic songs and ballads. It was not narrowly neo-classical since there was no attempt to revive any arbitrary code of mechanical rules or to denominate the classical epic as the only bona fide epic. Neither was it, all things considered, excessively "Romantic": it did not disparage time-tested opinion; it was not nostalgically primitivistic or stridently progressivistic. In criticizing Homer the Victorians may often have reverted to the old practice of divorcing form from content, but they realized that the form of the *Iliad* is no irrelevant matter. They recognized the unique virtues of the epic of action, its consistency of tone, its unity of plot, its purposeful discrimination between types of character, and above all, its depiction of the immutable nature of man. With respect to the *Aeneid,* they were at least willing to read this Roman work of wit with the same spirit that its author writ and to see that it was not a mere lunar reflection of the *Iliad*. There was rather less name-calling than there had been during the Age of Wordsworth, less insistence that Virgil was a dissembling and spineless courtier and that his hero, Aeneas, was a faithless paramour more fit for a hen-coop than for a battle. Virgil was sometimes credited, in fact, with a strong sense of the pathetic, with a genuine and rarely equalled understanding of the essential tragedy and sorrow of life. In estimating Dante, the Victorians did not concentrate, like the earlier Romantics, upon the nerve-shocking horrors of the *Inferno*. If too repeatedly concerned with episodes and obscure references in the *Divine Comedy,* they could on occasion view the poem as an organically conceived trilogy, as at once a summation of the poet's experience in its totality and of the ethical, spiritual, and political experience of a entire era, or possibly of mankind in general. Granted that little can be said for the criticism of Milton, that most of it was either repetitive or unnecessarily prejudiced, we can hardly fail to see that Victorian opinion of the epic reflects a higher degree of solidity, sanity, and tolerance than there had been some fifty years before. The pendulum had swung. Was it inevitably to swing again? Was there to be a reaction to the Victorian reaction? Were old objections to the epic to be revived or new ones to be found? The answers to such questions came, as we shall see, by the opening years of the new century.

6

Epic, Lyric, or Novel?
Intensification of a Rivalry
Around 1900

IN AN AGE OF steam it seems almost idle to speak of Dante.”[1]
To some extent Frederic Harrison was right: the great poets of
the past, even more than the minor poets of the present, appeared
to be alien to a world that was busily building machines, to one
that was keenly aware of the almost illimitable possibilities of
biology, chemistry, and physics. But there was actually no call
for pessimism as excessive as Harrison's. In periods of great
change men tend to look backwards as well as forwards, to re-
estimate their heritage as well as to predict their own prospects.
Often adopting the methodology of science themselves, the
scholars and critics at the turn of the twentieth century were
intent on examining the entire range of heroic poetry anew.
They studied the genesis of the epic; they tried to determine
its exact place in the long history of literature and the conditions
under which it had apparently thriven. In the thirty years from
1880 to 1910, in fact, more books and essays and journalistic
articles were written about epic poetry and poems than in any
other thirty-year span of time. Nor was all this work inconse-
quential and antiquarian. With Harrison, we today may look
askance at the valiant efforts to discover the name of the man
who married Milton's grandmother, or the houses in which the
poet resided, or the ailments that afflicted his first wife. But we
are obliged to concede that this historical-biographical-sociolog-
ical-philological study, though too often pursued as an end in

160

itself, was of great service to both the theoretical and practical criticism of heroic poetry in general. Providing a point of departure, a wealth of facts as a background for theory, it was instrumental in bringing about a thorough reassessment of traditional aesthetic opinion regarding the epic, of the views of the neo-classicist, the Romantic, and the early Victorian alike. Inevitably too, it led to an attempt to decide upon the relevancy of so early a type as the epic to an era of scientific progress.

How is "epic" to be defined and applied? As we have seen, theorists earlier in the nineteenth century had not been at all sure. So aware were they of the uniqueness and multiplicity of things, so hostile were they to the rigidity of the neo-classical system, that accurate definition of the literary kinds seemed almost out of the question. "Epic" was used as a generic term descriptive of any objective (therefore "unpoetical") verse or it was reserved for any verse that is not fundamentally lyrical or dramatic, for poems as opposite in nature as the *Iliad* and *Marmion*. At the end of the century, however, the situation was very different. To be sure, biological science had long recognized the particularity of the individual organism, but it was now emphasizing the fact that species and genera exist in nature, that in the process of time they develop and evolve according to pre-determined patterns, and that proper classification is one of the major goals of the empirical method. Taking their cue from the scientists, scholars and critics proceeded to study the evolution of literature with infinite care, approaching it from the point of view not of the conjectural historian of a century earlier but of the comparative anthropologist, the sociologist, and the archaeologist. They became convinced that there is a kind of verse one can rightly define as "epic," that there is a certain juncture at which poetry begins to assume an "heroic" character and a second juncture at which it begins to relinquish this character. In between the two points are the various stages of "epic," the later ones different from but potential in the earlier ones. Critics could not ascertain definitely the incipience of the whole epic process or describe with precision each of the stages. For the most part, however, they eschewed the Romantic practice of branding Southey's narrative poems as genuine epics and of speaking of the *Iliad* and *Odyssey* as noble effusions of the primitive mind. To all intents and purposes, every true epic now appeared to be an elaborate masterpiece of art, the product of a skilled genius or, in some cases, of several skilled geniuses working in collaboration. Thus C. C. Bradley declared that an "organizing and poetic power of a very high order is presumed in the case of any poem which the suffrage of the world has crowned as an epic."[2] Sketching the development of heroic poetry from beginning to end, Charles Gayley and Clement Young said that the epic is preceded by ballads, sagas, gestes, and romances, all of them relatively elementary forms of narrative that describe actions whose scope is limited. Much later comes the "folk-epic," a poem that does not somehow compose itself, as earlier critics had suggested, by a mysterious process of spontaneous generation, but that is "put together by a school of poets or an individual out of the naïve originals."[3] It is exceedingly complex, a summary of the life-philosophy of an organized people, a more or less unified agglomeration of history and myth or an accretion of true and fictitious tales around one central story. Eventually, as the communal spirit is lost, the folk-epic dies out and is replaced by new forms of art better adapted to a new state of society, or if conditions warrant it is transmuted into the "individual epic," a type of heroic poem which Gayley and Young describe as dealing with "a theme momentous . . . but not of the heart warm, nor leaping from the lips of the people,—rather sought out by the poet wherewith to lift his readers (hearers no longer) to a nobler view of life."[4] Properly speaking, the folk-epic would seem to set forth, in more or less objective fashion, the traditions of a whole nation and its interpretation of human life; the individual epic would seem to express the ideals of an age when the communal spirit is no longer vigorous and when a single genius is thus free to interpret those ideals more or less from his own point of view. In any event, each is an isolable species belonging to an isolable genus of poetry.

One must not assume, however, that the development of biological science was solely responsible for the revival of a system of genres. A second factor to be reckoned with was a reaction, far stronger than in the time of Carlyle, to Romantic and neo-Romantic vagueness, impressionism, and inattention to the matter of literary form. Disturbed by the chaotic and peripheral character of so much of nineteenth century criticism, many theorists endeavored to win credence for the view that an Aristotelian separation of the kinds, far from being merely arbitrary, is quite necessary and logical. Henry James averred that "kinds are the very life of literature, and truths and strength come from the complete recognition of them."[5] In an essay on the sonnet (1886), William Sharp declared that "any form of creative art, to survive, must conform to certain restrictions: would *Paradise Lost* hold its present rank if Milton had interspersed Cavalier and Roundhead choruses throughout his epic? What would we think of the *Aeneid* if Virgil had enlivened its pages with Catullan love-songs or comic interludes after the manner of Plautus or Terence?"[6] But the chief exponent of the segregation of the kinds was of course Irving Babbitt. Campaigning against Romantic dreaminess, illusion, and disregard of formal symmetry, Babbitt asserted that "an inquiry into the nature of the *genres* and the boundaries of the arts is far-reaching and involves one's attitude not merely towards literature but towards life."[7] "After all," he explained in another passage, "there is no mystery about this question of the *genres* and the boundaries of the arts if we consider it vitally and not formally. It reduces itself to this: a clear-cut type of person, a person who does not live in either an emotional or an intellectual muddle, will normally prefer a clear-cut type of art or literature. . . . He will desire each art and every *genre* to be itself primarily, and to give as Aristotle says of tragedy, its own special pleasure."[8]

The realm of the epic was thus circumscribed once again. For the first time in a hundred years heroic poetry appeared to stand apart as a legitimate species shading into but always distinct from other species of poetry. And for the first time in that hundred years almost every critic in England and in America ventured to reassess it boldly from an aesthetic point of view. Obviously an epic seemed in every way superior to its antecedents, to less artistic and complex forms like the primitive song, the heroic ballad, the geste and the saga, for the passion for crude and presumably impromptu sorts of poetry, a passion especially intense in Wordsworth's day, had by now virtually exhausted itself. But how did the epic compare with the literary types that sprang from or superseded it, and notably with those that were flourishing in the contemporary world? Could it minister to the needs, intellectual or emotional, of an age racing breathlessly down the grooves of change, an age busily exploiting the heathen and dreamily speculating about the future of the flying machine? Needless to say, there was a sharp difference of opinion, sharper perhaps than at any time since Swift wrote his *Battle of the Books.* One group of critics, led by Babbitt and Paul Elmer More, turned to the concept of the genres as hierarchical: the degree to which a type could present a full and significant interpretation of life was to determine its exact locus in the scale. A second group, among whom it is hard to find any principals as such, refurbished the familiar arguments to show that the epic as a kind now has rather more historical than aesthetic importance.

One is sorely tempted to give the latter group the traditional label "Moderns." Unquestionably some of them believed, just as the Moderns of Swift's day believed, not only that civilization tends to ameliorate but that literature, being at every stage its vehicle for recording and interpreting existence, also ameliorates at roughly the same pace. However, many of these critics at the beginning of the twentieth century were neither perfectibilitarians nor even ardent progressivists. A number of them held that the zenith of literature had been attained in the plays of Shakespeare, while others took the relativistic and uncritical point of view that, since art expresses the era, the most vital literature, for modern man at least, is the literature of his own day. But whatever the exact position of the individual critic, whether strongly or moderately progressivistic or whether purely relativistic, great importance was attached to the fact that the lyric was a living form while the epic was a dead one. In his essay "The Long Poem in Wordsworth's Age," A. C. Bradley said that since the modern world appears to the modern poet "uniform, ugly, and rationally regulated, a world of trousers, machinery and policemen," it cannot serve as the subject-matter for an epic; "it may suit the lyric or idyll, the monologue or short story, the prose drama or novel, but hardly the long poem or high tragedy. Even war, for reasons not hard to find, is no longer the subject that it was."[9] Ford Hueffer, on the other hand, attributed the absence of epic, and of real drama as well, to the fact that "we know too much," that the head of modern man is stuffed with too many unassimilated details. Dante, like every major poet until fairly recent times, was able to digest all knowledge available to him, and after synthesizing it, to serve with aplomb as philosopher and counselor; but, Hueffer continues, "until all the sciences have been so crystallized by specialists that one poet may be able to take them all in, and until we have that one poet, we cannot have any more poetry of the grand manner."[10] Arthur Symons brought together the views of both Bradley and Hueffer. In Dante's time, he said, it was no difficult matter for poetry to be representative of the age; now it is forced to take refuge "from the terrible improvements of civilisation in a divine seclusion, where it sings disregarding the many voices of the street."[11]

If the times did not encourage poets to write epics, neither did they encourage people to read them. "This age of ours is an impatient age," Alfred Ainger explained. "We like our poetry in small doses rather than long draughts."[12] Lionel Johnson spoke of it as the era of the "subtle-souled psychologists," one in which the lyric, the idyll, and brief dramatic study were "more in favour than works of prolonged elaboration."[13] Sidney Lanier, after making the peculiar comment that "trade has lengthened life by shortening leisure," stated that "the ideal of the lyric poem is a brief, sweet, intense, electric flashing of the lyric idea in upon the hurrying intelligence of men, so that the vivid truth may attack even an unwilling retina, and perpetuate itself thereupon even after the hasty eyelid has closed to shut out the sight."[14] "Hurrying," "unwilling," "hasty"—such words point to a tempo of living much too rapid for the enjoyment of the tra-

ditional epic of twelve or twenty-four books. Augustine Birrell
approved of the Johnsonian "heresy" that "nobody ever did wish
an epic longer," and it is probable that he considered the average
modern reader no exception to the rule.[15] Describing the Alex-
andrian age as an age that preferred lyrics and other brief poems,
John Churton Collins suggested that "no doubt they talked—
those degenerate, hurriedly living Alexandrians—of 'wading'
through the 'Iliad' and 'Odyssey' much as we talk of 'wading'
through 'Paradise Lost.' "[16] Similarly, Symons said that "we have
no longer the mental attitude of those to whom a story was a
story, and all stories good." Referring to Tolstoi's notion that
the Homeric epic is one of the few poems intelligible to the
masses, Symons asked his readers to imagine the reaction of a
modern laborer when confronted with such a passage from the
Iliad as this: "Upon the flaming chariot set she her foot, and
grasped her heavy spear, great and stout, wherewith she van-
quished the ranks of men, even of heroes with whom she of
the awful sire is wroth."[17]

But it was not simply that the times seemed to be out of joint
as far as the writing and reading of epics were concerned. Many
critics, mindful of what Poe and Mill had said, maintained that
the lyric is at least equal to the epic as a work of art. John
Bascom, an American, eulogized it as "less ambitious than other
forms" but "more close to the individual sentiment," more "wont
to be the refuge of the most genuine, simple and passionate
strains."[18] One suspects that George Saintsbury would not have
quarreled with this point of view, for in a discussion of the
critical proclivities of Dryden's time he observed that "while we
have treatises on Drama and Epic *ad nauseam,* their elder and
lovelier sister has been, 'poor girl! neglected.' "[19] Preferring Ten-
nyson to Milton, Lanier declared that modern poetry is "more
ethereal than that of the past times";[20] and Symons credited Poe
with having "proved" that the best epics are in reality only
collections of lyrical poems.[21] C. T. Winchester, claiming that
"the general evolution in society must make epic poetry rarer
in these later days, and give to it more and more an antiquarian
air," praised the lyric as "the most nearly universal form," "the

purest, most typical form."[22] Though a traditionalist in many respects, H. W. Mabie saw a definite indication of progress in the fact that "the remote epic themes have been succeeded by subjects more intimate and personal." Modern man, he explained, "has drank [sic] every cup of experience; won all victories and suffered all defeats; tested all creeds and acted all philosophies." As a consequence, the latter-day course of literature, with its ever-greater variety of moods, themes, and situations, seemed to Mabie both "inevitable and beneficent."[23]

Much more important than any of the above opinions were those of Walter Pater. In his *Studies in the History of the Renaissance,* Pater championed the organicist view that real poetry, good poetry, is not "made" but develops and unfolds from within. The supreme kinds, he said, are those in which the artist can achieve the most thorough fusion of form and content. Hence "lyrical poetry, precisely because in it we are least able to detach the matter from the form, without a deduction of something from that matter itself, is, at least artistically, the highest and most complete form of poetry. And the very perfection of such poetry often appears to depend, in part, on a certain suppression or vagueness of mere subject, so that the meaning reaches us through ways not distinctly traceable by the understanding."[24] Pater never singled out the epic for attack, and as the above phrase "at least artistically" may well imply, he was ready to acknowledge that types other than the lyric have important values of their own. But it is obvious that what he says here does not militate in favor of formal verse narrative, and neither do other passages in which he suggests that beauty rather than plot, or characterization, or ethical worth, should be the main concern of poet and critic alike; that music is the highest of the arts and that true poetry aspires to a condition of music. John Addington Symonds, himself believing that the lyric is "scarcely second" to the epic,[25] could not have been far wrong when he suggested that in Pater's opinion "drama and epic doff their caps before a song, in which verbal melody and the communication of a mood usurp upon invention, passion, cerebration, definite meaning."[26] However, it would seem that the chief importance of Pater as a critic lies not so much in what he actually thought and said as in what he prompted others to think and say. With Swinburne and Wilde, he was responsible for the revolt of the 1880's and 1890's "against exteriority, against rhetoric, against a materialistic tradition" (to quote Symons),[27] for the shift of attention from the moralistic, stylized verse of the early Victorians to the new lyric whose sole purpose was to be a thing of beauty. We must not suppose, however, that the aestheticism of Pater's generation posed any real threat to the prestige of heroic poetry. As we shall see, in fact, the championing of the messageless lyric may be said to have backfired: it was unquestionably one of the factors that inspired conservative-minded critics to demand a return to classical concepts and standards of literature.

For the first time in history, it was the novel rather than the lyric that became the principal challenger of the epic. In Wordsworth's day, we will recall, a reviewer here and there had cautiously intimated that prose fiction appeared to be invading the domain of the heroic poem; in the Age of Carlyle, though people were busily reading and writing novels, practically nothing was said about the relationship or the relative worth of the two literary types. The *fin de siècle,* however, was virtually forced to make comparisons. A full consciousness that an evolutionary principle governs all things, the widening of the abyss between the poet and the public, the mushrooming of simple, romantic fiction whose sole purpose was to narcotize the semi-literate or to appeal to their stock responses, the new passion for the artistic realism of the Flaubertians and for the positivistic realism or naturalism of Zola and his disciples, the intense interest in debates as to whether a slattern in the gutter is as proper a protagonist as Shakespeare's Rosalind—these are only a few of the developments which obliged the critic to inquire into the *raison d'être* of all creative narrative and especially to determine the objectives, methods, and values of each kind of narrative, of the ancient ballad and epic at one extreme and of the latest Parisian tale of perversion at the other.

That the man-in-the-street vastly preferred novels to epics

was of course obvious to every literary critic. Frederic Harrison, feeling that the trend towards prose fiction was unwarrantedly strong, scornfully commented that his generation was ready to welcome "M. Zola's seventeenth romance" but that it could "no more read Homer than it could read a cuneiform inscription."[28] But theorists generally believed that there was little sense in deploring the situation, that the flourishing of the novel was as inevitable as death and taxes. Resorting to the argument he had used in support of the lyric, J. A. Symonds said that art avoids the law of organic evolution "no more than does an oak." The epic is nationalistic, he declared, and it is "natural" in the early stages of civilization ("it is not given to any race under the conditions of conscious culture to create a genuine epic"); the novel, on the other hand, is a later and a "hybrid" form in which "both drama and epic for the modern world lie embedded."[29] Similarly, Frank Norris boldly announced that "to-day is the day of the novel": epics had not been written to celebrate the heroic fight at the Alamo and the even more heroic Civil War, and it was very doubtful whether a real epic poem would ever be written in the future.[30] In four key words Brander Matthews summed up the entire history of fiction: it dealt first with the Impossible, then the Improbable, then the Possible, and finally the Inevitable. Suggesting that William Dean Howells had sanctioned his views, Matthews went on to explain that "the modern novel is not only the heir to the epic" but that it has "despoiled" other types such as the drama and the lyric; it "may be likened to Napoleon at the very height of his power, when no other monarch could make sure of resting in peace upon the throne of his fathers."[31]

Where, then, are epic and novel to be stationed in the scale of aesthetic values? Once again the evolutionists brought forth their customary and metaphorical argument: the epic had been the healthy and vigorous sapling, the novel was now the fully grown tree in all its glory. Usually more of a traditionalist, Bliss Perry declared that "we talk of human nature being ever the same, but nothing is falser to the facts of life and the process of the world's growth." While brute nature, that of the ape and tiger, seemed to him to remain stationary (an odd view of evolution), he thought "the human spirit changes, widens, grows richer" in time, "and over against this wonderful process of development stands the novelist, himself a part of it all, and yet one of its interpreters."[32] Norris, after observing that each literary genre has had its day, suggested that the novel is the most admirable of the kinds because "it expresses modern life better than architecture, better than painting, better than poetry, better than music."[33] (Here Norris blends evolutionism with relativism.) Henry James, finding in prose fiction "all the varieties of outlook on life," said that "the Novel remains still, under the right persuasion, the most independent, most elastic, most prodigious of literary forms."[34] As a young man, George Moore entertained no illusions about the epic or about other forms of poetry, for he visualized "a new race of writers that would arise, and with the aid of the novel would continue to a more glorious and legitimate conclusion the work that the prophets had begun."[35] Walter Raleigh disliked Zola's writings and he saw fit to write a book on Milton, but he could not help complaining that the epic "is so like the deed itself. . . . Epic is dangerously near the deed."[36] Finally, Lanier denominated the novel as the supreme type because it represents "the meeting, the reconciliation, the kiss of science and poetry,"[37] while Richard Burton, vaguely intimating a progressivistic sense of values, pointed to "psychologic laws and sociologic conditions" as responsible for the fact that an early age is well-satisfied with the epic, "an age more sophisticate . . . favors the play," and "our own time, with its tremendously complex social needs and interrelations, finds in prose fiction, so flexible in form, so all-embracing in theme, its natural outlet of expression."[38]

To see how strong this new persuasion had become at the end of the century, one need only turn to two American critics, Garland and Hamilton, who synthesized the opinions of the others. Hamlin Garland, the earlier and less conservative, observes that when critics finally discovered a "definite succession in art and literature as in geologic change," it was no longer difficult for them to explain the "dominance of the epic in one age" and of other types in other ages. He argues like Whitman that the art of the past is feudalistic and obsolete while that of his own time is essentially democratic and is indicative of a yet more democratic art in the future; he disagrees with Whitman, however, in suggesting that prose fiction has once and for all ousted poetry in general (epic, lyric, and drama). With excessive self-assurance he proclaims that "this is our day. The past is not vital."³⁹ The "old idols are crumbling."⁴⁰ "The people can never be educated to love the past, to love Shakespeare and Homer. Students may be taught to believe they believe, but the great masses of American readers want the modern comment. . . . On higher planes of reading they want sincere delineation of modern life and thought, and Shakespeare, Wordsworth, Dante, Milton, are fading away into mere names,—books we should read but seldom do."⁴¹ If Garland is a relativist, Clayton Hamilton is both a relativist and a progressivist. In his *Materials and Methods of Fiction* (1908), Hamilton credits the epic with "a vaster sweep of vision" than any other type of literature, but he is quick to point out the ways in which it falls short of the modern novel. Since it is "communal" in the sense that it describes a great cause of undying interest to a whole people, an heroic poem is necessarily "inefficient" in displaying "the more intimate and personal phases of human character": Homer's heroes are for the most part "mere boys,"⁴² and it is only the cause for which they fight that lends them any real dignity at all; Virgil, mainly concerned with the founding of Rome, shows scant sympathy for the crushing miseries of deserted Dido. The theme of love, so popular with all novelists, seems to Hamilton to be totally ignored by the typical heroic poet. "The epic, in the ancient sense, is dead today. Facility of intercommunication between the nations has made us all citizens of the world." We have become tolerant of all religions, and since the French Revolution "we have grown to set the one above the many," to believe that society exists for the individual rather than the other way around. Summing up the situation, Hamilton declares that "the novel, which deals with individual personality in and for itself, is more attuned to modern life than the epic, which presents the individual mainly in relation to a communal cause which he strives to advance or to retard."[43]

As we have briefly suggested before, an impressive number of critics were strongly opposed to these latter-day tendencies in literary theory. If they saw grave danger in the emphasis upon sheer emotionalism regardless of quality, in "Romantic" vagueness and impressionism, they saw just as grave danger, and serious error as well, in the doctrine of literary progress and in critical relativism. Both appeared to coincide with the supposedly deplorable naturalism of the age, with an acceptance of scientific determinism as the underlying principle of life, with a confusion of human law with the law of organic nature. Relativism was often singled out as a target because it implied that an aesthetic code does not really exist at all, that the function of the critic is to elucidate and interpret rather than to criticize. Concentration upon a poem as a full or partial embodiment of the "culture" or life-philosophy of a given era seemed as mistaken and inutile as to concern oneself with some elusive and equivocal essence, the "poetical" essence, of that poem. As a result, these critics not only did their best to disentangle the genres once again but also to re-establish, on what they regarded as a sound and logical basis, a scale or hierarchy of kinds approximating that of the eighteenth century neo-classicists. Surely we today do not read modern novels simply because they portray our own eccentricities, it was said; surely we do not turn to earlier literary works merely to discover how well they "express" Greek or Roman or Medieval civilization.

This return to a more traditional concept of the hierarchy naturally led to a glorification of the heroic poem. But not all the critics arrived at the same estimate. Andrew Lang reminds one of earlier German theorists when he places the epic at the top of the scale because of its comprehensiveness: it is "the sum of all poetry—tragedy, comedy, lyric, dirge, idyll," each of these types being "blended in its great furnace into one glorious metal, and one colossal group."[44] Conversely, E. C. Stedman asserts that while the lyric is an inferior kind, drama is "more inclusive than the epic. There is little in Homer that is not true to nature, but

there is no phase of nature that is not in Shakespeare."[45] Though
Bayard Taylor makes no attempt to evaluate tragic drama as a
whole, he is at least certain that epic is superior to lyric. "The
broad and massive character of epic poetry, the deeper elements
with which it deals, give it an intrinsic dignity and authority
which cannot belong to the short flights of lyric song. The latter
may furnish the ornament of the temple, but the former con-
tributes the blocks and pillars which give it space and perman-
ence."[46] W. P. Trent, on the other hand, seems to think entirely
in terms of ethical value. "That there is a hierarchy of genres,"
he declares, "is a fact as well proved as that there is a hierarchy
of mental powers or of bodily functions." Because Homer, Virgil,
Dante, and Milton are "all not merely not immoral, but profound-
ly and positively moral"—"they stir our moral emotions"—every
schoolboy ought to regard the epic poets as greater than the
greatest of the lyric poets.[47] Oddly enough, however, even the
exponents of the new lyric sometimes made large concessions to
the heroic poem. Speaking out against relativist and progres-
sivist theory, Swinburne said that no important art of the past,
no true epic or romance "is obsolete yet, or ever can be; there
is nothing in the past extinct";[48] and on another occasion he
vaguely hinted at a preference for epic and drama when he re-
marked that "the man who attempts in an age of idyllic poetry
to write a heroic poem, or to write a dramatic poem in an age
of analytic verse, deserves at least the credit due to him who
sees and knows the best and highest, and strives to follow after
it with all his heart and might."[49] Similarly, there is evidence
of a compromise in Symonds' observation that "the best poetry
is that which reproduces the most of life, or its intensest mo-
ments."[50] Though he considered the epic as an almost primitive
type, Symonds did not quarrel with the fact that "the extensive
species of the drama and the epic, the intensive species of the
lyric, have been ever held in highest esteem."[51]

Of greater influence than any of these critics were of course
Babbitt and More. Having insisted that it is vital to make sharp
distinctions between the poetic kinds, Babbitt proclaims with
confidence as great as Trent's that a hierarchy is no fiction of

the critic's imagination. "The *genre* is to be ranked according to the intrinsic value and importance for man of the matter it treats. Because the neo-classicists turned this truth into mere conventionality there is no reason . . . why we should be like them."[52] Babbitt does not specifically rate "the matter" of the various types, but it is easy to deduce his view from his pronouncements about classical and modern literature in general. Ever belaboring the impressionists, sentimentalists, naturalists, and aesthetes, reiterating over and over again Arnold's concept of literature as a criticism of life, he sees the salvation of the latter-day world only through a re-dedication to Graeco-Roman standards of conduct. Classical art seems to him to exemplify and to inculcate these standards: it appeals "to our higher reason and imagination—to those faculties which afford us an avenue of escape from ourselves, and enable us to become participants in the universal life."[53] And Babbitt's belief in the important role of the ancient epic is apparent not only in his many allusions to Homer and Virgil as educators of mankind but also in his statement that "Greek literature at its best is to a remarkable degree a creative imitation of Homer."[54] Paul Elmer More was not unsympathetic with opinions like these, for he too ranked the genres according to their ethical and disciplinary values. The supreme kinds for him were of course the epic and the tragic drama. "The aim of the epic is breadth of view, the aim of tragedy is intensity; the one proposes to offer a large picture of life artistically disposed, the other to express a brief passion of conflict."[55] But More sometimes tends to soar on philosophic wing above the heads of Babbitt and the others. In another passage he says that drama and epic are pre-eminent because they sweep away the "clogging limitations" of the will and understanding so that "we feel ourselves to be acting and speaking the great passions of humanity in their fullest and freest scope." Hence, Achilles and Hamlet and Satan seem to us like absolute types, and we are led to believe that the poet himself had been "carried into a region above our vision" where he beheld "the great ideas of which our worldly life and circumstances are but faulty copies."[56] Such neo-Platonism could mean that More had

no great love for lyric poetry and none whatsover for the natur-
alistic novel. "The office of the novel—and this we see more clear-
ly as fiction grows regularly more realistic—is to represent life
as controlled by environment and to portray human beings as
servants of the flesh."[57]

Viewed as a whole, the rivalry of the genres at the turn of
the present century would seem to suggest that the reputation of
heroic poetry was no better than it had been in the Age of
Wordsworth. Certainly the pleas for modern literature were
more abundant and often more vigorous than those for the epic.
But broad generalizations about literary types have a way of
being misleading, of suggesting rather more than is intended, of
obscuring important exceptions to the rule. Jonathan Swift, it
will be remembered, once remarked that he heartily detested
mankind. People took Swift at his word and promptly classified
him as an utter misanthrope, apparently forgetting that the
Dean had gone on to say that he loved certain, perhaps many,
individuals—Peter and John and Paul and Lawyer Such-a-one.
Similarly, we would do an injustice to the literary critics around
1900 if we heeded only their more categorical statements about
the epic, the lyric, and the novel as genres. We would overlook
the fact that some theorists who were indifferent towards epics
in general were anything but indifferent towards this epic or
that one, and conversely, that other theorists who thought of
the epic as supreme could not abide certain chefs-d'oeuvre of the
species. Possibly more than at any time since the eighteenth
century, applied criticism failed to quadrate with criticism of a
theoretical sort. For this reason, it is necessary that we survey
with special care the consensus regarding folk-epics and indi-
vidual epics, particular heroic poems and poets.

The minor epics, those of minimal aesthetic importance, cer-
tainly received plenty of attention. English and American schol-
ars, many of them trained in German universities, studied the
vast multitude of these poems from every conceivable angle—
historical, prosodical, linguistic, sociological, psychological.
Learned journals were flooded with elaborate articles on the
Pharsalia, the *Kalevala,* the *Thebais,* the *Nibelungenlied,* the *Cid,*

the *Ramayana,* the *Araucana;* on Russian epics, Brazilian epics, Sanskrit epics, Icelandic epics, Babylonian-Sumerian epics; on poem after poem that contained certain elements of the epic: the *Táin Bó Cúalnge,* the *Mabinogion, Waldere* and the *Battle of Maldon*—folk tales, chansons de geste, animal fables, epical-lyrical romances, sagas and ballads. But if all this meticulous work was conducive to a better understanding of literary history, it certainly had no impact upon literary theory or upon the reading habits of the public. Even the old favorites of Wordsworth's contemporaries were almost totally neglected. Ossian had been relegated, very likely for all time, to the textbook of eighteenth century literature and to the dustier shelves of university libraries; his "grandiose and very monotonous rhapsodies," said Alfred Ainger, are "to us now unreadable."[58] The *Gierusalemme Liberata* and the *Orlando Furioso,* so often cited around 1800 as supreme examples of the "romantic epic," evoked no more than an honorable mention from the critics. W. P. Ker tells how surprised he was to discover that a friend had been reading and apparently enjoying one of the Italian epics during his vacation: "I cannot believe," Ker remarked, "that there were many others at the same time in the island of Britain engaged in a like pursuit: reading the *Orlando Furioso* or *Morgante;* the fashion is otherwise. Still, it is pleasant to find that the old fashion has not altogether died out."[59] Similarly, T. W. Higginson observed that while the cherished textbook of earlier readers of Italian had been one entitled *I Quattro Poeti,* "Ariosto and Tasso are now practically dropped out of the running."[60] Only slightly more popular, in fact, was the Anglo-Saxon epic, *Beowulf.* Saintsbury said that he enjoyed the fights between the hero and the monsters, A. S. Richardson detected "poetic touches" here and there, Gummere described the artistry as "highly developed," and Stopford Brooke called the poem "the English Genesis." However, Sidney Lanier was merely overstating the case when, in 1898, he made this remark about the reputation of *Beowulf*: "One will go into few moderately appointed houses in this country without finding a Homer in some form or other; but it is probably far within the truth to say that there are not fifty copies of *Beowulf* in the United States."[61] Elsewhere he suggested that there were perhaps ten thousand Americans who could read the Greek epics for each one able to master "our own English epic," that he doubted whether twenty copies of *Beowulf* were to be found "outside of the great libraries."[62]

Though Lanier deplored this attitude as "unpatriotic," the fact remains that Englishmen and Americans alike, the literary critics as well as the public, were far more interested in the masterpieces of heroic poetry. Homer, Milton, and Dante were widely read, explained, and compared. And as time went on, as the critical issues of the age became clearer, they began to assume a more and more vital role in literary discussions. Moralists and religious idealists stood firmly behind Dante. Theorists of almost every school disparaged Milton, though old-fashioned Romanticists and defenders of the English tradition decried the decriers. The humanists and the teachers of classical literature, while they gave Dante his due, averred that Homer was second to none. No group seems to have championed Virgil, but because of his importance both in earlier and later criticism, something should certainly be said about his reputation in the age with which we are now concerned.

Turning first to the estimates of the classical epic, we might well look for the waging of another campaign against both Homer and Virgil. Aside from the fact that the novel and the lyric were in the ascendancy, the era had its special reasons for feeling inimical towards ancient literature as a whole. E. L. Youmans, in an essay written two years after the end of the Civil War, raised a question that was not to go unheeded in either America or England: "Is the most thorough acquaintance with humanity to be gained by cutting the student off from the life of his own age, and setting him to tunnel through dead languages, to get such imperfect and distorted glimpses as he may of man and society in their antiquated forms; or by equipping him with the best resources of modern thought, and putting him to the direct and systematic study of men and society as they present themselves to observation and experience?"[63] Over and over again utilitarian educators and practical-minded per-

sons in all professions asseverated that present pedagogical meth-
ods were rendering the study of the classical languages an utter
waste of time, a luxury for the few; or that while a knowledge
of Greek and Latin literature might possibly be "broadening,"
it was far less "useful" than a solid grounding in biology and
physics or even in the "living" literatures of England, France,
and Germany. According to Professor Goldwin Smith, it was be-
ing argued that "six months of the language of Schiller and
Goethe will now open to the student more high enjoyment than
six years' study of the languages of Greece and Rome."[64] And
it was obviously a move in a new direction and a blow to the
vested interests of the classics when, in the middle 1880's, Har-
vard University decided to institute President Eliot's program
of electives.

For the time being, however, educational theory was to have
no appreciable effect upon criticism of the epic. Few critical
writers went as far as Garland in describing the greater poets
of the past as "crumbling idols"; fewer still expressly attacked
the heroic poems of Homer and Virgil. Gerard Manley Hopkins
spoke facetiously about the Homeric divinities: "at their best
they remind me of some company of beaux and fashionable world
at Bath in its palmy days of Tunbridge Wells or what not";[65]
and Robert G. Ingersoll observed that "the cloud-compelling
Jupiters, the ox-eyed Junos . . . are nothing to us," that they fail
to "touch the human heart."[66] Harry T. Peck agreed with
Andrew Carnegie that one is bored by Homer's wrangling gods
and by the "heroism of heroes who are invulnerable": "one feels
at last as if he had been listening to the banging of a brazen
kettle."[67] And various critics raised the traditional objections to
the imitativeness and uninspired tone of Virgil. But adverse
criticism of both these poets, though it had been still fairly
common in the Age of Carlyle, seems to have slackened appre-
ciably by 1900, seems almost to have dwindled out. On the
occasions when it did appear, it was inclined to be casual and
good-humored rather than earnest and intolerant.

Are we to assume, then, that the prestige of the classical epic
was once again high, higher perhaps than at any time since the

early eighteenth century? Towards Virgil the prevailing atti-
tude was actually neither *pro* nor *contra*. There was no special
reason to attack him, for his limitations as a poet had been
pointed out plainly enough by the Romantics of Wordsworth's
day; indeed they had been pointed out much too plainly. On the
other hand, there was no real call to go to the opposite extreme,
for the early Victorians, in wishing to see justice done, had said
all that could be said in favor of the exquisite artistry and the
quiet grandeur of Virgil's poetry. For the time being at least,
a state of equilibrium had been achieved: the *Aeneid,* if obviously
not the greatest of epics, seemed great enough to deserve a rea-
sonable measure of respect. Perhaps this was enough. But it is
also true that impartiality may be tantamont to indifference, and
in the era of which we are speaking, such appears to have been the
case. Only two critics, J. W. Mackail and George Woodberry,
were sufficiently interested in Virgil to make fresh and significant
appraisals of his epic.

In a series of lactures delivered at Oxford between 1907 and
1911, Mackail intimated that he was no believer in the doctrines
of the neo-classical, progressivist, and art-for-art's-sake schools.
Definitely favoring an organicist approach, he held that the
form and substance of a poem should be indistinguishable and
inter-determinative but that the primary object of all verse should
be to cast new light on important segments of human exper-
ience. "Poetry," he said in agreeing with Arnold, "is greater,
not as it purports to deal with a greater subject, but as it gathers
and absorbs into itself more of life."[68] Honoring the epic at
the expense of the lyric and possibly of the drama, this view of
poetry as at once organic and interpretative became the basis for
Mackail's exhaustive and novel analysis of the *Aeneid*. His meth-
odology, akin to and yet different from that of the Homeric and
Beowulf scholars, was that of tracing the gradual evolution of
the form and substance of the poem in the mind of the poet.
Initially, he affirmed, there was a kind of *Ur-Aeneis,* a story of
kings and battles, of the hero's arrival in Latium, and of the
founding of Rome. Then came an expansion of the theme. From
the *Odyssey* Virgil derived the idea of going back to narrate the

wanderings of Aeneas during the seven years after his departure
from Troy. This segment of the story was told in the opening
books of the final poem. But "poetry, being vital and organic,
never rests anywhere."[69] From the second theme evolved a third
one; hence we have the "engrafted epic of Aeneas and Dido," an
epic "even more wonderful and more enthralling than its parent
stem, the Italian epic of conquest and settlement."[70] In proceed-
ing in this manner, Virgil was of course running the risk of
making his poem as a whole too episodic. Being a true craftsman,
however, he then conceived the idea of inserting a book in the
very middle that was to become a keystone to lock the entire
structure. Book VI looks backward and forward. Presenting "an
impassioned vision of the whole of existence," it establishes the
mood or tone of the *Aeneid* as we now have it. "This trans-
mutation and spiritualisation of poetry was Virgil's final achieve-
ment; and it is this which, in the end, gives him his unique place
among the poets. . . . The function of art is to create and em-
body some image of perfection; and the image which Virgil
finally sets before us is of imperfection; the wistfulness, the
haunting trouble of his poetry, is of its inmost quality."[71] Hence
it is a unitary and integrated criticism of human experience,
"the very voice of mankind itself speaking, with majestic tender-
ness, of patience and obedience, of honour in life, of hope beyond
death," that gives deep meaning and an organic character to an
epic which would otherwise be a rambling account of fights and
strange adventures and a tragic love affair.[72]

Whether or not we agree with Mackail at all points, his
historical interpretation and critical estimate of the *Aeneid* would
seem to transcend—to come closer to the truth—than any that had
been made up to that time, and they were to set the pattern for
many later discussions of the poem. Very different were the views
of Woodberry. In an essay entitled simply "Virgil," Woodberry
might be described as consciously inverting the salient arguments
of the Romantics of Wordsworth's time, as earning the distinc-
tion, moreover, of becoming the first critic in at least a cen-
tury to think that Virgil could do no wrong. For him, Aeneas
is not the fawning hypocrite and the opportunistic rake but the

self-controlled and dutiful Roman, the ideal man of integrity outstripping in every way "creatures of self-will" like Turnus or Milton's Satan. He "gains, and is truly seen, in proportion as the mind is free from the allurements of individuality, free from the worship of the ungovernable human power in life, and all that makes against the ideal of patience, obedience, and rule."[73] He is a hero who ponders before he acts, who in being guided by his rational nature makes a strong appeal to one's sense of what is right. And if Woodberry is anti-Romantic in his views about Virgil's protagonist, he is not less anti-Romantic in his opinion that pathos rather than bathos permeates the entire *Aeneid,* a pathos "not . . . of individual lives but of the general lot." Describing three great defeats, and a final victory that actually amounts to a final defeat, the Roman poet has written "the saddest book of the world": *"Lacrimae rerum* seems almost the other name of the 'Aeneid.' "[74] Woodberry believes, in fact, that Virgil has barely managed to keep his poems within the bounds of the epic: "a thousand lines have the lyrical cry; they could, and do, stand alone, each one a poem,"[75] each an echo of all men's hearts. Reiterating his point, Woodberry says that " 'pain, pain, ever, forever,' rings through the poem like a Promethean cry."[76]

However interesting both these studies of the *Aeneid* may be, we must remember that they stood quite alone. The age of steam, as Harrison called it, did not seem to find any of its ideals of poetry or of life best exemplified by the epic poet of ancient Rome. But there was no such indifference towards Homer. As might be expected, words of high praise came from academicians intent on vindicating the prominence of the classics in the university curriculum, and from humanists urging a return to the ethical standards of the ancients. They also came, however, from the enemies of these men—from the exponents of the naturalistic novel and from the defenders and practitioners of aestheticism. Great as their zest for contemporary literature may have been, these latter groups did not hesitate to accord Homer a place of high honor, to speak of his poems as notable exceptions to the rule that the epic is obsolete or inferior to prose fiction or the lyric. Perhaps there is testimony to the good sense of the era, and to the imperishability of the Greek epic as well, in the fact that a wide divergence of basic critical theory did not preclude general agreement as to the greatness of Homer.

How were the *Iliad* and *Odyssey* composed? During most of the nineteenth century, this had not only been a vexatious and hotly debated question but also one which had borne directly and importantly upon judgments of Homer. Arguing for separatism, critics like Coleridge and Carlyle had denied the existence of a cohering, organic principle in either of the Greek epics; arguing for unitarianism, other critics had stressed the consistent spontaneity and naturalness or, more often, the craftsmanship implicit in the structural symmetry of the poems. By the 1880's and 1890's, however, the Homeric controversy had practically ceased to be a controversy at all. Separatism, never very popular in England and America, was yielding more and more ground because its novelty was gone, because it had been responsible for altogether too much bickering and airy, futile conjecturing, and because it had mistakenly emphasized the mechanical rather than the poetical aspects of the *Iliad* and *Odyssey*. In 1886 Gerard Manley Hopkins wrote to Robert Bridges that "the pendulum is swinging heavily towards the old view of a whole original Iliad";[77] and a year later E. C. Stedman pointed out that while some of the scholars appeared to doubt that Homer had existed, "we begin to see in his poems a single creation, rather than a growth, and again to conceive of his simple and poetic individuality."[78] Even Walter Leaf, the most confirmed separatist of the time, conceded that his theories of authorship were not more than theories. Delving into the *Iliad* in the spirit of the archaeologist, Leaf arrived at an opinion that sounds suspiciously Germanic, namely, that the poem is comprised of three distinct poetic strata. At the base, he said, is the story of the "Menis," the "Wrath of Achilles," dating to about 1000 B.C. Later, and over a long period of time, other narrative elements were assimilated by the original plot until it grew into the complex and extensive poem we now call the *Iliad*. Yet Leaf was willing to make the following admission: "It is no doubt possible that a poet, especially before the invention of writing, may have put together one long poem" during the course of many years "and that it may represent the gradual development of a long life."[79]

But if separatism was losing force in this era, so too was thoroughgoing unitarianism. Linguistic, archaeological, and sociological study had demonstrated, once and for all, that poems such as the *Iliad* and *Odyssey* could not be *entirely* the work of a single author, that a compromise should be made between separatist and unitarian points of view. Andrew Lang insisted that Homer's epics, though they have "all the fresh vivacity and unwearied zest of 'popular' poetry, are also master-pieces of conscious art."[80] In 1907 Thomas Seymour of Yale University explained that current opinion favored "the organic development of the Homeric poems," and that "many are now ready even to accept the necessary inference from the principle that a great poem implies a great poet, though no one doubts that the poet whom the Greeks and we call Homer used with absolute freedom the poetic material which he in common with other bards had inherited, and which had been gathering for generations by a process of gradual accretion."[81] Gilbert Murray stood midway between the separatist and unitarian points of view. The poems, he said, "are the products of a civilized age and of a long process of development."[82] "Instead of the primaeval and all-wise poet, Homer, we are left with a kind of saga-figure. . . . The name Homêros may conceivably be a name once borne by a living person. But if so, we know nothing of him, except indeed that he did not, in any complete sense, write the *Iliad* and *Odyssey*."[83] J. W. Mackail took much the same position as Murray. Waxing metaphorical, he declared that "both poems are vital organisms, and their growth was organic, whether we regard it as the slow age-long deposit of some coral forest under the sea, or as the bursting into flower, in a single lifetime, of what had been long maturing invisibly in root and stem and bud." A moment later he attacked the primitivistic conception of Homer that had been so prevalent early in the nineteenth century: "the old careless view, due partly to ignorance and partly to misunderstanding of ambiguous terms," that the Homeric epics "represent the birth of poetry in some fancied youth of the world, is as nearly as may be the reverse of the truth. They are not the birth of poetry; they are its full maturity."[84]

On the whole it would appear impossible to classify these critics either as separatists or unitarians, for in contrast to Coleridge and Gladstone, none of them made any positive claims that a Homer had or had not existed, that a single hand had or had not given final shape to the Greek epics. In fact all seemed to be agreed that the poems were not primitive, that while it had taken ages for them to attain their present form, they should be regarded first and foremost as masterly works of art. Nor did other critics differ with those whom we have just been discussing. An outspoken writer in the *London Spectator* justified his belief that Homer had composed the Greek epics by pointing out that "it is as impossible that a first rate poem or work of art should be produced without a great master-mind to conceive the whole, as that a fine living bull should be developed out of beef sausages."[85] W. J. Courthope observed that "even the age of Homer was one of considerable artistic refinement";[86] Gerard Manley Hopkins announced to a friend that he was "struggling to get together matter for a work on Homer's Art";[87] and W. C. Lawton, though he suspected that the Trojan War was a mythical war, referred to the "self-conscious art" of Homer and insisted that "the detailed story of Achilles' wrath is as clearly the conscious creation of a poetic mind as Prospero's enchanted island and its inhabitants."[88] Much the same was the opinion held by Irving Babbitt. The neo-classicists, he wrote in the *New Laokoon,* had been inclined to treat the epic as "a cold and deliberate concoction of the intellect." In violent reaction, critics in Wordsworth's time had gone to the other extreme by characterizing the Greek epics as wholly spontaneous and primitive: "the counter-exaggeration of the romanticists was to eliminate the element of conscious and deliberate art and make of the Homeric poems an almost unconscious emanation of the folk-soul." But, he continued approvingly, "the opinion is now gaining ground that the *Iliad* and *Odyssey* are not primitive but works of consummate art, though the word art, of course, is not understood in quite the same sense as by Le Bossu."[89]

How *was* "art" to be understood? Clearly, Babbitt and the others were not implying that there is no pathos, no intensity of emotion, no exuberance or sublimity discoverable in the Homeric epics: without such qualities, they knew well, the poems would be little more than versified tales or histories in verse. Murray, in fact, spoke of the "accumulated emotion" of the *Iliad*,[90] Jebb of the impetuosity and "the vehemence of dark passions,"[91] Lang of the "fresh vivacity and unwearied zest" of the Greek poet,[92] and Stedman went so far as to describe Homer as singing with the irrepressibility of a nightingale.[93] Yet it is striking how firmly resolved they all were to avoid overstressing the poetic features which the Romantics had stressed. If they did not quite treat the Greek epic as a "cold and deliberate concoction of the intellect," if they did not disassemble and fragmentize it in the manner of the earlier neo-classicists, they certainly emphasized strongly enough many of the characteristics which the neo-classicists had especially prized. W. J. Courthope, for instance, referred approvingly to the "judgment, knowledge of composition and proportion" manifested by the two epics;[94] More called the *Iliad* not a patchwork of rhapsodies but "the most perfectly constructed poem devised by man or men";[95] W. P. Ker said that such "strong" poets as Homer "have their strong reasoning" as well as grace and charm, and that it is the structure of the plot that "gives unity and harmony to the composition."[96] Like More, Mackail declared that the *Iliad* is "probably on the whole the greatest poem ever made": "what is put in or left out is in nearly all cases put in or left out for valid poetical reasons."[97] Jebb ascribed a large "mental grasp" to Homer,[98] while Murray proclaimed that "the *Iliad* is a definite poem, composed with great artistic elaboration for an artistic end, beginning in the middle of an action, and leading up to a skilfully prepared climax. Its methods are the methods not of conscientious pillar-to-post chronicle, but of artistic fiction."[99] Aside from dwelling on the architectonics of the Greek epics, Walter C. Perry exhibited a definite antagonism to the Romantic point of view when he asked, "may we not, after all, thank God we learn nothing of Homer even from himself? . . . One of the greatest vices of modern literature is the boastful display of the subjective feelings of the author."[100] "Judgment," "devised," "reasoning," "composed," "made," "mental"—it is illuminating to note how the critics were tending to use words such as these rather than the words commonly employed in the early nineteenth century, "sing," "efflux," "spontaneous," "inspired," "heartfelt," "extemporaneous."

Another much-discussed subject was the language and style of Homer. No longer were there suggestions that the poet's words were the first that had come to his mind under the pressure of tremendous emotion, or that their figurativeness was owing to the poverty of primitive language, to a want of precise and still more of abstract terminology. "To the long comparisons of Homer," Gummere wrote, "no wise man will now appeal as examples of the artless and natural in poetic style. Savages, like Mr. Shandy, may dearly love a comparison, but it is a logical process, a kind of incipient science, in any case subsequent to the unconscious stage of metaphors."[101] Homer may be "simple" in certain respects, said Oscar Wilde, but "simple in language he undoubtedly is not."[102] S. H. Butcher, censuring modern novelists for "inventorying" details of description, called attention to the conciseness and compression of Homer's language: "a single epithet will often open up to us the very heart of the object; its inmost and permanent character will stand out in clear-cut outline."[103] And in a highly original lecture on Greek poetry, Mackail said that the Homeric epics are full of traditional stylistic devices: poetry was not in a primitive condition; it "had become a matured art with its recognized symbols." Epithets like "wine-bright," "violet-coloured," and "unvintaged" were interchangeably applied to the sea because "each implies the others, and they convey (or any one of them conveys in the reflected light of the others) a complex image, not descriptive only but in the highest degree imaginative."[104] Nor did Mackail concur with Romantic opinion that Homer's repetitions are monotonous, awkward, and "unpoetic": they may be described as an "artifice," "an essential element in design,"[105] their purpose being to achieve an effect "like that of flowers in a tapestry or diapers in a painting."[106]

Naturally, these critics did not admire Homer simply because of his technique. In spite of all the talk about the organic nature of poetry, in spite of all the praise of the lyric for its intensity and of the novel for its faithful recording of life as it is lived, there was general agreement not only that the Homeric epics are immortal but also that they are immortal largely because of their "content." No matter to what particular school a critic belonged, he held that the great worth of Homer lay in his transcendence of the local and temporal, in his having embodied in the concrete some element or aspect of essential "truth." Sometimes Homer was especially valued for his sense of the eternally beautiful. Referring to the passages in which the poet describes the shield of Achilles and the household of King Alcinous, Walter Pater declared that the Homeric world was not a barbaric world at all but one "that would have charmed . . . our comparatively jaded sensibilities";[107] in the Greek epic he detected a "lively impression of delightful things recently seen. Genuine poetry, it is true, is always naturally sympathetic with all beautiful sensible things and qualities."[108] Oscar Wilde, another lover of beauty, thought Morris a capable translator of the *Odyssey* because "he has all the Greek's joy in the visible aspect of things, all the Greek's sense of delicate and delightful detail, all the Greek's pleasure in beautiful textures and exquisite materials and imaginative designs."[109] George Santayana agreed with these so-called aesthetes. "Nowhere else can we find . . . so uncompromising a dedication to beauty, and such a gift of seeing beauty in everything. Homer, the first of poets, was also the best and the most poetical." In contrast, "our poets are things of shreds and patches; . . . they have no total vision. . . . The comparatively barbarous ages had a poetry of the ideal; they had visions of beauty, order and perfection."[110]

At other times it was Homer's moral or ethical idealism that was stressed, the "rightness" and eternal validity of the lessons to be learned from his poems. Opposing the earlier notion that

Homeric concepts of human conduct are crude and anti-Christian, Butcher asked the question: "Does Homer indeed enfeeble the spirit and relax the moral fibre? or does he brace the mind to all strenuous and noble action?"[111] and was as sure of the answer as Sir Philip Sidney had been. T. S. Perry averred that the Greek poet "teaches great lessons without preaching";[112] Lang that "the Homeric poems are the best training for life. There is no good quality that they lack";[113] and Mackail that it is only in Homer and in some of the northern sagas that man is "so great, and the moral effect of the poetry, as distinct from its moral lesson, so uplifting and sustaining."[114] Likewise, Aubrey De Vere found "a general purity the more striking from its unguardedness," and he proceeded to show, as eighteenth century moralists had shown, that the poems not only exemplify a virtue like courage but even the many kinds and nuances of courage.[115] William James, though he condemned the imperialistic spirit of the early Greeks and their love of "war for war's sake,"[116] was delighted to find in Homer a "freedom from all moral sophistry and strain." Since the ancients believed that "good was good, and bad just bad," they would have discovered mere "silliness" in Whitman's opinion that "what is called good is perfect and what is called bad is just as perfect."[117]

More commonly, emphasis fell upon Homer's sound comprehension of life as a whole, upon his breadth of vision and his typicality. While some critics thought the naturalistic novel the best source for the study of human motivations, T. S. Perry called attention to the "unequaled psychological knowledge" displayed by Homer,[118] and W. C. Perry declared that the heroes of the two epics are "more real and better known to us than nine-tenths of the people with whom we live."[119] In "Intentions," Wilde and Vivian say that "all bad art comes from returning to Life and Nature," but elsewhere Wilde himself praised Homer for his "wonderful psychological knowledge of human nature."[120] Symonds described the poet as portraying "life in its breadth and largeness, eliminating what is accidental, trivial, temporary, local, or transmuting simple motives into symbols of the universal by his treatment."[121] With Aristotle ever in mind, Butcher observed that an interpretation of life underlies and is "essential" to the unity of Homeric poetry, that Penelope, Nausicaa, Andromache, and other women in Greek literature "are beings far less complex than the heroines of a dozen novels that come out in a single year. Their beauty and truth lie precisely in their typical humanity."[122] Leslie Stephen agreed wholeheartedly with Arnold that the Greek epic is important chiefly as a "criticism of life,"[123] and Paul Elmer More, sharing the very same view, eulogized the "large currents of life," the "depth of wisdom," and the "truthfulness" of Homer. The supreme artists, he said, are supreme not only because they have a sense for the perfection of form but also because they "embody more truth, more wise reflection—in short, because they present a fairer criticism of life" than one finds in lesser artists.[124] A few of the early Victorians had of course discovered this "wise reflection" in Homer, but almost every critic around 1900 seems to have directed attention to it. In the eyes of the poet, it was said, the world appeared to be a place in which much is to be endured, in which joy yields to grief and hope yields to disappointment. Thinking in terms of the *Iliad,* More observed that "there lay the greatness of the heroic epos for readers of old,—in the sense of human littleness, the melancholy of broken aspirations, swallowed up in the transcending sublimity of man's endurance and daring."[125] Lang remarked that Homer was deeply impressed with the sadness of human existence, that he is great in part because he was concerned with the very same problems that beset modern man, "the eternal problems of death and life, of war and peace, of triumph and defeat, of pleasure and pain."[126] Similarly, Butcher found a "large, human, universal" melancholy in Homer but none of the deplorable "parade of melancholy" so characteristic of later poets. The early death of Achilles "is the burden of the *Iliad*"; he fights on though he knows his days are numbered, and it is this foreknowledge that "lends a peculiar pathos to all he says and does."[127] Nor was T. S. Perry's interpretation essentially different from Butcher's. Protesting against Frederic Harrison's comment that there is no sense of care or doubt or decay in Homer, Perry says that "the world he beheld was one full of grief, disappointment, treachery, and the immortal charm of his portrayal lies in his recognition and expression of this truth. Was there no care in Troy, or in the Grecian camp? None in Penelope's heart as she waited for Odysseus? . . . Was there no doubt among the stalwart warriors that fought the immortal fight about Ilium? No decay?"[128]

Through the centuries critics have almost never characterized or judged Homer in the light of the entire body of Homeric poetry. Instead, they have based their impressions upon certain books, passages, characters, episodes, and manners, with the result that their interpretations have tended to differ widely. Homer has variously been described as spontaneous or self-possessed, natural or stately, barbarous or refined, warlike or domestic. In the troubled age with which we are here concerned, it was natural that "sad," "melancholy," and other adjectives of this sort should be added to the already lengthy list, that people should find their own outlook on life, their own feeling of disappointment, reflected by the Homeric epic. But as perhaps in every age from classical antiquity to the present, there were those to whom the world of Homer was a world far better than the one in which they were living, far happier or nobler or simpler. Believing that the vitality and the heroic spirit of man were rapidly evaporating, W. E. Henley looked back through the *Odyssey* to the distant and glorious "morning light" of the human race. "In a space of shining and fragrant clarity you have a vision of marble columns and stately cities, of men august in single-heartedness and strength of women comely and simple and superb as goddesses; and with a music of leaves and winds and waters, of plunging ships and clanging armours, of girls at song and kindly gods discoursing, the sunny-eyed heroic age is revealed in all its nobleness, in all its majesty, its candour, and its charm."[129] George Gissing, whose realistic novels testify not to any enthusiasm for modern life but rather to a strong distaste for it, said that to read Homer "is like standing in the light of sunrise and seeing the world renewed." He was fascinated by the *Odyssey* and especially by its happier domestic incidents and descriptions. Typical is his remark that "in some ideal common-wealth one can imagine the Odyssean bed, a normal institution, every head of a household, cottager or lord . . . lying down to rest, as did his fathers, in the Chamber of the Tree. This, one fancies, were a somewhat more fitting nuptial chamber than the chance bedroom of a hotel. Odysseus building his home is man performing a supreme act of piety."[130] Charles Dudley Warner, unsympathetic with the "stained-glass attitudes" of the aesthetes and the "wholly unidealized view of human society" shared by the naturalistic novelists, was at least as ecstatic as Gissing about the pictures of life in the *Odyssey*. He reminds one of critics like Madame Dacier, Joseph Warton, and Rousseau (certainly not of Romantics like Shelley) when he describes in the most glowing terms the meeting of Nausicaa and the Son of Laertes. "Is there any woman in history more to be desired than this sweet, pure-minded, honest-hearted girl, as she is depicted with a few swift touches by the great poet?— the dutiful daughter in her father's house, the joyous companion of girls, the beautiful woman whose modest bearing commands the instant homage of man. Nothing is more enduring in literature than this girl and the scene on the Corfu sands."[131] E.C. Stedman spoke of turning to Homeric poetry "as strong men wearied seek again the woods and waters of their youth";[132] while Murray said of the heroic age that "those were the days when a hero was really a hero and a princess a princess."[133] And Charles Eliot Norton, usually more scholar than critic, described the sanity and "healthiness of spirit" in Homer. "Have we gained in our modern civilization an equivalent for what the Greeks possessed and what is not ours? We seem to have eaten of the fruit of the Tree of Knowledge, and to have lost Paradise thereby. And, worse than this, the apples of the Tree are no better than apples of the Dead Sea."[134]

One sometimes hears it said that since about 1800 literary theorists have tended to equate "lyrical" and "poetical," thereby intimating that narrative verse, to the extent that it relates rather than expresses or suggests, cannot really be regarded as poetry at all. Admittedly this critical concept was stated and restated at intervals throughout the nineteenth century, and it was implicit, of course, in some of the judgments which we examined at the beginning of the present chapter. Nevertheless, everything points to the fact that after Wordsworth and before Croce the dominant approach to poetry, or at least the prevalent view as to the attributes of a truly great poem, was not pronouncedly different from what it had been in the time of Pope. The early Victorians had revived Aristotelian opinion; critics at the end of the century were intent on consolidating it. If the reputation of Homer was again almost unassailable, it was because the theorists later branded as "genteel"—the Babbitts, Mores, Stedmans, Woodberrys, and Mackails—all affirmed that the only possible rival of the ancient epic is the tragic drama. Moreover, as we have seen, even those who pleaded for naturalistic fiction or for art-for-art's-sake poetry, were not averse to joining with this group in paying tribute to Homer. Homer was reckoned supreme because of the symmetry of his poems, of a unity that was there no matter how resolutely the separatists had argued to the contrary. He was supreme because of the artistry displayed in the compression of descriptive detail, in the selection of effective images, in the reliance upon certain technical devices. He was supreme for many reasons but the chief one was simply this: that his two epics, as imitations of action, employed the guise of the particular to manifest the ineffable beauty of life and of objects, the indisputable and absolute truths of ethical conduct, and the nature and the potentialities of man.

In the 1880's and 1890's there was one fairly radical change of attitude towards Homer, one that was made possible largely by the indefatigable work of classical scholars and historians and sociologists. Many early Victorians, we will recall, had been inconsistent enough to speak of the Homeric epic as a work of consummate art and yet to assume that it was a primitive or "natural" sort of poem, to liken it to the communal ballad; others, fully convinced of its primitiveness, had treated it not really as a unified work of art at all but as groups of detachable poems that had accreted to a single master-poem; and still others had discovered differing degrees of craftsmanship in each of the two epics. At the end of the century, on the other hand, the Homeric epic was generally recognized as being neither wholly "primitive" nor wholly "artificial." It was said to represent an in-between stage in the history of poetry, an organic growth over generations and even centuries, to be a work that exhibits many traces of its primeval origin but at the same time much unmistakeable evidence of the shaping hand of a single genius to whom its immortality is essentially due. Nor is this change of attitude without important implications. Antiquarian pursuits often have a direct bearing on literary criticism, and the newer theory of Homeric origins, in gaining wide currency around 1900, put a quietus on the more extreme interpretations of the neo-classicist and the Romantic alike. At least there was no longer any proclivity to think of Homer as singing his woodnotes wild or to imagine, as Le Bossu had done, that he had concocted the two epics for the sole purpose of driving home a lesson in morality.

Notwithstanding Harrison's remark about Dante in the age of steam, the prestige of the Italian poet has perhaps never been higher than it was during the latter part of the nineteenth century. In England he was read by all who made any pretense of being liberally educated; he was the darling of the small but influential group known as the Pre-Raphaelites; and, as we saw in the previous chapter, he was the subject of eulogistic criticism by such writers as Church and Symonds. In America Dante's reputation was amazingly great; in this land of sudden and transitory enthusiasms, the *Divine Comedy* became such fashionable reading during the 1870's, 1880's, and 1890's that it is doubtful whether any native poem or novel received a comparable amount of attention. Partly responsible for the vogue was a trio of university professors: at one time or another Longfellow, Lowell, and Norton taught courses in Dante; they wrote about Dante and formed an influential Dante society. Two of them, Longfellow and Norton, publicized the Italian poet through English translations. Dante became a favorite topic for young ladies who were corresponding with one another, a favorite subject for the manufacturers of calendars, for lecturers at the

Chautauqua gatherings and at meetings of small town literary groups, and for enterprising college graduates intent on winning their spurs as scholars.

Needless to say, a prodigious amount of Dante literature was forthcoming each year on both sides of the Atlantic. Some of the scholarly essays and monographs—those by Paget Toynbee, for example—were really substantial contributions; but the vast majority of the things written managed to survive barely more than a decade or so. Certainly no one today is tempted to unearth any of the host of unpretentious and amateurish books that set forth in a patronising sort of way the facts of Dante's life, the relationship between Dante and Beatrice, the moral lessons to be gleaned from the *Divine Comedy,* the major differences between Guelph and Ghibelline, the state of the Church in the fourteenth century, and so on—books such as Elizabeth Harrison's *The Vision of Dante, a Story for Little Children and a Talk to Their Mothers* (1892); A. J. Butler's *Dante, His Times and His Work* (1895), with an appendix entitled "Hints to Beginners"; or the Reverend Mr. J. F. Hogan's "inspirational" *Life and Works of Dante* (1899). This kind of "literature," one suspects, was principally motivated by the hope for financial profit and by a desire to strengthen the religious faith of the public. Hardly less ephemeral were many, perhaps most, of the scholarly writings—works like D. J. Snider's *Commentary of the Divine Comedy* (1892-1893), a collection of miscellaneous historical data, and W. T. Harris' abstruse *The Spiritual Sense of Dante's Divine Comedy* (1899), a treatise that approached the poem as if it were little more than a labored study of the nature of sin. Irving Babbitt possibly had books of this type in mind when he observed, in 1908, that "the Cornell University library already contains, for the special study of Dante alone, over seven thousand volumes; about three fourths of which, it may be remarked in passing, are nearly or quite worthless, and only tend to the confusion of good counsel."[135]

Worthless or not, virtually everything written about Dante was eminently explicatory and analytical. Here and there, in introductions and prefaces, one may discover casual remarks about the value of the *Divine Comedy* as a literary work. But there was no substantial body of Dante criticism, hardly a single essay in which the author made an incisive examination of the purely aesthetic features of the poem. Among the Americans writing just after the Civil War, Norton has often been referred to as a leading critic of Dante, but influential as he was, the only semi-critical thing that he wrote was an essay that appeared in the *North American Review,* "Dante, and His Latest English Translators." Even this essay dealt in the familiar generalities: Dante was sincere, he epitomized the Middle Ages, he is a difficult poet to read and therefore requires close study. If Norton deserves credit as a Dante critic, it is largely because of certain passages in which he discussed the unity of the poem: he says, for example, that "in its general proportions, in the balance and harmony of its parts, in the subordination of its detail to the main effect, in freedom of expression within the limits of construction, the *Divine Comedy* stands supreme."[136] All very true, though even this seems rather superficial. As a critic of Dante, Lowell was certainly more important. His long essay in 1872 was often praised and quoted; it bespeaks a genuine love for the Italian epic. Yet it lacks originality and real focus. We read, as we have read before in earlier Romantic critics, that Dante is "subjective," that his vision of God has "imaginative grandeur," that it is the poet's sincerity which makes the poem "universal," that the scene is laid in the soul of man, that it embodies "the Christian idea of a triumphant life."[137] W. C. Brownell goes rather too far in saying that Lowell's essay is "uncritical" as well as "inartistic," but there would seem to be some truth in his comment that Lowell "does not express his general conception of Dante and he does not because he has not himself, one feels sure, thought it out into definition."[138]

Late in the century, English and American critics made observations about Dante that are hardly more illuminating than Lowell's. Some could do no justice at all to the *Divine Comedy.* The realist Howells, while approving of the Paolo-Francesca episode and the passage about Ugolino, found much that was "dull and tough and dry" in the poem.[139] He scorned the idea that one should regard a work in its entirety: "As a matter of fact, we see nothing whole, neither of life nor art. We are so made, in soul and in sense, that we can deal only with parts, with points, with degrees."[140] John Jay Chapman declared that the *Divine Comedy* "is a series of disconnected scenes," that it is "unrelieved by a single scene of comedy," that "Dante is most foreign to the genius of the English race";[141] Coventry Patmore thought the poem no better than Wordsworth's *Excursion;*[142] and Robert Ingersoll spoke of the "malignity and solemnity" of Dante's "revengeful lines," giving him credit only for having the courage "to see a pope in hell."[143] Even more severe was Swinburne. Irritated by the attitude of Rossetti and his friends, he held that "for these Unitarians or Mohammedans of Parnassus there is but one Muse, and Dante is her prophet. If we would not be reprobate in their eyes we must accept and worship as they do the idol, the whole idol, and nothing but the idol; we must not stop our noses in hell with loathing, nor distend our jaws with yawning in heaven; neither may we worship any other God."[144] These men, he says elsewhere, suffer from an "acute monomania."[145] But opinion of Dante was usually a great deal more favorable. To Santayana, he was much as he had been to Carlyle, a prophet on the order of Homer, a rare genius whose mission was to unveil hidden beauty.[146] To G. K. Chesterton, he stood for all that the aesthetes did not: these latter-day poets seemed to be of a mind "to write a 'Divine Comedy' in which heaven shall be under the floor of hell."[147] To Harrison, Dante's poem was "the great epic of Catholicism," a "Bible or Gospel," and at the same time "the review in one vast picture of human life as a whole, and human civilisation as a whole; all that it had been, was, and might become."[148] To Mackail, it was no "series of disconnected scenes" (as Chapman had said) but an organic whole, a work having "a single vast pattern," "a unity of progressive design."[149] Mabie combined the views of Santayana and Mackail: the *Divine Comedy* "flows together; it unfolds by virtue of an interior force which plays freely and masterfully through every part of it";[150] it is also an "interpretation," a prophecy that lays bare "the laws upon which life rests."[151] And there was a particularly significant comment by Walter Pater. However much he may have praised the lyric because it seemed to approach closely to the condition of music, Pater felt that the *Divine Comedy* was one of the few masterpieces of literature: "It is on the quality of the matter it informs or controls, its compass, its variety, alliance to great ends, or the depth of the note of revolt, or the largeness of hope in it, that the greatness of literary art depends."[152] This comment should not be overlooked by those interested in Pater's critical theory.

As intimated earlier, there is nothing very impressive about these estimates of Dante. Generally they seem repetitive and vague; generally they leave one with the feeling that the critics had not taken the trouble or had somehow been unable to formulate any precise ideas about the merits of the *Divine Comedy*. Possibly this is a chronic situation. Possibly the complexity and the obliqueness of the poem tend to embarrass the critic, to make it difficult for him to arrive at clear-cut judgments. But this does not entirely explain the matter. Around 1900 the ordinary reader and the literary theorist took rather different attitudes towards Dante's epic. Often the person of average tastes was inclined to emphasize and praise its "romantic" elements, its emotionalism and subjectivity, its platonic concept of love, its strangeness and its distance from the everyday world of the present. Women were usually the most avid readers of Dante. Furthermore, the general public was prone to stress the doctrine contained in the poem. In her study of the reception of Dante in America, Angelina La Piana says that "the essential Christian and moral content of the *Divine Comedy,* in spite of its symbolism and its medieval theology, seems to have been more attractive and more appreciated than either the mythological splendor of Homer or the cloudy, philosophical myth of Faust."[153] People of all religious denominations were reading Dante's epic in the same way that they were reading the Bible, in the same way that their forefathers had read *Paradise Lost* and *The Pilgrim's Progress*. The theologians of course encouraged such an approach. Referring to the *Divine Comedy* as a religious text, A. H. Strong asked whether there was "anything that our age needs more than this strengthening of conscience, this assertion of the claims of righteousness, this declaration that the soul that sinneth, it shall die."[154] And we find the same emphasis in a few of the critical writings of the time. Though he said that he read Dante's poem "for the poetry and humanity of it," Stopford Brooke observed that the Florentine was "nearer to the idea of Essential Divinity than any one is in this present hour of the world's history";[155] while Mabie, in contrasting the religious idealism of Dante with the skepticism of the moderns, averred that "we do not believe enough in God, in ourselves, and in the divine laws under which we live."[156] It is fully apparent, however, that the great majority of the literary critics did not share these enthusiasms with the public. Granted that they recognized the importance of Dante, they were of no mind to value the poem as an inspirational work, as a treatise on the nature of sin and righteous living. Nor were they willing to follow Hazlitt, Hunt, and Coleridge, and most contemporary readers as well, in praising its "romantic" features, its emotionalism and subjectivity. If their estimates of Dante were often unoriginal or vague and indecisive, one good reason, it would appear, was that most of them found their ideal of poetry not so much in the *Divine Comedy* as in the ancient classics. Their greatest enthusiasm was similar to what Arnold's had been: an enthusiasm for the epic of action, for the sanity and temperateness, the breadth and the grace and the sense of proportion which they associated with Homer, for all those virtues of life and of literature that the nineteenth century had tended to underrate.

Of the four major epic poets with whom we have been mainly concerned, Milton was clearly the one to be most frequently challenged. The reading public, though largely Protestant, could somehow overlook the Catholic doctrine of the *Divine Comedy;* it was not perturbed by the often puzzling allegory or by the many allusions to persons and events long since forgotten. But it could not tolerate *Paradise Lost,* the one great epic written in the mother tongue: strong objections were raised to the long and involved periods, the stateliness of manner, the obscure references to classical mythology, and above all, the unorthodox nature of Milton's religious beliefs. Actually, many of the literary critics shared the same feelings. Not reading *Paradise Lost* until late in life, Howells observed that "Milton is a trial of the spirit in three-quarters of his verse."[157] Alfred Ainger wondered how anyone could manage to read the poem through: "Will he ever achieve it, unless he be one day cast upon a desert island, and save a Milton from the wreck, as well as the salt beef and biscuit?"[158] Though far from sympathizing with popular opinion, Leslie Stephen allowed that "readers are generally bored when a poet is bored himself; and Milton, if not bored, is clearly writing under constraint, which has much the same effect."[159] In *The Way of All Flesh,* young Ernest was rather shocked to hear the "author" say that the five pounds which Milton received for *Paradise Lost* was more than he deserved: "I would have given him twice as much myself not to have written it at all."[160] And there was John Burroughs. Launching into a tirade, he declared that "Milton's poetry, for the most part, is to me a kind of London Tower filled with old armor, stuffed knights, wooden chargers, and the emblems and bedazzlements of the past. Interesting for a moment, but dead, hollow, moth-eaten. Not a live thing in one of his poems that I can find. . . . His 'Paradise Lost' is a huge puppet-show." Milton himself, Burroughs added, stands in English literature "like a great museum of literary archaeology."[161]

Many of the critics gave specific reasons why they disliked Milton, and the reasons were often the traditional ones. Again the poet was called a "Puritan," the term generally being used because of the unpleasant connotations now attached to it. Again it was said that he was too austere and cold and self-centered, a man standing apart from his fellow-men. A. C. Benson spoke of his "ghastly humor": he "had not himself emerged beyond the childish stage, which finds its deepest amusement in the disasters and catastrophes of stately persons."[162] W. E. Henley said that Milton was "in the mind's eye of Milton the noblest of created things and to Mr. Saintsbury almost as unpleasing a spectacle as the gifted but abject Racine."[163] Burroughs, forgetting about the poet's days at Horton and his later participa-

tion in political and religious affairs, remarked that Milton
"seems to have had no experiences of his own, and hardly to have
seen the earth and sky, or men and women, with his natural eyes.
He saw everything through the classic eyes of the dead past."[164]
Though himself not displeased with the personality of the poet,
Mark Pattison observed that "he had none of that sympathy with
which Shakespeare embraced all natural and common affections
of his brother men. Milton, burning as he did with a consuming
fire of passion, and yearning for rapt communion with select
souls, had withal an aloofness from ordinary men and women,
and a proud disdain of common-place joy and sorrow, which has
led hasty biographers and critics to represent him as hard, austere,
an iron man of iron mould."[165] But the bulk of the adverse
criticism of Milton was not directed at the character of the poet
or for that matter at the style and syntax of his epic or at his
Adam, Eve, and Satan. More and more, the attacks were concen-
trated upon the primary motive of *Paradise Lost,* upon the theme
and the way in which it is presented, upon the theological and
philosophical content. J. H. Shorthouse announced that "we can
only read parts" of the poem at all, "or at least with edifica-
tion, for such parts as are purely narrative are so gross in their
conceptions and so unworthy of the themes of which they treat,
that no amount of allegorical interpretation can render them
otherwise than disgusting."[166] John Churton Collins spoke of
the "hideous and revolting anthropomorphism of much of his
theology—an anthropomorphism not like that of the Greeks,
sanely, soundly, nobly symbolic, but *often* and more than *acci-
dentally un-*sane, unsound, not noble."[167] Agreeing with Ruskin,
W. P. Ker stated that "Milton in *Paradise Lost* does not believe
his own story; his world would have seemed to Dante as crazy
as his chaos, and more uncomfortable from its pretence of reason
and religion."[168] Paul Elmer More admitted that the "immediate
appeal of *Paradise Lost* has been dulled by the lapse of time. The
stories of Genesis do not strike us to-day as immediately and
literally true; they even leave the average reader colder than
the myths of ancient Greece, because they are drawn from a
more restricted field of our human nature."[169] To More's way

of thinking, Milton could not begin to compare with old Homer. John Bascom even refused to give the poet credit for having sometimes managed to conceal his intent to teach moral lessons: "Art is not only not didactic, it will not allow the didactic spirit to disguise itself under its work."[170] And Hugh Walker charged that Milton, great as he might be, was unable to rise above the narrow, "individualistic views of his time. . . . Even the visiting of the sins of the fathers upon the children is rather a theological mystery, an imputation of guilt by arbitrary will upon the person not guilty, than a profound fact in the constitution of the universe."[171]

Actually, the most comprehensive statements of the case against Milton were made by two men who had the highest respect for the Miltonic epic, George Woodberry and Mark Pattison. Woodberry held that the poet chose the older Ptolemaic scheme of the universe because of the "classical prepossession of his mind— his desire for a world limited, closed and clear, like a Greek temple." The result is that the poem "is apt to seem as antiquated as its celestial geography." Moreover, in tracing history back to the fall of Adam, Milton "gave an importance to its Biblical events, which they can only retain in a limited way. The centre and movement of history are now so differently conceived by the general modern mind that Milton's account of history has little essential interest to the reader."[172] And finally, Woodberry offered a new though minor objection, one that attests to the influence of the idea of evolution upon literary evaluation. Modern man is so pledged to the concept of progress, he explained, "that the notion of hell as a kind of sink and prison of the universe finds no place for itself in our minds." The only equivalent for the Miltonic hell is the latter-day jail, and society is determined that that shall not be "a place that leads nowhere, even for the most hardened." Woodberry proceeded to contrast the "Hebrew fixity of Milton's thought" with the theory of progress ultimately derived from the Greeks, and to suggest that the failure of *Paradise Lost* "to interest the modern mind in hell, except as a spectacle, is connected with the fundamental denial of progress in it, and its departure from the thought of development."[173] Pattison, in somewhat the same vein, observed that it would have been "a thing incredible to Milton" that the hold of the Old Testament over the imagination of Englishmen could ever become weaker. "This process, however, has already commenced." For many readers Milton's "angelology" is little more than poetic machinery, and the anthropomorphic theology causes considerable distress. "Were the sapping process to continue at the same rate for two more centuries, the possibility of epic illusion would be lost to the whole scheme and economy of the poem." Thinking that Milton took a plan of life for life itself, Pattison says that he should have remembered the principle laid down by Aristotle, namely, "that men in action are the poet's proper theme." Had Milton done so, "he would have raised his imaginative fabric on a more permanent foundation; upon the appetites, passions, and emotions of men, their vices and virtues, their aims and ambitions, which are a far more constant quantity than any theological system."[174]

"Malt does more than Milton can to justify God's ways to man." Certainly the reading public and some of the men-of-letters could sympathize with the view expressed in Housman's famous line. But were there not things to be said in favor of *Paradise Lost?* In the face of all this depreciation, was there no one who was willing to rise to its defense? Actually, many theorists felt that the defects of the poem— defects existed, to be sure—were being treated with far too great severity, that in the final analysis Milton's epic remained one of the masterpieces of literature. Henry A. Beers declared that "when all has been said that can be said in disparagement or qualification," *Paradise Lost* is still "the foremost of English poems and the sublimest of all epics."[175] With true enthusiasm, John Bright averred that there is nothing in ancient literature that can compare in value "with the unsurpassable grandeur and beauty of Milton." "If all existing Greek and Latin books were destroyed, is there not in our English classics sufficient material whereon to build a future of which our successors need not be ashamed?"[176] Richard Garnett, apparently regarding the much-praised *Iliad* as a mere folk-epic like the *Nibelungenlied,* came to the rescue of Milton by pointing out that "to evolve an epic out of a single incident is a greater intellectual achievement than to weave one out of a host of ballads."[177] As in the case of Bright, English critics sometimes defended *Paradise Lost* because of their loyalty to everything English, because Americans and Germans and Frenchmen like Taine and Scherer were attacking it with such malice. For example, Augustine Birrell stoutly declared that "no other poem can be mentioned which has so coloured English thought as Milton's, and yet, according to the French senator whom Mr. Arnold has introduced to the plain reader, '*Paradise Lost* is a false poem, a grotesque poem, a tiresome poem.' It is not easy for those who have a touch of Milton's temper though none of his genius to listen to this foreign criticism quite coolly."[178] Everyone, Birrell added, should learn "to enjoy great things greatly."[179]

Supporters of Milton usually tried to give more definite and logical reasons for their praise of *Paradise Lost*. Now and again it was the organic nature of the poem that they chose to stress. "Composed in darkness, brooded over in memory, dictated in fragments, it all fell into place," wrote J. W. Mackail. "We can hardly imagine any material alteration if, like Virgil," Milton had retained the manuscript for a long time and had given it "day by day, the final touches of a patient and fastidious hand."[180] Similarly, Arthur Symons stated that Milton "becomes the great poet whom he is universally admitted to be, because he is almost always successful in the fusion of substance and form."[181] More frequently, however, these critics sought to rebut the chief arguments of their opponents, to defend the general theme and the intellectual content of the poem, or to interpret them in a more favorable way, or to minimize their significance. Though he did not underestimate the difficulty of so doing, Leslie Stephen said that "we must not only 'suspend disbelief' but get rid of our positive beliefs; then it is perhaps possible to read *Paradise Lost* without a shock."[182] John Morley was inclined to put the case rather more strongly. The poet's ethics and theology and "his so-called Platonical metaphysics, have as little to do with the power of his poetry over us, as the imputed Arianism of any other aspect of the theology of *Paradise Lost* has to do with the

strength and the sublimity of Milton, and his claim to a high
perpetual place in the hearts of men."[183] Birrell rejected Arnold's
contention that one is obliged to take the poem literally: like
the world of the *Arabian Nights,* Milton's world is an ideal world,
and his fable and characters are not from Holy Scripture but
from "a legend, ancient and fascinating."[184] Praising the poet
as "a daring thinker," Edward Dowden emphasized the "intel-
lectual effort" that he exerted in constructing his own theology:
the creation of *Paradise Lost* and its sequel "was a far bolder and
vaster undertaking than is commonly supposed."[185] Mackail be-
lieved that it is the "flawless excellence of workmanship" which
gives Milton's major epic its enduring value: "it is independent
of any view which later generations have taken, or may take,
of the quality of its subject";[186] and Garnett expressed an opinion
shared by many critics when he claimed that "the vital question
for the poet is his own belief, not the belief of his readers."
"If the *Iliad* has survived not merely the decay of faith in the
Olympian divinities, but the criticism which has pulverized
Achilles as a historical personage, *Paradise Lost* need not be
much affected by general disbelief in the personality of Satan,
and universal disbelief in that of Gabriel, Raphael, and Uriel."[187]
Likewise, Sir Walter Raleigh insisted that the poem is, after all,
a poem and not a disquisition on theological views which we
must accept or reject. In fact, "the less it will endure the trial as
a system or theory of the universe, the more wonderful does it
appear as a work of art." Raleigh compared Milton's epic to a
"gigantic filamented structure," to an "enchanted palace" raised
by such "careful engineering science" that "it just stands, and
no more."[188] Finally, there is Paul Elmer More's novel interpre-
tation of *Paradise Lost.* Most readers dislike the poem, he says,
because they misunderstand Milton's purpose in writing it, be-
cause they assume he wished to justify God's ways, to expatiate
on the nature of good and evil. "The true theme is Paradise it-
self; not Paradise Lost."[189] It is a theme traceable to "that
ancient ineradicable longing of the human heart for a garden of
innocence, a paradise of idyllic delights, a region to which come
only 'golden days fruitful of golden deeds.'" "It is, the world

over, youth's vision and age's dream of a happiness that never was on land or sea; it is the glimmering of those 'trailing clouds of glory' which, to Wordsworth's fancy, follow us from somewhere afar off into the darkness of our birth."[190] Appropriately enough, says More, the pastoral scenes are portrayed in the middle of *Paradise Lost;* they are preceded by descriptions of all the forces antagonistic towards human contentment and are followed by a picture of "the reality of life set like a shadow against the brief and golden dream of Paradise."[191] Though Milton gives a religious significance to his theme, what is vital to us "who merely read and seek the exalted pleasures of the imagination" is "that perfect and splendid vision of pastoral bliss."[192]

Before Arnold wrote his essay "A French Critic of Milton," discussions of *Paradise Lost* had tended to focus upon the "content" of the poem, upon the theme and the underlying ideology. In the last decades of the century, however, literary theorists often seemed to think that the emphasis had been too strong, that (to use Mackail's terminology) "execution" was at least as vital as "conception." Hence the supporters of Milton, and indeed many who scoffed at his theme, were more and more inclined to regard the technique of Paradise Lost—its versification, imagery, and diction—as an attribute that made it deserving of the highest commendation. Beers said that "Milton's blank verse in itself is enough to bear up the most prosaic theme, and so is his epic English, a style more massive and splendid than Shakspere's"; like many of the early Romantics, Beers was ecstatic about "the countless single beauties that sow" the pages of the poem.[193] Garnett described Milton's diction as "the delight of the educated": "every word seems instinct with its own peculiar beauty, and fraught with its own peculiar association."[194] "That the theme of 'Paradise Lost' should have evoked such grandeur is a sufficient compensation for its incurable flaws and the utter breakdown of its ostensible moral purpose."[195] Edmund Gosse cited the variable pattern of the blank verse as the reason why "no one with an ear can ever have found Milton dull";[196] while A. S. Richardson, having little patience with the common feeling that the poem is "tiresome," declared that the "poetic measure" of Milton "has never been equalled in English verse from Chaucer to this day."[197] W. M. Dixon spoke for Hopkins and Bridges as well as himself when he said that "Milton is the central man of the world for style: not only of England, but of all the world, ancient & modern."[198] Severely critical of Milton in almost every possible way, Pattison devoted many pages to praise of his imagery and especially of his ability to choose words that, "over and above their dictionary signification, connote all the feeling which has gathered round them by reason of their employment through a hundred generations of song."[199] Likewise, Saintsbury was most displeased with the content of *Paradise Lost* but he was highly enthusiastic about the "poetical jewels" in the poem. Taking the cue from Arnold, he even wrote a long and rather tenuous essay entitled "The Grand Style of Milton."[200] Stedman announced that "the world has well agreed that what is fine in 'Paradise Lost' is the poetry; what is tiresome, the theology."[201] But most laudatory of all the estimates of Miltonic technique was the one made by Sir Walter Raleigh. After praising "the measured roll" of the verse, "the artful distribution of stress and pause," the "choice character" of the diction, and the "wealth of vaguely emotional epithets," Raleigh stated that Milton had "attained to a finished style of perhaps a more consistent and unflagging elevation than is to be found elsewhere in literature."[202] On another occasion he compared the style to "a satin brocade, stiff with gold, exactly fitted to the body." And we can well imagine what Poe would have said about Raleigh's opinion that Milton "packs his meaning into the fewest possible words, and studies economy in every trifle."[203]

Was Satan the hero of *Paradise Lost*—noble, self-sufficient, and proud; or did he represent goodness deteriorating by slow stages and transforming itself into evil? This was another warmly debated issue around 1900. By and large, however, Miltonic criticism was concerned with the two matters we have been discussing—with the theme and the ideology on the one hand and with the literary style and expression on the other. Clearly the content presented greater problems, more insurmountable difficulties, than did the technique. It was not very convincing to say that Milton's cosmology or his theory of evil could be neglected, for they play too large a part in shaping the action of the poem: it is obvious, if Milton can be taken at his own word, that he was writing *Paradise Lost* with the express purpose of justifying God's ways, and justification implies the marshalling of arguments that seem likely to persuade. It was hardly more convincing to claim that this content is not at all dated or that Milton's outlook, religious and moral, was ever at heart the outlook of more than a small segment of mankind. Increasingly, the critics felt obliged to concede that the views expressed or intimated by the poem were in the main Milton's own views, and indeed that, as time went on, his theories of good and evil, like his speculations about free will and predestination, would be treated with less and less sympathy even by educated readers. Nor did reinterpretation of the theme appear to offer much promise. To assert, in the manner of Paul Elmer More, that the scenes in the Garden are the core of the poem and that everything else serves merely as a foil was clearly to neglect the obvious, to invite still greater embarrassment by transforming secondary motives into primary ones. But how much was to be gained by all the emphasis upon style and expression? Did it not again suggest evasiveness? "Style alone will never confer enduring and cosmopolitan fame upon a poet," said John Addington Symonds, looking at the matter broadly; "if one thing is proved with certainty by the whole history of literature down to our own time, it is that the self-preservative instinct of humanity rejects such art as does not contribute to its intellectual nutrition and moral sustenance."[204] Certainly it would seem ridiculous, as in fact it did seem to later critics, to honor Homer largely because of his universal representations of ethical and human truths, and yet to honor Milton almost as much simply because he was a master at putting the right words in the right places or because with his keen sense of harmony he had composed verse with the musical perfection of a Beethoven symphony. Thus no defense of *Paradise Lost* appeared to be really air-tight; no approach appeared to minimize the glaring deficiencies of the poem. Whether new arguments could be found, or whether Milton's prestige was to be endangered still further—this remains to be touched upon in the final part of our study.

Before we glance at the epic criticism of the twentieth century, of a century that has been remarkable for the development of many new theories of literature, it might be well to survey briefly the major shifts that occurred in the extensive span of time between the *Lyrical Ballads* and Croce's *Estetica*. For the Romantics, we will recall, the epic was to be associated with neo-Aristotelianism, with a critical code that appeared to (and did) overstress the purely architectural aspects of art. In theory at least, an epic poem seemed to many of Wordsworth's contemporaries not to be truly poetical at all, to be an artificial construction of the intellect, a work lacking in inspiration and imagination, one that exhibited merely the externalities of objects and of man. It was often thought to be relatively antiquated, if not quite obsolete, both in its intention and in its poetic method. In practice, however, critics around 1800 either tended to lose sight of the nature of epic (hence to compare Homer as a poet with Shakespeare or Chaucer as a poet) or to make rule-of-thumb distinctions between kinds of epic poems, between "classical" and "romantic," pagan and Christian, early and modern. Virgil was always denounced as artificial, insincere, and "unromantic"; he was given credit, with some reluctance, only for his style and versification. Occasionally Homer too was censured for being "classical" and artificial: Coleridge described him as "objective" and pedestrian, his characters as abstractions and automatons. Generally, however, Homer was classed with Ossian as a "primitive" poet—primitive either in the sense that he was "early," "rhapsodic," "pathetic," "imaginative," and "natural," or in the sense that his vision was limited, that his comprehension of life and of poetry as an art was narrow, crude, and perhaps even childish. The "romantic" or Christian epic, on the other hand, was almost universally admired, and admired for reasons that would hardly have occurred to the neo-classicist of the preceding century. Critics around 1800 did not think of Milton and Dante, or Ariosto and Tasso, as exhibiting man in action, the central passions and motives that lead to action. These poets were said to be great simply because they were, in the language of the day, so thoroughly "poetical." Ariosto was acclaimed primarily for his supramundane creations and his element of magic, Tasso for his sublimity of expression and the element of love, Dante and Milton for their egoism, their rebelliousness and lofty idealism, their revelations of basic religious truths. In every case the prestige of the "romantic" epics was enhanced by the application of some distinctively Romantic criterion.

The early Victorian period brought significant shifts in literary theory. If Romantic approaches were not entirely discarded— are they not, in fact, still with us today?—the chief measure of an epic poem was less likely to be its intangible "beauties" or its supposed exuberance or its expression of personality, and more likely to be the truth or scope of its treatment of human nature and the conscious artistry displayed in its structure, language, and versification. Hence Homer was once again prized for his universality and his craftsmanship while Virgil was honored for his technique and for his understanding of the essential tragedy of life, of the unattainability of man's highest aspirations. For the same reason Milton was accused of ignoring what is central in human experience, of being both too individualistic and too theological. But if the early Victorians were often inclined to view the epic with broad perspective, one nevertheless has the feeling that their estimates rarely indicate any incisive thinking about the place of heroic poetry in the realm of literature. Few critics bothered to consider how "epic" should be defined or how an epic should be compared with other poetic types; fewer still showed true insight in their discussions of the *Iliad* as a folk-epic and yet a consummate work of art. With some notable exceptions, comments on Homer and Virgil tended to be brief and superficial, to sound much like early eighteenth century comments shorn of their extreme dogmatism and standard phraseology. Similarly, the grumblings about the obsolescence of Milton's cosmology and his religious beliefs, as well as the many random remarks about the *Divine Comedy,* do not suggest a determination to get at the essence of poetry, to focus upon the very qualities that make a poem a poem. Granted that Victorian theory was relatively free of many of the deplorable emphases of the preceding age, that it was less subjective and peripheral, one must nevertheless conclude that it reflects a kind of instinctive reaction to Romantic excesses rather than a conscientious effort to reappraise the basic nature and function of art.

By the end of the nineteenth century, literary criticism had become as complex as life itself; it had become so complex that generalization about it seems almost out of the question. But if there was no homogeneity of opinion, there was at least a propensity to come to grips with the central problems in aesthetics, hence to inquire sedulously into the prime features and the worth of epic poetry. A major reason for this was of course the ever-gathering momentum of science. Disturbed by the implications of determinism, revolting against the positivistic approach to human nature and experience, a smallish band of literary theorists were bent on divorcing poetry from life. For them the messageless lyric, as a thing of beauty unto itself, became a more vital form than the extensive and often prosaic epic of action or of spiritual aspiration. No less disturbed than the aesthetes, the humanists and indeed all who shared a deep respect for the wisdom of past ages, sought to withstand both scientific doctrine and the new "fad" of art-for-art's-sake by reaffirming more vigorously than the early Victorians the existence and the logicality of a hierarchy of literary kinds. These conservative critics, more numerous than any other group, cared little for lyrics of any description and openly abominated the naturalistic novel. For them the ideal of poetry was the classical epic; for them Homer was the supreme genius by virtue of his artistry but even more by virtue of his profound ethical wisdom and his full comprehension of the godlike potentialities of human nature. But epic theory around 1900 does not reflect merely an antagonism to the scientific approach. Believing that the era of important poetry was past, that prose fiction was the only type of literature destined to flourish in a machine society, many critics came to regard the latter-day novel as the most pertinent if not necessarily the greatest of all the kinds. They were condescending towards Homer and Dante, sometimes even highly respectful, but they were only too ready to broach the relativistic point of view that the modern novel was most nearly in tune with the modern world, that it derived its meaning and value from the patent fact that it pursued the method and attitude of contemporary science.

Granted that acceptance of and reaction to the larger issues of the times prompted a good deal of serious pondering about epics and epic poets—we find a mirroring of the scientific approach, incidentally, even in the new theory of the evolution of the epic through its communal, communal-individual, and individual stages—it can hardly be claimed that actual criticism of Homer, Virgil, Dante, and Milton was vastly superior to the kind of criticism dominant during the earlier part of Victoria's reign. Clearly the estimates of the Greek epic mark a decided advance: they imply a searching investigation into basic principles rather than a parroting of eighteenth century opinion, a return to Aristotle rather than to the neo-Aristotelians. But as we have suggested in the course of this chapter, there was an inclination to overlook Virgil because of all of the idolization of Homer. There was also an inclination to treat Dante in an altogether too superficial fashion, to expatiate on the beauty and loftiness of the *Divine Comedy* or about its spiritual inspiration or its vividness or its earnestness or its individuality. Few were the attempts to consider the poem as an organic whole and to point out how it could be significant for an age that was rapidly becoming irreligious. Can we be far wrong when we say that the critics were too much awed and perhaps puzzled by Dante's poem to approach it with the assurance and painstaking care that they exhibited in their appraisals of the *Iliad?* In any event, the most glaring weakness in epic theory around 1900 manifested itself in the criticisms of *Paradise Lost.* The debate about Milton's epic had of course been incipient in the time of Carlyle, but as it waxed hotter and hotter, less and less effort was apparently made to regard the poem in its entirety.

Disapprobation of Milton's personality, overemphasis upon the scientific inaccuracy of the Miltonic universe and of its origin, preoccupation with the role of Satan—these led in many cases to the erroneous assumption that *Paradise Lost* is a meaningless anomaly, an outright failure as an epic. On the other hand, it is plain that the defenders of Milton did not take to solid ground. To argue *ad nauseam* about the poet's style, to prize *Paradise Lost* (as Saintsbury did) exclusively for its striking images and "poetical jewels," was tantamount to reducing poetry to a matter of technique, to a condition in which form as well as content must seem altogether immaterial. Returning to the point that was made a few moments ago, we find ourselves in no position to offer a telling generalization about epic theory at the end of the nineteenth century. Perhaps all that can be said is simply this: that it was traditional and anti-traditional, penetrating and superficial, scientific and humanistic, exhibiting the diverse ways in which men were bound to react to the contending demands and pressures of the most complex of all societies except our own.

EPILOGUE

The Epic in an Age of
Disillusionment, 1910-1950

In the victorian age it was still possible for a literary critic confidently to assert that "the future of poetry is immense." Science, Arnold held, will hereafter be completed not by religion and philosophy but by poetry. For an understanding of life mankind must turn to the best poetry, the quality of which can be sensed even in a few lines of Homer, Dante, Shakespeare, or Milton.

Certainly this prophecy has shown few signs of fulfillment. In our age of science and technology, the further dissolution of "what passes with us for religion and philosophy" has been accompanied by a marked decline of public interest in poetry—especially in the great epics and dramas Arnold had in mind. The public taste has been satisfied by the realistic-sentimental-sensational novels of the day, by utilitarian prose in books, magazines, and newspapers, by the soap-operas, "westerns," and gangland dramas of the cinema and television. If the Homeric epics are still read outside educational requirement, they are not read as "best poetry" but, in prose, as exotic novels of adventure. The exalted ethos of the Classical and Christian traditions which informed all the major epics makes small impression upon a skeptical public seeking casual recreation rather than "high poetic truth and seriousness."

Indifference toward epic poetry has often been shared by the literary critics themselves. Many have agreed with Croce and

Spingarn that "we have done with the genres," with any hierarchy of kinds; that each poem is an entity unto itself, an "expression" subject to no imposed pattern or law, deriving its worth solely from its degree of "completeness." Terms like *epic, lyric, pastoral* are merely convenient abstractions; they do not identify distinct species or higher and lower types of poetry. In practical criticism, writers like Brooks and Warren have tended to concentrate upon the lyrical poem: its governing intent and internal character, the manifold elements entering into its success or failure—rhythm, images, allusions, attitude, tone, ambiguity, innuendo, irony, paradox, determinative symbol. Aesthetic analysts have found the tight economy of the lyric a congenial and sufficient challenge. They have shown scant concern for the vast epic, its varied characters and slowly unfolding story, its ethical confrontation of human nature and life, its "great argument" reaching toward the ultimate mysteries.

In the eyes of some critics the epic and the lyric alike have fallen into disesteem. The epic, it appears, is "primitive" and artificial, and the lyric, typically "metaphysical," has grown over-subtle. Such critics have preferred the drama: its immediacy and directness, its special capacity to explore certain kinds of conflict within man and between men. Or they have preferred the novel, as a truly living, healthy form, best suited to the complexities of the mind, the tragic (more often pathetic) impact of environment on individuals, the causes and results of social tension, the baffling problems of industrial societies, racial prejudice, national passions, and the like. Is not the novel the most flexible and diversified type of literature, and does it not concern itself with a complex world far more interesting to modern man than that of Homer or even Chaucer?

In view of such forces inimical to the epic, one would expect to look in vain for more than an occasional spokesman or apologist. Yet actually, in the best-informed and substantial criticism of our time, opinion of the epic has perhaps never been higher.

In the first place, intensive historical study has led to a fuller understanding of the major poems, has left little doubt, for example, that only a master craftsman, using primitive poetic materials, could produce so complex and coherent a work as the *Iliad;* that Virgil, under fierce attack as an imitator a century or so ago, was nearly as original and skillful as Homer. In the second place, if the New Criticism has tended to shift attention to the lyric, it has on the other hand impressed upon critics the need of concentrating first of all upon the aesthetic principles operative in the major epics, upon the basic intent and organic nature of these poems. In the third place, many responsible judges of literature—principally men with academic affiliations— have strongly advocated a return to a more or less traditional concept of poetry. Edmund Wilson has assailed the "touch-stone" method proposed by Arnold and employed by later critics in order to exalt the lyric. Allen Tate has deplored Croce's repudiation of the genres. And others, in the face of modern relativism and determinism, have boldly reasserted the view that great literature is that which symbolizes, through variety of action and characters, some broad and significant interpretation of human experience. Believing that the epic, along with the tragic drama, can accomplish this best, humanists like Irving Babbitt have regarded the older lyric as too slight, the modern as esoteric, and have derided the specialized theories of imagism, expressionism, and pure aestheticism. Joseph Wood Krutch has found latter-day poetry to be "provisional, fragmentary, and barbarous," lacking the synthesis of the epic, its portrayal of a "complete and possible world." Repeatedly critics have averred that, as imaginative fiction, the epic is superior to the novel. Poets like Homer and Virgil, it is said, hit upon vital truth when they represent self-fulfillment coming to man only when he struggles heroically against tremendous odds. By contrast the typical novel seems to them peripheral, exploiting the local and transitory, often displaying only the lowest common denominator in human behavior. Grierson, for example, complains because Joyce "travestied the nobility of the *Odyssey* into that dreary *reductio ad absurdum* of itself, *Ulysses,* while Paul Elmer More, remembering Homer, brusquely dismisses *Manhattan Transfer* as an "explosion in a cesspool."

Perhaps the best way to clarify the high status of the epic in our time is to turn directly to the criticism of some of the major epic poets. There is no need to consider here Ariosto and Tasso and Ossian, whose stars declined long ago, nor *Beowulf,* a favorite during the heyday of Germanic scholarship, nor even Virgil, rightly cherished by students of Roman civilization. While these still have their devoted champions, it will suffice for our purpose to glance at the reputation of Homer, Dante, and especially Milton, representing the ancient world, the Middle Ages, and the Renaissance.

Homer and Dante have perhaps never been more warmly received. Not since the time of Pope have the Homeric epics been rated so high in terms of both aesthetic and human values. They have been widely admired not only for their musical language, color, and imaginative vigor but also for qualities uncommon in our world today—sanity, serenity, profound idealism. Here, said Irving Babbitt, is "normal human nature *in action*." Homer, said Sir Richard Livingstone, embodies "simple, central nature" whereas moderns like Yeats insist on leading us "into the bypaths of the human soul." Others have agreed with C. S. Lewis that the *Iliad* is a "human and personal tragedy," having as its dominating theme a great assertion: that man's salvation lies (as Abercrombie put it) in a "turning of the dark, hard condition of life into something which can be exulted in."

Dante's Christian masterpiece has been praised for substantially new reasons. Earlier critics, we will recall, often focused their attention upon isolated elements of the "Inferno," singling out certain episodes for adulation (invariably the one about Francesca) or dwelling upon and, like as not, condemning the body of religious doctrine. Today, theorists are inclined to regard the *Divine Comedy* as a whole and to marvel at Dante's success in fusing its multitudinous and disparate materials into a single poetic conception. T. S. Eliot, in an early essay, spoke of the poem as "one vast metaphor," in which each image reinforces the last, each episode and each allusion becomes part of the "same reality." Similarly, Mark Van Doren has said that "the poetry is the allegory; the allegory is the poetry," and Allen Tate that "the didactic element is in solution with the other elements of the poem."

More than a glance seems called for by Milton. *Paradise Lost,* the epic most widely read "in the original," has been a focus of controversy among scholar-teachers and critics in the last thirty or forty years. One group, while recognizing that the theology of Dante was fully assimilated by the poetry, has found no such synthesis in Milton. His ideas, they maintain, rarely become anything more than ideas; the raw materials remain distinct, even tend to jostle one another, because no compression, no transmutation of thought by emotion has occurred. Herbert Read has declared that Milton's thinking "was a system apart from his poetic feeling," Grierson that the argumentative part of the poem is entirely "adventitious." Moreover, though Arnold and other Victorians could agree that the "grand style" fully atones for the didacticism of *Paradise Lost,* some theorists in our day have not been willing to go even that far. They feel that whereas the diction of poets like Donne and Marvell is perfectly attuned to their emotion and thought, Milton's is arbitrary, unnatural, inorganic, in a word rhetorical rather than poetical. Eliot, leading this attack, was soon joined by Pound, who spoke of the "abominable dog-biscuit of Milton's rhetoric," by Leavis, who branded the style "magniloquent" and "orotund," by Wilson Knight, who found it an "imposition" on the material.

This attack has lost much of its power in recent years. Once Eliot had succeeded in freeing contemporary verse from the spell of Milton, he retracted his derogatory statements about *Paradise Lost.* Moreover, the detractors of Milton have met with strong opposition. Taking issue with the charge that the style is unnatural and often bombastic, Gilbert Murray and Douglas Bush have maintained that the great epics—*Paradise Lost* like the *Iliad* —all demand a diction and syntax far removed from those of everyday speech. Is it not obvious, they have asked, that without its Latinities and complex syntactical patterns *Paradise Lost* could never have achieved the effect intended? As C. S. Lewis has pointed out, Milton saw the need of using long and involved "sentences" in order to create in the reader a necessary feeling of expectancy, an "all-important sense that *something* out of the *ordinary*" is about to occur.

For the most part, however, the successful defense of Milton has concerned not the stylistic art of *Paradise Lost* but its essential theme. Ever since Edwin Greenlaw affirmed, in 1917, that its theme is the struggle between basic elements in man's nature rather than between man and God, critics have characterized Milton less as a religious polemic and more as a Renaissance humanist exploring the causes and effects of wise and unwise moral choices. As a result, emphasis has shifted from the earlier books of *Paradise Lost* and the dominating personality of Satan to the later books and the meaning and implications of the Fall. Some theorists have suggested that Milton uses myth to symbolize the tragic conflict between individual will and universal necessity, a struggle that admits of no solution because the demands of each must be recognized. The majority, however, think of the poet as illustrating through fiction what happens when man allows his natural self to rule, even briefly, his rational self. Thus, E. M. W. Tillyard attributes the Fall to an irrational "going against the nature of things," Merritt Hughes to sheer intemperance ("Men suffer from their impulse to overreach themselves"), James Holly Hanford to a lack of inner discipline, and Babbitt to a neglect of Milton's own awareness that "he who reigns within himself and rules passions, desires, and fears is more than king."

In *The Cycle of Modern Poetry* G. R. Elliott attempts to show why Milton's masterpiece, far from obsolescent owing to its religious doctrines, has greater pertinence in our time than a century or two ago by virtue of its poetic truth. The future of poetry *could* be immense if we were able to regain Milton's perception of the dual consciousness of man: "the unexampled union of peace and strenuousness in his style comes from his unexampled belief in 'Satan' and the 'Son of God' as the prime facts of human nature." He achieved a "final concentration" of the theme that had appeared intermittently in Spenser and in Shakespeare, the eternal conflict between "human passion and human peace." Loss of vital awareness of this conflict has impoverished modern thought, one-sided in its naturalism, and modern poetry, wandering on sundry by-paths. "The highway of poetry ahead of us passes through the centre of Milton's poem."

How does our latter-day opinion of the epic compare with that of the preceding periods, now somewhat clarified by the passage of time? In the eighteenth century, it was commonly assumed with good reason that literature must bear importantly upon life, that literary types are real and not necessarily equal in value, and that there must be objective standards if art and criticism are not to fall into chaos. But the virtues of neo-classical theory and practice appear to have been offset by a constant tendency to treat an epic like the *Iliad* as a kind of treatise on morality, as an inorganic structure to be disassembled and subjected to mechanical examination, as an artifact devised by reason. One cannot think, however, that the Romantic revolt brought a sounder type of epic criticism, for if the bad features of neo-classicism were discarded so too were its good ones. True, a few critics after 1800 did recognize the organic character of great poetry, of the major epics as well as the select lyrics; but most of them appear never to have considered or judged a work like *Paradise Lost* as a whole. Some assailed the major epics as too "objective" and too formal, because they preferred the poetry of personal emotion. Others, less hostile towards the epic, dwelt upon and rhapsodized over isolated episodes and passages— Milton speaking of his blindness, Hector taking his leave of Andromache, Nausicaa playing ball beside the river. Again and again there were idle effusions over the lot of Ossian and all but meaningless generalizations about the "beauty" of Dante's poem or the "truth" and "idealism" of *Paradise Lost*.

Victorian criticism was perhaps more substantial, certainly less peripheral. Granted, theorists frequently explained rather than criticized the *Divine Comedy*. Granted also, they rarely saw Milton's epic as a whole: they were concerned with its poetic style, and with the question whether Darwinian science had rendered *Paradise Lost* obsolete. Occasionally there was some real critical grasp, some realization that Dante's poem is one poem, not three—at any rate not a hodgepodge of episodes; that, whatever their origin, the Homeric poems are works of supreme art and, like the *Aeneid,* reflect enduring human values. It was because of these values that a critic here and there waged war on the growing assumption that the lyric and the novel had eclipsed the epic.

This glance back at the earlier periods may suffice to suggest that epic criticism rarely displayed the range and penetration it has attained in the twentieth century. Not without reason have the first four or five decades of this century been called an "Age of Criticism." The fortunes of the epic during these years owed little to the impressionist approach, but much to an historical method grown more mature, to the neo-humanist emphasis on the ethical imagination, and to a "New Criticism" engaged in close aesthetic analysis. The last of these, despite its concentration on the lyric, had a fructifying influence on the study of the epic as a work of art. Increasingly there was an interplay of the aims and methods of these very different approaches. More fully than ever before, the epic was understood in relation to time and place, was interpreted in its aesthetic aspects, and was esteemed for its ethical truth—its vision of an eternal human reality not limited to the relativities of time and place.

When our contemporary period has been completed and clarified by perspective—become a unit of history—it may well be seen, surprisingly enough in an age of science, to have been more broadly and soundly favorable to the epic than were the neo-classic, romantic, and Victorian periods.

NOTES

CHAPTER 1

1. *Essays of John Dryden,* ed. W. P. Ker (Oxford, 1926), II, 154.
2. *Ibid.,* II, 137.
3. *Ibid.,* II, 154.
4. *Ibid.,* II, 43.
5. *Ibid.,* II, 158.
6. *Ibid.,* II, 160.
7. *Ibid.,* II, 167.
8. *Ibid.,* II, 177.
9. *Ibid.,* II, 12-13.
10. *Ibid.,* II, 27.
11. *Ibid.,* II, 29.
12. *Ibid.,* I, 150.
13. *The Iliad of Homer,* tr. Alexander Pope (London, 1715-20), I, Preface.
14. *Ibid.* Since the pages of the Preface are not numbered, it seems unnecessary to supply footnotes for other quotations from the Preface.
15. *The Spectator,* ed. G. Gregory Smith, Everyman's Library (London, New York, 1933), IV, 84.
16. *Ibid.,* IV, 128, 130.
17. See *Essays of Dryden,* II, 166 ff.
18. *The Elements of Criticism* (New York, 1823), II, 263.
19. *Works* (London, 1807), X, 365.
20. *The Letters of Sir Thomas Fitzosborne, on Several Subjects* (London, 1784), p. 183.
21. *Rasselas* (Oxford, 1816), p. 43.
22. *Lives of the English Poets,* Everyman's Library (London, New York, 1925), I, 100.
23. *Ibid.,* I, 100 ff.
24. *The Divine Legation of Moses Demonstrated* (London, 1846), I, 245.
25. *An Essay on Original Genius, and Its Various Modes of Exertion in Philosophy and the Fine Arts, Particularly Poetry* (London, 1767), pp. 283-284.
26. *Critical Observations on the Writings of the Most Celebrated Original Geniuses in Poetry* (London, 1770), p. 247.
27. *Hurd's Letters on Chivalry and Romance, with the Third Elizabethan Dialogue,* ed. Edith J. Morley (London, 1911), p. 118.

28. *Ibid.*, 126.
29. *Lectures on Rhetoric and Belles Lettres* (Philadelphia, 1784), p. 412.
30. *An Essay on the Writings and Genius of Shakespeare* (Dublin, 1769), p. 115.
31. XL (1785), 55.
32. *Lectures*, p. 411.
33. *Critical Review*, Second Series, II (1791), 369.
34. *Lectures*, p. 411.
35. *A Dissertation on the Rise, Union, and Power, the Progressions, Separations, and Corruptions, of Poetry and Music* (London, 1763), p. 190.
36. *Letters of Literature* (London, 1785), pp. 146-147, 149-150.
37. *Six Dissertations upon Different Subjects* (London, 1755), p. 214.
38. XXII (1760), 126.
39. Brown, ... *Poetry and Music*, p. 81.
40. *An Enquiry into the Life and Writings of Homer* (London, 1735), p. 288.
41. *Ibid.*, p. 55.
42. *Ibid.*, p. 47.
43. *Ibid.*, p. 80.
44. *Ibid.*, p. 120.
45. *Ibid.*, p. 345.
46. Wood, *An Essay on the Original Genius and Writings of Homer* (London, 1775), p. 280.
47. See my book, *Homer in English Criticism* (New Haven, 1947), chapter 6.
48. *Letters of Literature*, p. 4.
49. *An Essay on the History of Civil Society* (Edinburgh, 1767), p. 266.
50. Duff, *Essay on Original Genius*, pp. 269-270.
51. *A Critical Dissertation on the Poems of Ossian, the Son of Fingal* (London, 1765), p. 63.
52. *Ibid.*, p. 53.
53. Ewen Cameron, *The Fingal of Ossian, an Ancient Epic Poem, in Six Books* (Warrington, 1776), p. 33n.
54. *Ibid.*, p. 190n.
55. *Temora* (London, 1763), p. 4n.
56. *Ibid.*, p. 3n.
57. *Critical Dissertation*, p. 41.
58. *Ibid.*, p. 44.
59. *Ibid.*, p. 43.
60. *Ibid.*, p. 42.

CHAPTER 2

1. A. W. Schlegel, *A Course of Lectures on Dramatic Art and Literature* (London, 1846), p. 43.
2. *Prose Works of William Wordsworth*, ed. A. B. Grosart (London, 1876), II, 132.

3. *Critical Essays of the Early Nineteenth Century,* ed. R. M. Alden (New York, 1921), p. 298.

4. VIII, 149.

5. *Ibid.,* VIII, 150.

6. *Introduction to the Literature of Europe,* 3rd ed. (London 1847), III, 475.

7. *Coleridge's Miscellaneous Criticism,* ed. T. M. Raysor (London, 1936), p. 13.

8. *Lectures on the Truly Eminent English Poets* (London, 1807), II, 499-500.

9. *Biographical, Literature, and Philosophical Essays* (New York and Philadelphia, 1844), p. 332.

10. *Poems* (London, 1802), I, xliii-iv.

11. *Essays and Tales in Prose* (Boston, 1853), II, 147.

12. *The Reflector,* ed. Leigh Hunt (London, 1811), II, 269.

13. Hallam, *op. cit.,* III, 474.

14. *Diary, Reminiscences, and Correspondence,* ed. Thomas Sadler (New York, 1877), I, 301.

15. *Letters* (Edinburgh, 1811), VI, 226-228.

16. *Quarterly Review,* VI, 223.

17. *Letters on the Character and Poetical Genius of Lord Byron* (London, 1824), pp. 440-441.

18. Thomas Medwin, *Conversations of Lord Byron* (London, 1824), pp. 247-248.

19. *Alfred: an Epic Poem* (Newburyport, 1814), Preface.

20. "Lectures on Poetry," *New Monthly Magazine,* Ser. II, Vol. XVI, p. 527.

21. XXVIII, 179.

22. *Works of Samuel Taylor Coleridge* (New York, 1853), IV, 116 ff.

23. *Letters,* V, 13-14.

24. *Quarterly Review,* XXV, 428.

25. *The Lusiad,* trans. Musgrave (London, 1826), p. xvi.

26. Medwin, *op. cit.,* p. 107.

27. *The Letters of William and Dorothy Wordsworth, The Later Years,* ed. Ernest de Selincourt (Oxford, 1939), p. 1010.

28. XV, 40.

29. *Quarterly Review,* XXXIV, 519.

30. *Blackwood's Edinburgh Magazine,* II, 269-270.

31. *Quarterly Review,* XXXIV, 400.

32. *The Lusiad,* trans. W. J. Mickle (Dublin, 1791), p. ccclvii.

33. "Evils of Measurement in Literature," *New Monthly Magazine,* Ser. II, Part II, Vol. XXIII, p. 205.

34. *Essays,* pp. 332-333.

35. *Imagination and Fancy* (London, 1846), p. 62.

36. *Introductions to the Study of the Greek Classic Poets* (Boston, 1842), p. 112.

37. I, 254.

38. *The Divina Commedia of Dante Alighieri,* trans. Henry Boyd (London, 1802), I, Preface.

39. *Critical Essays of the Early Nineteenth Century,* ed. Alden, p. 299.
40. *Coleridge's Miscellaneous Criticism,* p. 161.
41. See *ibid.,* p. 162.
42. *The Complete Works of William Hazlitt,* ed. P. P. Howe (London and Toronto, 1930), V, 52.
43. *Essays and Marginalia* (London, 1851), I, 5.
44. *Quarterly Review,* XXXVI, 45, 50.
45. *Lectures,* II, 502.
46. *Edinburgh Review,* XXXV, 55.
47. *Works,* V, 17.
48. *Divina Commedia,* p. 5.
49. *Imagination,* p. 64.
50. *The Writings of Arthur Hallam,* ed. T. H. Vail Motter (New York, 1943), p. 256.
51. *Works,* VI, 479.
52. *Coleridge's Miscellaneous Criticism,* p. 164.
53. *Writings,* p. 256.
54. *Life of Geoffrey Chaucer* (London, 1803), I, 223.
55. XLVII, 20.
56. *Works,* IV, 43.
57. *Lectures,* II, 484.
58. *Critical Essays of the Early Nineteenth Century,* p. 290.
59. *Critical and Miscellaneous Essays* (Philadelphia, 1842), I, 329.
60. *Works,* V, 57.
61. *An Essay on English Poetry* (London, 1848), pp. 97-98.
62. *Evenings in Autumn* (London, 1822), II, 286.
63. *The Ruminator* (London, 1813), I, 200-201.
64. *The Prelude* (1805-06), III, 284.
65. *Imagination,* p. 18.
66. *Works,* V, 63-64.
67. *The Complete Works of W. S. Landor,* ed. T. Earle Welby (London, 1927), V, 238.
68. *Coleridge's Miscellaneous Criticism,* p. 146.
69. *Essays of the Early Nineteenth Century,* p. 298.
70. *Essays,* II, 160-161.
71. *The Life of Milton* (Dublin, 1797), p. 290.
72. *Lectures,* II, 315.
73. *Essays,* II, 163.
74. *Works,* V, 67.
75. There are many remarks on Dante throughout the *Life of Chaucer.*
76. *Pursuits of Literature* (London, 1798), p. 128.
77. *Diary,* II, 139.
78. *Works,* V, 280.
79. See especially *Works,* VI, 302-303.
80. *Memoir of Henry F. Cary, by His Son,* Henry Cary (London, 1847), I, 43.
81. *Greek Classic Poets,* p. 90.
82. *Quarterly Review,* XXXV, 518.

83. *Ibid.*, XXXVI, 47.
84. *Diary*, I, 270.
85. John B. Trotter, *Memoirs of the Latter Years of the Rt. Honourable Charles James Fox* (Philadelphia, 1812), p. 324.
86. Medwin, *op. cit.*, p. 106.
87. *Literature of Europe*, III, 473.
88. *Essays and Marginalia, by His Brother* (London, 1851), I, 374.
89. *Writings*, pp. 235-236.
90. *Imagination*, pp. 327-329.

CHAPTER 3

1. *Letters*, p. 586.
2. *Poems* (London, 1802), p. xiv.
3. *Letters*, p. 817.
4. *Works*, V, 18.
5. *Evenings in Autumn*, II, 4, 189.
6. *Poems by Hartley Coleridge, with a Memoir by His Brother* (London, 1851), I, clvi.
7. Cyrus Redding, *Literary Reminiscences and Memoirs of Thomas Campbell* (London, 1860), I, 112.
8. *The Iliad of Homer*, ed. W. M. Trollope (London, 1827), I, xviii.
9. *The Poems of Ossian in the Original Gaelic* (London, 1807), I, lxvii-lxviii.
10. William Taylor, *A Historic Survey of German Poetry* (London, 1830), I, 291.
11. *Introductions to the Study of the Greek Classic Poets* (Boston, 1842), pp. 79-80, 125.
12. *Evenings in Autumn*, pp. 13-14, 23.
13. *The Life and Correspondence of Robert Southey*, ed. C. C. Southey, (New York, 1851), p. 98.
14. "Lectures on Poetry," *New Monthly Magazine*, Ser. II, Vol. I, p. 137.
15. *Reminiscences* (New York, 1825), I, 13.
16. *Ruminator*, I, 57.
17. *Letters*, IV, 265, 267.
18. *Fragments in Prose and Verse* (London, 1809), I, 7-8.
19. *Blackwood's Magazine*, XXIX, 829; XXX, 125.
20. *New Monthly Magazine*, Ser. II, Vol. XX, p. 8; Vol. II, p. 12.
21. *Works*, III, 168.
22. *Imagination and Fancy*, pp. 5-6.
23. *Fragments*, I, 137.
24. *Works*, V, 15, 22.
25. *The Iliad of Homer* (London, 1715-20), Preface.
26. *Ruminator*, I, 57.
27. *Evenings in Autumn*, II, 194.

28. *The Letters of Percy Bysshe Shelley,* ed. Roger Ingpen (London, 1909), II, 833.
29. *Essays and Marginalia,* II, 51.
30. *Ibid.,* II, 51.
31. *Recollections of the Table-Talk of Samuel Rogers* (London, 1856), p. 62.
32. *Reminiscences,* I, 14.
33. *New Monthly Magazine,* Ser. II, Vol. II, p. 15.
34. *Imagination and Fancy,* pp. 27-28.
35. *Blackwood's Magazine,* XXXI, 179.
36. *New Monthly Magazine.* Ser. II, Vol. II, p. 13.
37. *Blackwood's Magazine,* XXXI, 178 ff.
38. *Winter Nights* (London, 1820), II, 3.
39. *Athenaeum,* I, 34.
40. *Peacock's Four Ages of Poetry,* ed. H. F. B. Brett-Smith (Boston and New York, 1921), p. 7.
41. *Essay on the Authenticity of the Poems of Ossian* (Edinburgh, 1807), p. 122.
42. *New Monthly Magazine,* Ser. II, Vol. XX, Part II, pp. 8-9.
43. *Imagination and Fancy,* p. 62.
44. *Works,* V, 70.
45. *Keble's Lectures on Poetry, 1832-41,* tr. E. K. Francis (Oxford, 1912), I, 88.
46. *Ibid.,* I, 90.
47. *Ibid.,* I, 146.
48. *Ibid.,* I, 242.
49. *Occasional Papers and Reviews* (Oxford and London, 1877), p. 6.
50. *Edinburgh Review,* XVI, 281.
51. R. P. Gillies, *Memoirs of a Literary Veteran* (London, 1851), I, 245.
52. *The Critical Opinions of William Wordsworth,* ed. M. L. Peacock, Jr. (Baltimore, 1950), p. 303.
53. *Ibid.,* p. 305.
54. *An Analytical Inquiry into the Principles of Taste* (London, 1805), p. 287.
55. *History of Scotland* (London, 1804), IV, 492.
56. *Ibid.,* IV, 429-430.
57. *Ibid.,* IV, 446.
58. H. Weber, R. Jamieson, *Illustrations of North Antiquities, from the Earlier Teutonic and Scandinavian Romances* (Edinburgh, 1814), p. 249.
59. *Works,* VI, 312. James Fenimore Cooper tells of an incident that reveals Coleridge's keen interest in the Wolfian hypotheses. At a social gathering in England, after-dinner talk turned to Homer. "Some one remarked that Mr. Coleridge did not believe in his unity, or rather that there was any such man. This called him (Coleridge) out, and certainly I never witnessed an exhibition as extraordinary as that which followed. It was not a discourse, but a dissertation. Scarcely any one spoke besides Mr. Coleridge, with the exception of a brief occasional remark from Mr. Sotheby, who held the contrary opinion; and I might say no one *could* speak. At moments he was surprisingly eloquent, though a little

discursive, and the whole time he appeared to be perfectly the master of his subject and of his language. As near as I could judge, he was rather more than an hour in possession of the floor, almost without interruption." *Gleanings in Europe,* ed. R. E. Spiller (New York and London, 1930), II, 161-162.

60. XLIV, 124.

61. *Lectures,* II, 497.

62. "General Observations," in *The Iliad of Homer,* trans. Alexander Pope, a new ed. (London, 1817), I, clxxvii.

63. Weber and Jamieson, *Illustrations of Northern Antiquities,* p. 249.

64. XXX, 41.

65. *Miscellanies of Literature,* a new ed. (London, 1840), p. 268n.

66. *Edinburgh Review,* XXIV, 41.

67. *Historic Survey,* I, 291.

68. *Literature of Europe,* III, 473.

69. *Greek Classic Poets,* p. 79.

70. *Historical and Critical Essays* (Boston, 1856), I, 266.

71. *Miscellaneous Criticism,* pp. 160-161.

72. *Works,* V, 238.

73. See his *Examination of the Primary Argument of the Iliad* (London, 1821).

74. *Quarterly Review,* XLIV, 150.

75. T. J. Mathias, *Observations on the Writings and on the Character of Mr. Gray* (London, 1815), p. 78.

76. Isaac Disraeli, *Amenities of Literature* (New York, 1841), II, 144.

77. *Edinburgh Review,* XXIII, 232.

78. *The Works of Thomas De Quincey* (New York, 1878), IV, 457.

79. *Lectures,* II, 20.

80. *Letters from a Father to His Son* (London, 1838), p. 12.

81. *Letters,* pp. 506-507.

82. *Divina Commedia,* p. 7.

83. *Alfred,* p. 22.

84. *Life of Chaucer,* I, 323-324.

85. *Works,* VI, 312-313.

86. *Ibid.,* VI, 313.

87. *Ibid.,* VI, 400.

88. *Ibid.,* VI, 494.

89. *Reminiscences,* I, 12.

90. *Extracts from the Diary of a Lover of Literature* (Ipswich, 1810), p. 209.

91. *Ibid.,* p. 209.

92. *Specimens of the Classic Poets* (London, 1814), II, 74-75.

93. *Edinburgh Review,* XXV, 150.

94. *Essays and Marginalia,* I, 23.

95. *Specimens,* III, 6.

96. *Table-Talk,* p. 209.

97. *Works,* VI, 276.

98. *Lectures,* II, 375.

99. *Ibid.,* II, 377-379.

100. *Ibid.,* II, 418.
101. *Ibid.,* II, 393.
102. *Lectures on Dramatic Art and Literature,* trans. John Black, 2nd ed. (London, 1909).

CHAPTER 4

1. "Manuductio ad Ministerium," in *American Poetry and Prose,* ed. Norman Foerster, 3rd ed. (Cambridge, Mass., 1947), p. 66.
2. *The Works of Thomas Jefferson,* ed. P. L. Ford (New York and London, 1904), II, 36.
3. See Karl Lehmann, *Thomas Jefferson, American Humanist* (New York, 1947).
4. *North American Review,* XLII, 99.
5. *Literary Criticisms and Other Papers* (Philadelphia, 1856), p. 434.
6. From an essay in *Time-Piece* (Oct. 9, 1797) quoted in Lewis Leary, *That Rascal Freneau* (New Brunswick, N.J., 1941), pp. 295-296.
7. *The Writings of Hugh S. Legaré,* ed. by his sister (Charleston, S.C., 1845), II, 322.
8. "Library of Old Authors" (1858-64), *Literary Essays* (Boston and New York, 1891), I, 293.
9. *Letters,* ed. C. E. Norton (New York, 1894), p. 243.
10. *The Function of the Poet, and Other Essays* (Boston and New York, 1920), p. 4.
11. See XVIII, esp. p. 104.
12. XXXVII, 364.
13. LV, 123.
14. See the preface to his translation of the *Iliad* (Boston, 1833).
15. *Literature of the Early Republic,* ed. Edwin H. Cady (New York, n.d.), p. 464.
16. *Ibid.,* p. 466.
17. For examples see *The Journals of Ralph Waldo Emerson* (Cambridge, Mass., 1909), III, 329, and IV, 36. Also: "Homer's is the only Epic. How great a deduction do all the rest suffer from the fact of their imitated form. It is especially fatal to poetry." (*Ibid.,* IV, 439-440).
18. *Ibid.,* IV, 36.
19. *Ibid.,* III, 530.
20. *Complete Works of Ralph Waldo Emerson* (Boston and New York, 1903), XII, 72.
21. *Literary and Historical Miscellanies* (New York, 1855), p. 125.
22. *Biographical and Critical Miscellanies* (Philadelphia, 1861), p. 571.
23. *Literary Essays* (Boston and New York, 1891), III, 293.
24. "Epic Poetry," *Essays and Poems* (Boston, 1839), p. 29.
25. *Writings,* II, 44n.
26. *Literary Essays,* IV, 161.

27. *Literary World,* VI, 535.
28. *Works of Henry Wadsworth Longfellow* (London, 1886), I, 284.
29. *North American Review,* XVI, 234.
30. *The Essays of Henry Timrod,* ed. E. W. Parks (Athens, Ga., 1942), p. 112.
31. *North American Review,* LXXXII, 241.
32. *Ibid.,* LXIX, 203.
33. *Ibid.,* XLVIII, 367.
34. *Alexander H. Everett, Critical and Miscellaneous Essays* (Boston, 1845), I, 192.
35. *Literary World,* II, 432.
36. *Essays,* p. 3.
37. *Writings,* II, 38.
38. *Orations and Speeches on Several Occasions* (Boston, 1850), II, 223.
39. *North American Review,* LXX, 268.
40. *Complete Works of Edgar Allan Poe,* ed. James A. Harrison (New York and Chicago, 1902), XVII, 173.
41. *North American Review,* VI, 36-37.
42. Edward Everett, for example, suggests (*Orations,* II, 218-220) that modern astronomy was opening the way for imagery far better than that of Milton, Homer, and Virgil. Looking into the future, he says that if man can ever "penetrate that mysterious temple of the Infinite," all previous art "will be as nursery tales."
43. From a review dated 1853 in Parke Godwin, *Out of the Past* (New York, 1870), p. 186.
44. Excerpt from a letter in Parke Godwin, *A Biography of William Cullen Bryant* (New York, 1883), I, 295.
45. III, 1.
46. I, 459.
47. *Dramas, Discourses, and Other Pieces* (Boston, 1839), II, 95.
48. Thomas S. Grimké, *Reflections on the Character and Objects of All Science and Literature* (New Haven, 1831), p. 48.
49. *Orations,* I, 65.
50. *Works,* III, 38.
51. *Ibid.,* VI, 180.
52. *North American Review.* LXXXII, 273.
53. *Literary Essays,* II, 149-150.
54. *Complete Prose Works of Walt Whitman* (New York, 1914), p. 353.
55. *Ibid.,* pp. 233, 288, 393.
56. *Democracy in America,* ed. H. S. Commager (New York and London, 1947), p. 290.
57. *Journals,* I, 376.
58. See *Works,* XII, 151, and *Letters of Edgar Allan Poe,* ed. J. W. Ostrom (Cambridge, Mass., 1948), I, 239.
59. *Essays upon Authors and Books* (New York, 1849), p. 42.
60. *Ibid.,* p. 40.
61. *Essays,* p. 68.
62. *North American Review,* LXXI, 100.
63. *The Optimist* (New York, 1850), pp. 103-109.

64. *Journals*, VI, 268-269.

65. *Democracy*, p. 296.

66. *The Journals of Charles K. Newcomb*, ed. J. K. Johnson (Providence, 1946), p. 123.

67. *The Letters of Lydia Maria Child* (Boston, 1883), pp. 192-193.

68. *North American Review*, LXXIII, 266-267.

69. *Out of the Past*, p. 156.

70. XXXVIII, 168.

71. *Ibid.*, LXIX, 384.

72. *Literature and Life* (Boston, 1871), pp. 52-53.

73. *American Writers, a Series of Papers Contributed to Blackwood's Magazine (1824-25)*, ed. F. L. Pattee (Durham, N. C., 1937), pp. 249-250.

74. *North American Review*, XXVIII, 130.

75. *Essays and Reviews* (Boston, 1851), I, 413.

76. *North American Review*, LXXIII, 475.

77. *The Letters of Ralph Waldo Emerson*, ed. Ralph L. Rusk (New York, 1939), IV, 196-197.

78. Samuel Longfellow, *The Life of Henry Wadsworth Longfellow* (London, 1886), II, 86.

79. *People's Edition of the Entire Works of William Ellery Channing* (Belfast, 1843), I, 3.

80. *Ibid.*, I, 8.

81. *Ibid.*, I, 10.

82. *Literary Recreations and Miscellanies* (Boston, 1854), p. 430.

83. *Miscellanies*, p. 273.

84. *Writings*, II, 387.

85. *North American Review*, XLVII, 71.

86. III, 481.

87. *The Gathering of the Forces*, ed. Cleveland Rogers and John Black (New York and London, 1920), I, 288.

88. *Southern Review*, II, 456.

89. *Works*, VIII, 57; II, 24.

90. *Journals*, V, 133.

91. *Ibid.*, III, 328.

92. *Letters*, VI, 52n.

93. *Sunny Memories of Foreign Lands* (Boston, 1854), I, 207-208.

94. *The Literary Remains of W. B. O. Peabody*, ed. Everett Peabody (Boston, 1850), p. 15.

95. *Writings*, II, 44n.

96. *Out of the Past*, p. 125.

97. *Shakespeare: His Life, Art, and Characters* (Boston, 1872), I, 252-253.

98. *Life of Longfellow*, I, 11.

99. *Literary Essays*, I, 369.

100. *Memoirs of Margaret Fuller Ossoli* (Boston, 1852), II, 180.

101. *North American Review*, XLII, 58.

102. *Reflections*, p. 161n.

103. *Critical Essays*, I, 192.

104. "Lectures on Poetry," in *Representative Selections of William Cullen Bryant*, ed. Tremaine McDowell (New York, 1935), p. 199.

105. *Works,* VI, 197.
106. *Journals,* II, 234.
107. *Works,* II, 26.
108. *Journals,* III, 490.
109. *North American Review,* LXXIII, 478.
110. *Literary Miscellanies,* pp. 194-195.
111. *The Writings of Henry David Thoreau,* Riverside ed. (Boston and New York, n.d.), II, 98-99.
112. *Ibid.,* VII, 47.
113. *Ibid.,* II, 159.
114. *Ibid.,* II, 178.
115. *Ibid.,* I, 94.
116. *Literary Recreations,* p. 428.
117. *Views and Reviews in American Literature, History and Fiction* (New York, 1845), p. 104.
118. *North American Review,* VI, 36.
119. *Life of Longfellow,* I, 68.
120. *Writings,* I, 431.
121. Godwin, *Biography of Bryant,* II, 272.
122. *Out of the Past,* p. 297.
123. *Essays,* I, 317.
124. II, 431.
125. *Essays,* pp. 5, 8.
126. *Ibid.,* p. 12.
127. *Ibid.,* pp. 13, 15.
128. *Ibid.,* pp. 18 ff.
129. *Ibid.,* pp. 29-30.
130. *Ibid.,* p. 26.
131. *Ibid.,* p. 25.
132. *Ibid.,* p. 31.
133. *Ibid.,* p. 33.

CHAPTER 5

1. *An Introduction to the Study of Dante,* 4th ed. (London, 1906), p. 97.
2. Letter to George Lewes, March 1, 1841, in Anna T. Kitchel, *George Lewes and George Eliot* (New York, 1933), pp. 31-32.
3. J. S. Mill, *Dissertations and Discussions* (London, 1859), I, 85.
4. *Fragments from Old Letters, E. D. to E. D. W., 1869-92* (London and New York, 1914), p. 92.
5. *P. Vergili Maronis Opera* (London, 1884), II, xxxii.
6. LXIX, 516.
7. Francis Darwin, *Charles Darwin* (New York, 1893), pp. 53-54.
8. *An Autobiography* (London, 1904), I, 261-262.
9. *A Manual of English Literature* (Boston, 1885), p. 343.
10. James A. Froude, *Short Studies on Great Subjects* (New York, 1883), p. 410.

11. *A History of Greece,* Amer. ed. (Boston, 1855), p. 42.

12. See his *Remarks on Prof. Mahaffy's Account of the Rise and Progress of Epic Poetry* (London, 1881).

13. LXIX, 55.

14. *An Account of the Life, Opinions, and Writings of John Milton* (London, 1855), p. 408.

15. *A History of Greece* (London, 1904), II, 95, 137.

16. *Lectures on the History of Literature,* ed. J. Reay Greene (London, 1892), pp. 16, 19.

17. *The Works of Thomas Carlyle,* Edinb. ed. (New York, 1905), XXVI, 245.

18. *Lectures,* pp. 22, 20.

19. *Ibid.,* p. 150.

20. *Ibid.,* p. 19.

21. Fitzgerald wrote to Frederic Tennyson in 1878 that with respect to the *Iliad* "I could never care for the original, with its brutal Gods and Heroes. I am sure my Taste must be defective in this: and that all the rest of the World has not been mistaken this two or three thousand years. But so it is." *Letters and Literary Remains of Edward Fitzgerald* (London, 1902-1903), IV, 43.

22. See pp. 66 and 108 above.

23. *A Critical History of the Language and Literature of Ancient Greece* (London, 1854), I, 199-200; II, 130.

24. LXXXVI, 237. (Amer. ed.).

25. LXXXI, 409, 413.

26. LXXXII, 181-182.

27. *Homer and the Iliad* (Edinburgh, 1866), I, 244.

28. Quoted by Blackie, *Homer and the Iliad,* I, 245.

29. *Guesses at Truth* (London, 1867), p. 427.

30. *P. Vergili Maronis Opera,* II, xliii.

31. CII, 216.

32. *Athens: Its Rise and Fall* (London, 1837), I, 271.

33. *Homer* (New York, 1879), p. 25.

34. *Landmarks of Homeric Study* (London, 1890), p. 106.

35. *Homer and the Iliad,* I, 215.

36. *Ibid.,* I, 263.

37. *Ibid.,* I, 407.

38. *History of Greece,* I, 235.

39. *Blackwood's Edinburgh Magazine,* CXVI, 371.

40. *The Collected Works of William Morris* (London and New York, 1910-1915), XXIII, 262.

41. *The Letters of George Meredith,* ed. A. G. Meredith (New York, 1913), I, 234.

42. *History of Greece,* I, 230.

43. *Homer and the Iliad,* I, 155, 158.

44. *Short Studies,* p. 412.

45. *Homer,* p. 5.

46. LXXXII, 178.

47. Froude, *Short Studies,* p. 412.

48. See *History of Greece*, I, 274-275.
49. *The Works of Walter Bagehot* (Hartford, Conn., 1891), I, 66.
50. *Homer*, pp. 128-129.
51. *Blackwood's Edinburgh Magazine*, LXXXII, 178.
52. *Quarterly Review*, CII, 247.
53. *Guesses at Truth*, p. 357.
54. Most British critics seem to have regarded the nature-myth theory as ridiculous, as evidence of the fantasticality of German scholarship.
55. *History of Greece*, II, 44.
56. *Studies on Homer and the Homeric Age* (Oxford, 1858), I, 6-7; *Homer*, p. 153.
57. Quoted in L. C. Collins, *Life and Memoirs of John Churton Collins* (London and New York, 1912), p. 88.
58. *Short Studies*, p. 417.
59. *Studies of the Greek Poets* (New York, 1880), II, 397-398.
60. *The Works of John Ruskin* (Boston and London, n.d.), X (Part II), 118.
61. *Robert Browning and Julia Wedgwood*, ed. Richard Curle (New York, 1937), p. 50.
62. Though the reference was originally made by Julia Wedgwood, Browning quoted it with approval. See *Browning and Wedgwood*, p. 60.
63. For example, see Morris' comments in *Collected Works*, XXIII, 199-200, 262.
64. *Homer and the Iliad*, I, 166.
65. *Guesses at Truth*, pp. 69, 48-49.
66. *Homer and the Iliad*, I, 148, 154.
67. *Aspects of Poetry* (Oxford, 1881), II, 405-406.
68. Quoted in E. L. Youmans, *The Culture Demanded by Modern Life* (New York, 1867), p. 144.
69. In the opening chapter of his *Studies on Homer and the Homeric Age*, Gladstone discusses the new emphasis upon Greek literature.
70. See John Forster, *Walter Savage Landor* (Boston, 1869), p. 545.
71. *Lectures*, p. 50.
72. *Ibid.*, p. 52.
73. *Homer and the Homeric Age*, I, 503.
74. *Browning and Wedgwood*, p. 115.
75. George O. Trevelyan, *The Life and Letters of Lord Macaulay* (London, 1876), I, 371.
76. *Lectures*, pp. 50-51.
77. *Essays* (London, 1882), pp. 209-210.
78. *Homer and the Homeric Age*, III, 506.
79. *Roman Poets of the Augustan Age: Virgil* (Oxford, 1897), p. 76.
80. *Ibid.*, p. 75.
81. *Ibid.*, p. 60.
82. *Ibid.*, pp. 300, 360, 280.
83. *Ibid.*, p. 324.
84. *Ibid.*, p. 356.
85. *Ibid.*, p. 83.
86. *Ibid.*, p. 91.

87. See F. W. H. Myers, *Essays Classical* (London, 1883), pp. 122, 125.

88. *Ibid.,* p. 144.

89. *Ibid.,* p. 144.

90. *Aspects of Poetry,* I, 160.

91. *Ibid.,* I, 161.

92. *Ibid.,* I, 179.

93. *Ibid.,* I, 164.

94. *Ibid.,* I, 167.

95. *Ibid.,* I, 165.

96. *Ibid.,* I, 162.

97. CXVI, 24.

98. *P. Vergili Maronis Opera,* II, xxviii.

99. *Lectures and Essays,* 2nd Ser. (Oxford, 1895), p. 195.

100. *Milton* (New York, 1879), p. 94.

101. "To Virgil," VI and X.

102. *Homer and the Iliad,* I, 272.

103. Quoted in E. T. Cook, *The Life of John Ruskin* (New York, 1911), II, 24.

104. *Letters of Fitzgerald,* II, 219, 215.

105. *Blackwood's Edinburgh Magazine,* LVII, 408.

106. Sir Archibald Alison, *Some Account of My Life and Writings,* ed. Lady Alison (Edinburgh and London, 1883), I, 26.

107. *The Works of Virgil,* tr. James Lonsdale and Samuel Lee (London, 1871), p. 81.

108. *P. Vergili Maronis Opera,* II, xxxv.

109. See Carlyle, *Works,* XXVII, 271.

110. *The Language and Literature of the Scottish Highlands* (Edinburgh, 1876), p. 234.

111. *Critical and Historical Essays* (Boston and New York, 1900), I, 20.

112. *The Letters of Elizabeth Barrett Browning,* ed. F. G. Kenyon (New York, 1910), p. 118.

113. *Ibid.,* p. 125.

114. *Life and Letters,* II, 146.

115. *Homer and the Homeric Age,* III, 543.

116. *Letters of Fitzgerald,* I, 280.

117. Trevelyan, *Life of Macaulay,* II, 22.

118. For excerpts from reviews of Rossetti's writings see Paget J. Toynbee, *Dante in English Literature from Chaucer to Cary* (London, 1909), II.

119. LV, 551. The same reviewer comments: "We hope that Signor Rossetti will persevere in the task which he has undertaken. . . . But where is his system of interpretation to end?"

120. *Critical and Historical Essays,* I, 11.

121. *Ibid.,* I, 12.

122. *Ibid.,* I, 17, 18.

123. *Ibid.,* I, 21.

124. *Ibid.,* I, 108.

125. *Ibid.,* I, 107.
126. *Ibid.,* I, 105.
127. *On Heroes, Hero-Worship, and the Heroic in History* (London, 1870), pp. 98, 96.
128. *Ibid.,* p. 99.
129. *Ibid.,* p. 107.
130. *Ibid.,* p. 109.
131. See F. W. Roe, *Thomas Carlyle as a Critic of Literature* (New York, 1910), p. 142.
132. *Dante and Other Essays* (London, 1891), p. 59.
133. *Ibid.,* p. 63.
134. *Ibid.,* p. 109.
135. *Ibid.,* p. 75.
136. *Ibid.,* p. 181.
137. *Ibid.,* p. 187.
138. *Ibid.,* p. 185.
139. *An Introduction to the Study of Dante,* 4th ed. (London, 1906), p. 103.
140. *Ibid.,* p. 105.
141. *Ibid.,* p. 112.
142. *Ibid.,* pp. 116-117.
143. See Preface to *The Comments of John Ruskin on the Divina Commedia,* ed. G. P. Huntington (Boston and New York, 1903).
144. *The Poetical Works of John Milton,* ed. David Masson (London, 1890), II, 77.
145. *Ibid.,* II, 99.
146. *Milton,* p. 94.
147. *Homer and the Iliad,* I, 6.
148. *John Milton: The Patriot and Poet. Illustrations of the Model Man* (London, 1852), p. 177.
149. George L. Craik, *A Compendious History of English Literature, and of the English Language, from the Norman Conquest* (New York, 1877), II, 94.
150. *Works of Milton,* II, 97.
151. *Homer and the Iliad,* I, 283.
152. See *The Three Devils: Luther's Milton's and Goethe's* (London, 1844).
153. *John Milton,* pp. 171-172.
154. *Critical and Historical Essays,* I, 90-91.
155. *Ibid.,* I, 93.
156. *Ibid.,* I, 94.
157. *Works,* I, 339.
158. *Ibid.,* I, 342.
159. *Essays and Tales,* ed. J. C. Hare (London, 1848), I, 75-76.
160. *Lectures on Literature,* p. 158.
161. *Fragments,* p. 117.
162. *Collected Works,* XXII, xvn.
163. *Lectures and Essays* (London, 1870), p. 138.
164. *Works,* X (Part II), 116.

165. *Lectures*, p. 139.
166. For Arnold's comments on Milton see his *Manual of English Literature*, pp. 346 ff.
167. Review of Masson's *Life of Milton*, in *National Review*, IX, 184-185.
168. *Homer and the Iliad*, I, 286.
169. *Works*, I, 334-335.
170. *Tennyson and His Friends*, ed. Hallam, Lord Tennyson (London, 1911), p. 146.
171. *Guesses at Truth*, p. 433.
172. *Lectures*, p. 142.
173. *Lectures on Literature*, p. 158.
174. Edward Dowden, *Studies in Literature, 1789-1877* (London, 1892), p. 90.
175. *Ibid.*, pp. 103-104.
176. *Life, Opinions, and Writings of Milton*, pp. 416-417.
177. *Works of Milton*, II, 100.
178. Thomas H. Huxley, *Science and Hebrew Tradition* (New York, 1897), p. 52.
179. *Ibid.*, p. 69.
180. *Works*, I, 223.
181. *The Works of Matthew Arnold* (London, 1903-1904), III, 120.
182. *Ibid.*, III, 324.
183. *Ibid.*, III, 332.
184. *Ibid.*, IV, 103.
185. *Ibid.*, V, 161-162.
186. *The Iliad of Homer*, tr. F. W. Newman (London, 1856), p. iv.
187. *Works*, V, 197.
188. *Ibid.*, III, 331.
189. *Ibid.*, IV, 26, 46.
190. *Ibid.*, V, 130.
191. *Ibid.*, X, 254.
192. *Ibid.*, X, 233.
193. European scholarship may well have encouraged some of these tendencies. Increasingly since the time of Wolf, students of literature had been disposed to adopt the methodology of science, to treat an epic such as the *Iliad* as a kind of well-preserved organism that should be examined with microscopic care and should be explained. Hence, the influential Lachmann insisted that it is a primary duty of the scholar to "criticize" a text (that is, to investigate the author's personality and the original form of his work), then to analyze his feelings and thoughts and the circumstances that gave rise to them. Many of the Continental scholars (Köchly, Haupt, Ritschl, Dindorf, Nauck, etc.) concentrated upon textual criticism; others, like K. O. Müller, were largely historians and antiquarians. Granted that the Germans, and to a lesser extent other Europeans, did valuable work that certainly needed to be done, it is not difficult to see how this work might prompt many of the critics with whom we have been concerned in this chapter to pay less attention to the larger aesthetic questions and to pay more attention to peripheral matters—historical backgrounds, biographical data, and the like.

CHAPTER 6

1. *The Choice of Books* (New York, 1908), pp. 139-140.
2. *On the Distinction between the Art-Epic and the Folk-Epic* (Berkeley, 1906), p. 4.
3. *English Poetry, Its Principles and Progress* (New York, 1911), p. xciv.
4. *Ibid.*
5. *The Art of the Novel* (New York, London, 1934), p. 111.
6. *Studies and Appreciations* (New York, 1912), p. 16.
7. *The New Laokoon* (Boston, New York, 1910), p. 252.
8. *Ibid.*, pp. 247-248.
9. *Oxford Lectures on Poetry* (London, 1926), p. 191.
10. *The Critical Attitude* (London, 1911), pp. 178-180.
11. *Studies in Prose and Verse* (London, n.d.), pp. 5-6.
12. *Lectures and Essays* (London, 1905), I, pp. 297-298.
13. *Post Liminium: Essays and Critical Papers* (London, 1912), p. 125.
14. *Works*, Centennial Edition (Baltimore, 1945), V, 330.
15. *Collected Essays and Addresses, 1880-1920* (London, Toronto, 1922), I, 30.
16. *Greek Influence on English Poetry* (London, 1910), p. 65.
17. *The Symbolist Movement in Literature* (New York, 1908), p. 134; *Studies in Prose*, p. 180.
18. *Philosophy of English Literature* (New York, 1874), p. 224.
19. *A History of Criticism* (New York, 1906), II, 376.
20. *Works*, V, 297.
21. *Symbolist Movement*, p. 134.
22. *Some Principles of Literary Criticism* (New York, 1899), p. 275. Elsewhere, however, Winchester says that while the epic is not as popular as the lyric, it is a higher form (*Ibid.*, p. 97).
23. *Essays in Literary Interpretation* (New York, 1892), pp. 1, 12, 5.
24. *The Renaissance* (London, 1910), p. 137.
25. *Essays Speculative and Suggestive* (London, 1890), I, 163.
26. *Ibid.*, I, 192.
27. *Symbolist Movement*, pp. 8-9.
28. *Choice of Books*, pp. 48-49.
29. *Essays*, II, 89; I, 240-241.
30. *The Responsibilities of the Novelist* (New York, 1903), pp. 5, 64.
31. *The Historical Novel and Other Essays* (New York, 1914), pp. 80-81.
32. *A Study of Prose Fiction* (Boston, New York, 1902), pp. 358-359.
33. *The Responsibilities of the Novelist*, p. 6.
34. *The Art of the Novel* (New York, London, 1934), p. 326.
35. *Confessions of a Young Man* (New York, 1901), pp. 64-65.
36. Letter to W. P. Ker, 1900, in *The Letters of Sir Walter Raleigh, 1879-1922*, ed. Lady Raleigh (London, 1926), I, 222.
37. *Works*, IV, 61.
38. *Forces in Fiction and Other Essays* (Indianapolis, 1902), pp. 19-20.

39. *Crumbling Idols* (Chicago and Cambridge, 1894), pp. 43, 190.

40. *Ibid.*, p. 187.

41. *Ibid.*, pp. 53-54.

42. *Materials and Methods of Fiction* (New York, 1908), pp. 157-158.

43. *Ibid.*, p. 159.

44. *Homer and the Epic* (London, 1893), pp. 6-7.

45. *The Nature and Elements of Poetry* (New York, Boston, 1892), p. 106.

46. *Studies in German Literature* (New York, 1879), p. 61.

47. *The Authority of Criticism* (New York, 1899), pp. 17, 132.

48. *Complete Works* (London, New York, 1925-1927), ed. Edmund Gosse, T. J. Wise, XIII, 248.

49. *Ibid.*, XV, 463.

50. *Essays*, II, 145.

51. *Ibid.*, II, 145.

52. *The New Laokoon*, pp. 245-246.

53. *Literature and the American College* (Boston, New York, 1908), p. 173.

54. *Ibid.*, p. 233.

55. *Shelburne Essays, First Series* (Boston, New York, 1904), II, 159.

56. *Shelburne Essays, Third Series* (Boston, New York, 1905). p. 84.

57. *Ibid.*, p. 86.

58. *Lectures and Essays* (London, 1905), I, 291.

59. *Collected Essays*, ed. Chas. Whibley (London, 1925), I, 337-338.

60. *The New World and the New Book* (Boston, 1892), pp. 186-187.

61. *Works*, IV, 291.

62. *Ibid.*, III, 10, 26.

63. *The Culture Demanded by Modern Life* (New York, 1867), p. 50.

64. *Ibid.*, p. 450.

65. *The Correspondence of Gerard Manley Hopkins and Richard Watson Dixon*, ed. C. C. Abbott (London, 1935), p. 146.

66. *Works* (New York, 1900), III, 78.

67. *Studies in Several Literatures* (New York, 1909), p. 9.

68. *Lectures on Poetry* (London, 1914), p. 37.

69. *Ibid.*, p. 84.

70. *Ibid.*, pp. 84-85.

71. *Ibid.*, p. 90.

72. *Ibid.*, p. 92.

73. *Literary Essays* (New York, 1920), p. 226.

74. *Ibid.*, pp. 226, 227.

75. *Ibid.*, p. 227.

76. *Ibid.*, pp. 232-233.

77. *The Letters of Gerard Manley Hopkins to Robert Bridges*, ed. C. C. Abbott (London, 1935), p. 251.

78. *Genius and Other Essays* (New York, 1911), p. 226.

79. *Companion to the Iliad* (London, 1892), p. 27.

80. *Homer and the Epic*, p. 7.

81. *Life in the Homeric Age* (New York, 1907), pp. 14-15.

82. *The Rise of the Greek Epic* (Oxford, 1924), p. 94.

83. *Ibid.,* p. 238.
84. *Lectures on Greek Poetry* (London, New York, 1910), p. 26.
85. Quoted in Augustus H. Strong, *The Great Poets and Their Theology* (Philadelphia, 1897), p. 20.
86. *The Liberal Movement in English Literature* (London, 1885) p. 27.
87. *Further Letters of Gerard Manley Hopkins,* ed. C. C. Abbott (London, New York, Toronto, 1938), p. 111.
88. *Art and Humanity in Homer* (New York, 1896), p. 7.
89. *The New Laokoon,* pp. 242-243.
90. *The Rise of the Greek Epic,* p. 260.
91. *Homer, Introduction to the Iliad and the Odyssey* (Glasgow, 1887), p. 18.
92. *Homer and the Epic,* p. 7.
93. *The Nature and Elements of Poetry,* p. 96.
94. *The Liberal Movement in English Literature,* p. 27.
95. *Shelburne Essays, First Series,* I, 171n.
96. *Epic and Romance* (London, 1926), p. 29.
97. *Greek Poetry,* pp. 37-38.
98. *Homer,* p. 117.
99. *The Rise of the Greek Epic.* p. 169.
100. *The Women of Homer* (New York, 1898), pp. 42-43.
101. *The Beginnings of Poetry* (New York, 1901), p. 447.
102. *Complete Writings* (New York, 1907), IV, 216.
103. *Harvard Lectures on Greek Subjects* (London, 1904), pp. 82-83.
104. *Greek Poetry,* p. 66.
105. *Ibid.,* p. 62.
106. *Ibid.,* p. 63.
107. *Works* (London, 1900-1901), VII, 198.
108. *Ibid.,* VII, 199.
109. *Complete Writings,* IV, 153.
110. *Interpretations of Poetry and Religion* (New York, 1900), pp. 167-168.
111. *Harvard Lectures,* p. 207.
112. *A History of Greek Literature* (New York, 1890), p. 122.
113. *Essays in Little* (London, 1891), p. 84.
114. *Greek Poetry,* p. 71.
115. *Essays Chiefly Literary and Ethical* (London, 1889), p. 28.
116. F. O. Matthiessen, *The James Family* (New York, 1947), p. 637.
117. *Ibid.,* p. 496.
118. *Greek Literature,* p. 122.
119. *The Women of Homer,* p. 42.
120. *Complete Writings,* VII, 55; IV, 218.
121. *Essays Speculative,* I, 159.
122. *Some Aspects of the Greek Genius* (London, 1891), p. 340.
123. See Noel G. Annan, *Leslie Stephen, His Thought and Character in Relation to His Time* (Cambridge, Mass., 1952), p. 255.
124. *Shelburne Essays, Second Series* (Boston, New York, 1904), II, 189.
125. *Ibid., Third Series,* p. 173.
126. *Homer and the Epic,* p. 11.

127. *Aspects of the Greek Genius,* pp. 133-134.
128. *History of Greek Literature,* p. 119.
129. *Views and Reviews* (New York, 1890), p. 92.
130. *The Private Papers of Henry Ryecroft* (New York, 1927), p. 234.
131. *Complete Writings* (Hartford, 1904), XV, 82.
132. *The Nature of Poetry,* p. 97.
133. *Rise of the Greek Epic,* p. 120.
134. *Letters of Charles Eliot Norton* (Boston and New York, 1913), II, 329.
135. *Literature and the American College,* pp. 153-154.
136. *North American Review,* CII, 511.
137. See, for example, *Literary Essays* (Boston, New York, 1891), IV, 161.
138. *American Prose Masters* (New York, Chicago, Boston, 1923), pp. 254-255.
139. *My Literary Passions* (New York, London, 1895), pp. 149, 151.
140. *Ibid.,* p. 151.
141. *Emerson and Other Essays* (New York, 1898), pp. 173, 175, 174.
142. Quoted in Basil Champneys *Coventry Patmore* (London, 1900), II, 98.
143. *Works,* III, 79.
144. *Complete Works,* XIV, 109.
145. *Ibid.,* XIV, 115.
146. *Interpretations of Poetry,* p. 286.
147. *Heretics* (London, New York, 1905), p. 19.
148. *The Choice of Books,* pp. 85-87.
149. *Lectures on Poetry* (London, 1914), p. 161.
150. *Essays in Literary Interpretation,* p. 190.
151. *Ibid.,* pp. 106, 179.
152. *Works,* V, 38.
153. *Dante's American Pilgrimage* (New Haven, 1948), p. 140.
154. *Great Poets and Their Theology,* p. 134.
155. L. P. Jacks, *Life and Letters of Stopford Brooke* (London, 1917), p. 510.
156. *Essays in Literary Interpretation,* p. 204.
157. *Imaginary Interviews* (New York, London, 1910), pp. 25-26.
158. *Lectures and Essays,* II, 323-324.
159. *Studies of a Biographer* (London, 1902), IV, 114.
160. Samuel Butler, *The Way of All Flesh,* Everyman's edition, (New York, 1916), p. 409.
161. Clara Barrus, *The Life and Letters of John Burroughs* (Boston, New York, 1925), I, 344.
162. *At Large* (New York, London, 1909), p. 77.
163. *Views and Reviews,* p. 129.
164. Barrus, *Life of Burroughs,* I, 345.
165. *Milton* (London, 1926), p. 176.
166. *Literary Remains* (London, 1905), II, 127.
167. *Posthumous Essays of John Churton Collins,* ed. L. C. Collins (New York, London, 1912), p. 101.

168. *Collected Essays,* I, 318.

169. *Shelburne Essays, Fourth Series* (London, New York, 1922), p. 242.

170. *Philosophy of English Literature* (New York, 1874), p. 132.

171. *The Greater Victorian Poets* (London, 1895), p. 248.

172. *The Torch* (New York, 1905), p. 159.

173. *Ibid.,* pp. 154-155.

174. *Milton,* p. 200.

175. *An Outline Sketch of English Literature* (New York, 1886), pp. 153-154.

176. Letter quoted in L. C. Collins, *Life and Memoirs of John Churton Collins* (London, New York, 1912), pp. 106-107.

177. *Life and Writings of John Milton* (London, n.d.) pp. 152-153.

178. *Collected Essays and Addresses,* I, 29-30.

179. *Ibid.,* I, 33.

180. *The Springs of Helicon* (London, 1909), p. 170.

181. *Studies in Prose and Verse* (London, n.d.), p. 194.

182. *Studies of a Biographer,* IV, 117-118.

183. *Studies in Literature* (London, 1907), p. 46.

184. *Collected Essays and Addresses,* I, 31.

185. *Puritan and Anglican: Studies in Literature* (New York, 1901), p. 184.

186. *The Springs of Helicon,* p. 179.

187. *Life of Milton,* p. 153.

188. *Milton,* p. 123.

189. *Shelburne Essays, Fourth Series,* p. 244.

190. *Ibid.,* pp. 244, 246.

191. *Ibid.,* p. 251.

192. *Ibid.,* p. 252.

193. *Outline of English Literature,* p. 154.

194. *Life of Milton,* p. 165.

195. *Ibid.,* p. 161.

196. *A Short History of Modern English Literature* (New York, 1898), p. 168.

197. *Familiar Talks on English Literature* (Chicago, 1892), p. 198.

198. *Correspondence of Hopkins and Dixon,* p. 17.

199. *Milton,* p. 207.

200. See vol. III of *The Collected Essays and Papers of George Saintsbury, 1875-1920* (London, 1923).

201. *Victorian Poets* (New York, Boston, 1887), p. 353.

202. *Milton,* pp. 238-239.

203. *Ibid.,* p. 197.

204. *Essays Speculative and Suggestive,* I, 153.

INDEX

242